The ABS Undergraduate
Directory of Business
Schools
1999/2000

The ABS Undergraduate Directory of Business Schools 1999/2000

Postgraduate and post-experience courses

BUTTERWORTH
HEINEMANN

OXFORD   BOSTON   JOHANNESBURG   MELBOURNE
NEW DELHI   SINGAPORE

Butterworth-Heinemann
Linacre House, Jordan Hill, Oxford OX2 8DP
225 Wildwood Avenue, Woburn, MA 01801-2041
A division of Reed Educational and Professional Publishing Ltd

A member of the Reed Elsevier plc group

First published 1998

British Library Cataloguing in Publication Data

A catalogue record for this book is available
from the British Library

ISBN 0 7506 3955 5

Printed and bound in Great Britain by Biddles Ltd, Kings Lynn & Guildford

Contents

Foreword

The managerial workplace of the mid-nineties is challenging and competitive. The explosion in demand for business and management-related qualifications from undergraduates, postgraduates and experienced managers reflects their need for study which combines academic rigour with practical relevance. The Higher Education Statistics Agency released figures in 1998 showing a record number of students – 220,000 – enrolled on Business and Management related courses in 1996/97. This accounts for 12.5 per cent of the total higher education student population.

For practising managers, business and management qualifications are seen as a passport to gaining new challenges and responsibilities in their careers and to achieving greater competence in the wide-ranging roles demanded of them by their employers. A recent Institute of Management/Ashridge survey showed that more than 70 per cent of a sample of 700 experienced managers said qualifications improved their career prospects.

Helping students and experienced managers to gain qualifications is only one indication of the valuable contribution business schools make to the development of a world-class managerial workforce. Leaner management structures, new methods of working, new technologies and the internationalisation of business continue to place unprecedented pressures on organisations and their managers to adapt and operate successfully. Employers also look to business schools to help them improve their organisational effectiveness and this is underlined by the dramatic growth in demand for customised development programmes and for consultancy services.

Employers, recognising the calibre of graduates educated by business schools, actively recruit them for their knowledge and skills. Research has shown that the top three requirements of human resource professionals when recruiting graduates are teamworking, leadership and business awareness. No other discipline taught at UK universities fulfils these particular needs so directly.

Britain is a world leader in management education and training. Each year business schools attract more than 36,000 EU and overseas students to the UK. In addition to their work with overseas students, UK business schools are active in other countries providing qualification programmes, executive education, research and consultancy in developed and developing nations worldwide.

I am very pleased to have this opportunity to present the *The ABS Undergraduate Directory of Business Schools* and to commend the continued commitment to the quality of business and management development which it represents.

Professor Chris Greensted
Chair, Association of Business Schools
1998

Introduction to The ABS Undergraduate Directory

The ABS Undergraduate Directory of Business Schools lists annually updated information about the full range of undergraduate level business and management courses offered by ABS member schools. No other publication provides the same level of detailed relevant information.

Each school's entry includes:

○   The key information about each school and its programmes.
○   Quality ratings for teaching and research from the Higher Education Funding Councils.
○   Contact information.
○   Full-time and associate/part-time staff numbers.

About the ABS

The Association of Business Schools (ABS) is the sole representative body of the business schools of the United Kingdom. Its membership covers all of the major UK higher education providers of business and management education, at first degree, postgraduate degree, nd post-experience levels.

The primary object of ABS is: to advance the education of the public in business and management in particular through the promotion of business and management education training and development so as to improve the quality and effectiveness of management in the United Kingdom.

ABS is widely recognised within the UK as the authoritative advocate of the business schools and the interests of their clients. It engages in representations and discussions with the principal UK funding bodies for higher education, the Higher Education Funding Councils for England (HEFCE), Wales (HEFCW), and Scotland (SHEFC), and with the quality assurance body for the UK universities, the Quality Assurance Agency for Higher Education (QAA). ABS also meets the representative body of the universities, the Committee of Vice-Chancellors and Principals (CVCP) on related issues.

Representative work on behalf of the business schools is also conducted with the Management Charter Initiative (MCI), the Confederation of British Industry (CBI), and government in the form of the Department for Education and Employment (DFEE). Representative meetings are also held with all of the political parties.

ABS is increasingly active at the European level of management education by working with other national associations and the European Foundation for Management Development (EFMD) particularly in the development of pan-European accreditation arrangements for schools and MBA programmes.

The Association has set up the Management Veritication Consortium (MVC), in conjunction with the Institute of Management to award National and Scottish Vocational Qualifications (N/SVQs). The MVC is currently the largest single awarding body for management and related N/SVQs in Higher Education in the UK.

Membership of ABS currently stands at one hundred and is restricted to the following:

O   institutions accrediting their qualifications through the UK higher education system.

O   distinct units with significant core staff engaged in business and management education.

O   provision of at least two of the following - undergraduate programmes, postgraduate programmes, post-experience programmes, and research programmes.

O   institutions providing appropriate information about themselves to ABS, and, where required, facilitating a visit by the ABS Membership Sub-Committee.

Enquiries about any of the above should be made to the ABS offices:
Association of Business Schools,
344/354 Gray's Inn Road,
LONDON, WC1X 8BP

Telephone: +44 (0) 171 837 1899
Fax: +44 (0) 171 837 8189
Email: abs@thembs.org.uk

Explanation of the Teaching and Research ratings

The ratings for teaching quality and research quality (see key to icons) arise from the work of the Higher Education Funding Councils, which separately cover England, Scotland and Wales, Northern Ireland is also covered.

The ratings for teaching quality of business and management stem from the 1994 exercise. In England, Northern Ireland and Wales there were only three possible ratings namely: excellent, satisfactory and unsatisfactory. In Scotland there was an additional category of higher satisfactory. Although the Funding Councils have now changed their ratings systems to a points/profiling methods, the subject of business and management will not be reviewed under the new system until at least 1998.

The ratings for research quality of the business and management area stem from the 1996 exercise.

O   A rating of 5' shows that the research assessed was of international excellence in a majority of sub-areas and at least of national excellence in all others.

O   A rating of 5 shows international excellence in some areas and national excellence in virtually all others.

O   A rating of 4 shows national excellence in virtually all sub-areas.

O   A rating of 3a shows national excellence in a substantial majority of sub-areas.

O   A rating of 3b shows national excellence in a majority of sub areas.

O   A rating of 2 shows national excellence in up to half the sub-areas.

O   A rating of 1 shows national excellence in no. or virtually no. sub-areas.

Aberdeen Business School

Aberdeen Business School

Address:	Garthdee Road
	Aberdeen
	AB10 7QE
Area:	Scotland
Phone:	01224 262000
Fax:	01224 263838
Email:	**rgu.ac.uk**
Website:	**www.rgu.ac.uk**
Email Application Available?	No
How to apply by email:	
Total Number of Teaching Staff:	40
Staff Teaching Undergraduate Courses	25
Research Rating:	3b
Teaching Rating:	Highly Satisfactory
Additional Rating Information	
Male:Female Student Ratio	50:50
Head of Business School	Hector Douglas
Head of Undergraduate Studies	Bob Gammie
Admissions Contact	Bob Gammie

About the School:

Aberdeen Business School is located in a new "state of the art" building at Gathdee on the bank of the River DEE. The building was designed by Sir Norman Foster and partners and incorporates a Library designed to utilise all the modern forms of electronic data access. The library incorporates 2,000 terminals connected to an internal network with access to the WEB
The School has very strong links with the local and international business community which are used to inform teaching quality and to promote work based projects for postgraduate courses.

About Undergraduate Studies:

Course offered:
BA/BA(Hons) in Business Studies
BA/BA(Hons) in European Business Administration with Languages
BA/BA(Hons) in Accounting and Finance
BA/BA (Hons) in Business Administration
All courses apart from BA/BA (Hons) Business Administration include a work placement including the BA/BA(Hons) in Accounting and Finance

Facilities:

The University has a very active Student Association and Union based in the centre of Aberdeen. The new building at Garthdee is the first stage of the process of developing the University on one site and offers students an extremely attractive environment in which to study and live.

Departments/Faculties:

Accountancy
Finance and Economics
Human Resource Management
Marketing and Corporate Strategy
Information and Operations Management

Links with Academic Institutions:

The School has extensive links with Institutions in France and Germany who partner us in the student and teaching exchange.
The School also has strong links with local further education colleges

Links with Industry:

The School has recently established a Commercial Liaison Group to formalise the many and diverse links with the local business community. The Group will serve to inform the future direction of the School and also to develop and extend the strong international profile of the School

General Undergraduate Courses

BA (Hons) Business Studies

Four years Honours degree, with paid 48 week placement during year 3. Career opportunities in Accountancy, Finance, HRM, Marketing, Operations Management, Logistics, Stockbroking, Banking and Insurance.

Modular Course?	Yes
Qualifications:	BA; BA Hons; Diploma HE
Application Deadline:	15/12/97
Commencement Date:	16/9/98
Entry Requirement:	SCE 5 subjects, 4 at H grade (BBCC), GCE 5 subjects 3 at A level
Applications to Places:	10:1
Registered:	110
Awards:	90

	Duration	EC Fees	Non-EC Fees
Full time	4 years		
Part time	4.5 years		
Sandwich	4 years		

BA/BA (Hons) Business Administration

Four year Honours programme. Students with an HNC with passes at a good standard may be admitted to Year 2. Students with an HND of a good standard may be admitted to Year 3. Career opportunities in Accountancy, Finance, HRM, Marketing, Logistics, Operations Management, Banking and Insurance.

Modular Course?	Yes
Qualifications:	BA; BA Hons; Diploma HE
Application Deadline:	15/12/97
Commencement Date:	16/9/98
Entry Requirement:	SCE 5 subjects, 4 at H Grade, (BBCC), GCE 5 subjects 3 at A level (CCC)
Applications to Places:	5:1
Registered:	50
Awards:	40

	Duration	EC Fees	Non-EC Fees
Full time	4 years		
Part time	4.5 years		
Sandwich	n/a		

BA/BA (Hons) Accounting and Finance

This course is fully accredited with ICAS, and receives excellent exemptions from CIMA, and ACCA. The course includes a twelve month paid placement for students progressing down the Honours route. Career opportunities exist in all sectors and disciplines of accountancy and finance, with particular emphasis on further accountancy qualifications.

Modular Course?	Yes
Qualifications:	BA; BA Hons; Diploma HE
Application Deadline:	15/12/97
Commencement Date:	16/9/98
Entry Requirement:	SCE 5 subjects, 4 at H grade (BBCC), GCE 5 subjects 3 at A level (CCC)
Applications to Places:	4:1
Registered:	60
Awards:	20

	Duration	EC Fees	Non-EC Fees
Full time	4 years		
Part time	n/a		
Sandwich	4 years		

BA (Hons) European Business Administration with Languages

The special features of this course are the study of one or two European business languages and the placement year spend in an established Business School abroad. Students attain a broadly-based business education and develop the qualities essential for operating effectively in the wider European business environment.

Modular Course?	Yes
Qualifications:	BA Hons; Diploma HE
Application Deadline:	15/12/97

Commencement Date:	16/9/98
Entry Requirement:	SCE 5 subjects, 4 at H grade (BBBC), GCE 5 subjects 3 at A level (CCC).
Applications to Places:	3:1
Registered:	30
Awards:	20

	Duration	EC Fees	Non-EC Fees
Full time	4 years		
Part time	n/a		
Sandwich	4 years		

BA/BA (Hons) Management

This course is taught on a part time basis two evenings per week and is assessed by continuous assessment and end of semester examinations. The opportunity exists to transfer between part time and full-time mode of delivery.

Modular Course?	Yes
Qualifications:	BA; BA Hons; Diploma HE
Application Deadline:	flexible
Commencement Date:	16/9/98
Entry Requirement:	SCE, 5 subjects 3/4 at H grade, GCE 5 subjects, 2 at A level
Applications to Places:	
Registered:	20
Awards:	n/a

	Duration	EC Fees	Non-EC Fees
Full time	n/a		
Part time	4.5 years		
Sandwich	4.5 years		

Anglia Business School

Anglia Business School

Address:	Danbury Park Campus
	Danbury
	Plus locations in Cambridge and Chelmsford
	Chelmsford
	CM3 4AT
Area:	London and South East England
Phone:	01245 225511
Fax:	01245 224331
Email:	**absinform@ford.anglia.ac.uk**
Website:	**http://abs.anglia.ac.uk**

Email Application Available?	Yes
How to apply by email:	Complete appropriate form on web site
Total Number of Teaching Staff:	85
Staff Teaching Undergraduate Courses	55
Research Rating:	2
Teaching Rating:	Satisfactory
Additional Rating Information	
Male:Female Student Ratio	50:50
Head of Business School	Professor Hugh Jenkins
Head of Undergraduate Studies	Don Burton
Admissions Contact	Admissions Office

About the School:
Anglia Business School is one of the best known in the UK and has in excess of 85 academic staff. The mission of the School is to be an institution of international standing providing a high quality, financially viable, vocationally relevant and flexible service of educational and training opportunities, research and consultancy.

About Undergraduate Studies:
The School's conception of business and management is of a multi-disciplinary, applied study of an eclectic nature closely related to the needs of organisations and managers in a variety of settings.

Facilities:
The University has a full range of facilities for students which include:
On-campus halls of residence.
Separate undergraduate and postgraduate student lounges.
All day refectory services serving hot meals and snacks.
Sports and recreational facilities, including a multi-gym and tennis courts.

A multi-faith Chaplaincy which allows students of all religions to engage in their spiritual life on campus.

Departments/Faculties:
Field of Business and Economics (Cambridge); Field of Business Studies (Chelmsford); Field of Management Development (Cambridge and Danbury). Plus three Research & Development Centres: Centre for Business Transformation; Centre for Educational Policy and Leadership; Centre for International Business & Economics Research.

Links with Academic Institutions:
Anglia Business School has widespread and well established partnership agreements with higher education institutions across Europe, in North America and Malaysia, and these support the School's distinctive international mission. Specific European relations exist with Business Schools in Holland, France, Germany and Spain. The MBA programme is delivered in Germany and Belgium, both generally and specifically for Ford Europe.

Links with Industry:
Anglia Business School pursues active links with local and national industry to develop essential managerial competencies, to develop organisational capabilities, and to develop strategic transnational skills. Particular features of our provision include tailored in-house programmes and Teaching Company Programmes. ABS further provides programmes that link NVQ with academic awards.

General Undergraduate Courses

BA (Hons) Business Economics; BA (Hons) European Business; BA (Hons) Business; BA (Combined Hons) Business; BA (Combined Hons) Economics

The Field of European Business Economics in Cambridge offers, within the University Modular System, single honours degree courses in European Business, Business and Business Economics. Both Business and Business Economics can also be taken in combined honours courses with a wide range of other disciplines from across the campus.

The modular programme allows students to move between courses if necessary. All courses contain some options from within the Business School, together with the opportunity to take modules from other departments on the campus. These courses provide a general business education from which students can progress towards career specialisation as graduates. The single honours courses have a common core curriculum which develops the essential business skills. The core includes modules in Business Decision Making, Economics, Finance, Information Technology, Human Resource Management, Marketing and, in the final year, Strategic Management. Combined Honours students also take the bulk of this core and are encouraged to use their options on the remaining core modules. All students write a dissertation in their final year. A distinctive aspect of the programme is the close co-operation with other European centres in dual award programmes. BA (Hons) Business Economics aims to prepare students for careers in business where an economic training has particular relevance, for example in financial services. BA (Hons) Business currently admits students with 120 or more credits. BA (Hons) European Business aims to develop the business, language and cultural skills needed to work in businesses operating across national boundaries. Language study is an integral part of the programme and students study for a year in one of our partner centres and complete a business placement in the partner country. BA (Combined Hons) Business enables students to combine the study of business with another discipline chosen from across the campus. Business may be taken as a major, minor or equal subject. BA (Combined Hons) Economics is also available as a major, minor or equal subject

Modular Course?	No
Qualifications:	BA Hons
Application Deadline:	UCAS deadline
Commencement Date:	
Entry Requirement:	5 GCSE passes with at least 2 at A-level or 4 GCSE passes with at least 3 at A-level, to include GSCE Maths and English at C or above, or Advanced Level GNVQ Merit. European Business requires one European language, preferably at A-level, although GCSE German, French or Spanish is acceptable.
Applications to Places:	5:1
Registered:	
Awards:	

	Duration	EC Fees	Non-EC Fees
Full time	3 years	£1000	£5750
Part time			
Sandwich	4 years	£1000	£5750

BA (Hons) Business Administration; BA (Hons) Business Studies; BA (Hons) Accounting

The Field of Business Studies in Chelmsford offers these three awards which are integrated within a modular structure. This means that it is possible for students to transfer from one award to another during their programme of study. The programmes have a strong vocational orientation and include significant option choice which allows students to follow pathways in specific vocational areas. These include: Marketing; Human Resource Management; Corporate Administration; Financial Services; Leisure Management. Students in choosing a particular route have the opportunity to maximise credit recognition with a number of professional bodies.

Modular Course?	Yes
Qualifications:	BA Hons
Application Deadline:	UCAS deadline
Commencement Date:	
Entry Requirement:	5 GCSE passes with at least 2 at A-level or 4 GCSE passes with at least 3 at A-level, to include GSCE Maths and English at C or above, or Advanced Level GNVQ
Applications to Places:	5:1
Registered:	550
Awards:	

	Duration	EC Fees	Non-EC Fees
Full time	3 years	£1000	£5750
Part time			
Sandwich	4 years	£1000	£5750

Aston Business School

Aston Business School

Address:	Aston University
	Aston Triangle
	Birmingham
	B4 7ET
Area:	Midlands
Phone:	0121 359 3611
Fax:	0121 359 6384

Email: abspg@aston.ac.uk

Website:

Email Application Available?	No
How to apply by email:	
Total Number of Teaching Staff:	100
Staff Teaching Undergraduate Courses	73
Research Rating:	4
Teaching Rating:	Satisfactory
Additional Rating Information	
Male:Female Student Ratio	50:50
Head of Business School	Professor John Saunders
Director of Undergraduate Studies	Mr D Johnson
Admissions Contact	Mr M Hussey

About the School:

Aston Business School is one of the largest and best regarded centres for business study in Europe with acknowledged strengths in teaching research and management activities. An outstanding academic portfolio, excellent facilities, innovative international programmes and strong industrial links, combine to offer students a rich and rewarding experience.

The School is part of Aston University which is located in the heart of Birmingham - an exciting and cosmopolitan city offering a wide range of social, sporting and cultural facilities.

About Undergraduate Studies:

The School's degree programmes all offer the opportunity of an industrial placement in their third year, and this is enormously valuable both in terms of academic development and real world experience. Many undergratuates now spend this year abroad. Opportunities for projects and placements overseas exist through the School's links with other leading business schools in Europe, Canada, the USA, Brazil, China and other Asian countries.

Facilities:

The School is located within walking distance of Birmingham's cultural, recreational and shopping facilities and mainline station, with easy access to the motorway system and Birmingham International Airport. The School has its own residential facilities including self-contained study bedrooms, lounge, bar and restaurant and is adjacent to the University's sporting and library facilities.

There are excellent sports facilities available to Aston students. Our city centre campus is the base for two leisure centres including a swimming pool, multi-gym and a synthetic all-weather sports pitch.

Further out of the city, the Recreation Centre spans 95 acres and is mainly used by our students for outdoor sports, either to train, compete or socialise. A number of classes and instructional courses are also on offer on campus including aerobics, life-saving, swimming and yoga.

Links with Academic Institutions:

The postgraduate programme offers study visits to Lille and Barcelona. There is also the possibility for MBA students to study one term in Maastricht.

Links with Industry:

Aston Business School has established links with industry, commerce and the public sector in the United Kingdom and around the world. This has enabled us to develop a real understanding of the relationship between academic study and practical management, and is a key factor in the excellent graduate recruitment record.

General Undergraduate Courses

BSc Accounting for Management

After a broad-based first year, students explore finance and accounting in depth in the second and final years. Professional recognition is available. Both three year and four year degrees are available, with integrated industrial/professional experience in the four year programme.

Modular Course?	Yes
Qualifications:	BSc
Application Deadline:	UCAS deadlines
Commencement Date:	
Entry Requirement:	GCE A-level 24 points
Applications to Places:	n/a
Registered:	25
Awards:	

	Duration	EC Fees	Non-EC Fees
Full time	3 years	£1000	£6700
Part time			
Sandwich	4 years	£1000	£6700

BSc Business Computing and IT

After a broad-based first year, students follow a number of compulsory and some optional courses. The aim is to produce hybrid managers of the future who will be computer literate and able to pass on their knowledge within the organisation. Both three and four year degrees are available, with integrated industrial/professional experience in the four year programme.

Modular Course?	Yes
Qualifications:	BSc
Application Deadline:	UCAS deadlines
Commencement Date:	
Entry Requirement:	GCE A-level 24 points
Applications to Places:	n/a
Registered:	15
Awards:	

	Duration	EC Fees	Non-EC Fees
Full time	3 years	£1000	£6700
Part time			
Sandwich	4 years	£1000	£6700

BSc Law with Legal Practice Management

Specialist studies in law follow a broad-based first year. The programme focuses on the crucial role which legal principles play in core legal fields and in business law. The programme is a qualifying law degree for the purposes of accreditation by the Law Society and Council of Legal Education. Full exemption is given from the academic stage of training. Both three and four year degrees are available, with integrated industrial/professional experience in the four year programme.

Modular Course?	Yes
Qualifications:	BSc
Application Deadline:	UCAS deadlines
Commencement Date:	
Entry Requirement:	GCE A-level 24 points
Applications to Places:	n/a
Registered:	30
Awards:	

	Duration	EC Fees	Non-EC Fees
Full time	3 years	£1000	£6700
Part time			
Sandwich	4 years	£1000	£6700

BSc Managerial and Administrative Studies

Aston Business School's main undergraduate programme in Management, this degree offers a wide range of optional subjects grouped in specialist streams, which are followed after the broad-based first year courses.

The six specialist streams currently offered are: finance and accounting; business computing; legal studies; marketing; operations management; personnel and organisational studies. A year of industrial/professional training (the third year of study) is a compulsory feature of this degree programme.

Modular Course?	Yes
Qualifications:	BSc
Application Deadline:	UCAS deadlines
Commencement Date:	
Entry Requirement:	24 points at A-level
Applications to Places:	n/a
Registered:	723
Awards:	

	Duration	EC Fees	Non-EC Fees
Full time	4 years	£1000	£6700
Part time			
Sandwich			

BSc Marketing

Students study in depth a number of key areas of marketing, after a broad-based first year. This is a four year degree, with a compulsory year of integrated industrial/professional experience.

Modular Course?	Yes
Qualifications:	BSc
Application Deadline:	UCAS deadlines
Commencement Date:	
Entry Requirement:	GCE A-level 24 points
Applications to Places:	n/a
Registered:	50
Awards:	
Full time	£1000 £6700
Part time	
Sandwich	4 years £1000 £6700

BSc Operations Management

After a broad-based first year, students explore in depth he methods by which organisations design, plan and control their operations. Both three year and four year degrees are available, with integrated industrial/professional experience in the four year programme.

Modular Course?	Yes
Qualifications:	BSc
Application Deadline:	UCAS deadlines
Commencement Date:	
Entry Requirement:	GCE A-level 24 points
Applications to Places:	n/a
Registered:	10
Awards:	

	Duration	EC Fees	Non-EC Fees
Full time	3 years	£1000	£6700
Part time			
Sandwich	4 years	£1000	£6700

BSc Sociology and Psychology in Business

This degree focuses on the part played by individuals and groups in the organisational process. Following a broad-based first year the second and final years develop critical and analytical skills. Both three year and four year degrees are available, with integrated industrial/professional experience in the four year programme.

Modular Course?		Yes
Qualifications:		BSc
Application Deadline:		UCAS deadlines
Commencement Date:		
Entry Requirement:		GCE A-level 24 points
Applications to Places:		n/a
Registered:		10
Awards:		

	Duration	EC Fees	Non-EC Fees
Full time	3 years	£1000	£6700
Part time			
Sandwich	4 years	£1000	£6700

BSc International Business and Modern Languages

This programme is offered jointly by Aston Business School and the Department of Languages and European Studies. The languages, societies and cultures of France and Germany are studied in an integrated manner together with business components (policy, finance, economics, marketing, operations etc). A comparative and international approach is developed throughout, with international business as the focus of the final year. The third year is spent in a major business school in France or University in Germany. Alternatively, some students spend the year in a 12 month work placement in industry.

Modular Course?		Yes
Qualifications:		BSc
Application Deadline:		UCAS deadlines
Commencement Date:		
Entry Requirement:		GCE A-level 24 points (B in language)
Applications to Places:		n/a
Registered:		325
Awards:		

	Duration	EC Fees	Non-EC Fees
Full time			
Part time			
Sandwich	4 years	£1000	£6700

BSc Psychology and Management

This joint honours programme took its first students in 1993. Students study a selection of related topics in psychology and management, included integrated work in each year. Psychology and Management may be studied as a three year degree or as a four-year sandwich programme.

Modular Course?		Yes
Qualifications:		BSc
Application Deadline:		UCAS deadlines
Commencement Date:		
Entry Requirement:		GCE A-level BBC
Applications to Places:		n/a
Registered:		119
Awards:		

	Duration	EC Fees	Non-EC Fees
Full time	3 years	£1000	£6700
Part time			
Sandwich	4 years	£1000	£6700

BSc (Combined Honours) Public Policy and Management

Part of the University's Combined Honours degree scheme, this subject is concerned with the management of the public sector Britain. It examines some of the fundamental issues facing local and central government - the environment, the health service, housing - and looks at what is being done by public sector managers to tackle these issues. Students may follow a three or four year sandwich programme.

Modular Course?		Yes
Qualifications:		BSc Hons
Application Deadline:		UCAS deadlines
Commencement Date:		
Entry Requirement:		GCE A-level 18/20 points
Applications to Places:		n/a
Registered:		159
Awards:		

	Duration	EC Fees	Non-EC Fees
Full time	3 years	£1000	£6700
Part time			
Sandwich	4 years	£1000	£6700

BSc (Combined Honours) Business Administration

Part of the University's Combined Honours scheme, Business Administration is a popular subject, taken by over 100 students each year. Business policy, financial management, marketing and human behaviour in work organisations are amongst the areas studied. Students may follow a three year or a four year sandwich programme.

Modular Course?	Yes
Qualifications:	BSc Hons
Application Deadline:	UCAS deadlines
Commencement Date:	
Entry Requirement:	GCE A-level 18/20 points
Applications to Places:	n/a
Registered:	462
Awards:	

	Duration	EC Fees	Non-EC Fees
Full time	3 or 4 years	£1000	£6700
Part time			
Sandwich			

BSc (Combined Honours) Sociology

Aston Business School offers three subjects within the University's Combined Honours degree scheme. In this scheme students study two subject side-by-side to honours degree level. Sociology addresses a range of important contemporary issues such as class, race and gender, and social policy issues concerned with the media, education, crime and deviance. The focus is primarily on British society, but international comparisons are involved as are historical and contemporary dimensions. Students may follow a three or four year sandwich programme.

Modular Course?	Yes
Qualifications:	BSc Hons
Application Deadline:	UCAS deadlines
Commencement Date:	
Entry Requirement:	GCE A-level 18/20 points
Applications to Places:	n/a
Registered:	228
Awards:	

	Duration	EC Fees	Non-EC Fees
Full time	3 or 4 years	£1000	£6700
Part time			
Sandwich			

BSc International Business and Economics

This programme combines business orientated applied economics with complementary international business subjects. The economics component aims to develop skills required for making assessments of the economic environment of businesses and their strategies within the contexts of national and international environments. The international business component aims to develop knowledge and skills to enable the assessment and development of international strategies and operations of business.

Modular course:	Yes
Qualification:	BSc
Applications deadline:	UCAS
Commencement date:	
Entry requirement:	GCE A-level 24 points
Applications to places:	n/a
Registered:	New programme
Awards:	

BSc Sociology and Public Policy

Providing an understanding and competence in sociological analysis and research with particular reference to issues of public policy is the particular aim of this programme. Additionally, to provide a thorough grounding in the principles and practice of public service management through the application of the sociology of administration and organisations.

Modular course:	Yes
Qualification:	BSc
Application deadline:	UCAS
Commencement date:	
Entry requirement:	GCE A-level 18 points
Applications to places:	n/a
Registered:	New programme
Awards:	

School of Management

Address:	Claverton Down
	Bath
	BA2 7AY
Area:	South West England
Phone:	+44 (0) 1225 826742
Fax:	+44 (0) 1225 826473
Email:	**recep@management.bath.ac.uk**
Website:	**http://www.bath.ac.uk/**
Departments/Management	

Email Application Available?	No
How to apply by email:	
Total Number of Teaching Staff:	50
Staff Teaching Undergraduate Courses	50
Research Rating:	5
Teaching Rating:	Excellent
Additional Rating Information	
Male:Female Student Ratio	55:45
Head of Business School	Professor Brian Bayliss
Head of Undergraduate Studies	Dr Alan Butt Philip
Admissions Contact	Ray Brockington

About the School:

The School is one of seven business schools to achieve top ratings for both teaching and research in the HEFCE assessments. Bath is one of eighteen British MBA providers accredited by the Association of MBAs for all their MBA programmes. The MBA which Bath runs jointly with the Malaysian Institute of Management is the first international collaborative MBA in the world to be accredited by the Association. Research is issue-based and multi-disciplinary covering: International Regulation and Policy; Work and Employment; Organisations, Culture and Change; Logistics, Supply and Strategic Networks; Decision and Information Systems. Research income in 1996-7 was £2.1m.

About Undergraduate Studies:

Our 4-year BSc degrees attract some of the best students in the country in terms of A level scores and have excellent records of graduate employment. Business Administration students spend two 6 month placements in two different organisations and also conduct a team consultancy project in their final year. International Management and Modern Languages students spend a year in France or Germany, the majority in a 12 month work placement.

Facilities:

The University of Bath has some of the best sporting facilities of any UK university with an Olympic standard swimming pool and sports village. In 1995 it hosted the European Youth Olympics. Other facilities include a Library and Learning Centre (the only one in the UK to open 24 hours a day during term time), a range of new restaurants and cafes and a new Arts Theatre. Over 100 clubs and societies are supported by Bath University Students' Union whose Welfare and Education units provide student support on a range of issues.

Departments/Faculties:

Research Centres:
Work and Employment Research Centre
Centre for Research into Strategic Information Systems
Centre for Research into Strategic Purchasing and Supply
International Centre for the Environment
Centre for Action Research in Professional Practice
Centre for Regulated Industries

Links with Academic Institutions:

The School has agreements with over 20 highly rated business schools in seven countries in mainland Europe and in North America. Since 1987 the School has been running a 2-year Executive MBA with the Malaysian Institute of Management (MIM) designed for experienced executives. In October 1997 it became the first international MBA to receive AMBA accreditation.

Links with Industry:

The School's industrial links range from well over 100 different employers in the UK and overseas who take undergraduate students on placement to companies such as Balfour Beatty and AT Kearney who are sponsors of major research projects and research centres. We also have close links with local companies, including many SMEs, who commission final year team projects as part of our undergraduate programme.

Student Testimonials:

I chose the Bath DBA for one very simple reason: the School of Management asked for the highest entrance requirements out of all the UK undergraduate business schools. The very close relationships which the School fosters with blue-chip companies helped me to land my first six-month placement with Coopers & Lybrand.. I developed a keen interest in corporate finance which led to a second placement with the investment banking arm of HSBC with whom I also arranged our final year team project.

My most memorable experience was the exchange at McIntire School of Commerce at the University of Virginia where I was able to experience an international setting and make many close friends. Four years and nine different addresses later I have joined Bankers Trust Company, an international investment bank. The School of Management gave me more than an education - it enabled me to pursue my own interests and to build up a set of skills which have proved invaluable now that I have joined the real business world.

General Undergraduate Courses

BSc in Business Administration

Four years including two six month work placements, a final year team consultancy project and an optional overseas exchange in mainland Europe or North America in year 4

Modular Course?	No
Qualifications:	BSc Hons
Application Deadline:	15 December
Commencement Date:	21 Sept 1998
Entry Requirement:	3 A levels at ABB or equivalent
Applications to Places:	12:1
Registered:	135 (total registered:460)
Awards:	102

	Duration	EC Fees	Non-EC Fees
Full time			
Part time			
Sandwich	4 years	£1000 p.a.	£6450 p.a.

BSc in International Management and Modern Languages

Four year fully integrated management and language (French or German) degree including the 3rd year spent on work placement, at business school or a combination of the two

Modular Course?	No
Qualifications:	BSc Hons
Application Deadline:	15 December
Commencement Date:	21 Sept 98
Entry Requirement:	ABB including min B in French or German
Applications to Places:	12:1
Registered:	66 (total registered: 236)
Awards:	54

	Duration	EC Fees	Non-EC Fees
Full time			
Part time			
Sandwich	4 years	£1000 p.a.	£6450 p.a.

The Birmingham Business School

The Birmingham Business School

Address:	Priorsfield,
	46 Edgebaston Park Road
	Birmingham
	B15 2RU
Area:	Midlands
Phone:	0121 414 6693
Fax:	0121 414 3553
Email:	**mba@bham.ac.uk**
Website:	**http://www.bham.ac.uk**

Email Application Available?	Yes
How to apply by email:	www.bham.ac.uk
Total Number of Teaching Staff:	68
Staff Teaching Undergraduate Courses	63
Research Rating:	4
Teaching Rating:	Satisfactory
Additional Rating Information	
Male:Female Student Ratio	50:50
Head of Business School	Professor John Samuels
Head of Undergraduate Studies	Dr JP Hanlon
Admissions Contact	

About the School:

The University of Birmingham, the original Redbrick university, is the oldest provider of management education in England. From 1902 onwards, the degrees of Bachelor of Commerce and Master of Commerce have attracted students from all over the world to its spacious campus. The tradition continues with a range of full-time and part-time MBA programmes that continually evolve in terms of quality and content to meet the changing needs of the International Manager. The Birmingham Business School is an accredited member of the association of MBA's.

Facilities:

Accommodation is guaranteed for all postgraduate students in purpose-built apartments both on and off campus. The University has excellent sporting facilities, including a swimming pool, sport's centre, athletics track, and rugby, hockey and football pitches.

Bolton Business School

Bolton Business School

Address:	Bolton Business School
	Bolton
	BL3 5AB
Area:	North West England
Phone:	01204 528 851
Fax:	01204 900 516
Email:	AK3@bolton.ac.uk
Website:	acs.bolton.ac.uk
Email Application Available?	No
How to apply by email:	
Total Number of Teaching Staff:	72
Staff Teaching Undergraduate Courses	65
Research Rating:	2
Teaching Rating:	Satisfactory
Additional Rating Information	
Male:Female Student Ratio	60:40
Head of Business School	Professor Alan Kitson
Head of Undergraduate Studies	J Hall
Admissions Contact	John Blower

About the School:

Created in 1990, the School has developed strong international links, in Europe, the Far East and the Middle East. It is leading major European projects related to the development and use of telematics in delivering management education. Strong links with the local business community are based on focusing on the needs of SMEs and the development of good working arrangements with Bolton/Bury TEC, Business Link, the Chamber of Commerce. The School values collaboration with practitioner and academic peers. Research focuses on management development, organisational behaviour, the night time economy, small business and business ethics.

About Undergraduate Studies:

The School offers a wide range of degree programmes - Accountancy, Business Information Systems, Business Studies, Marketing, Human Resource Management, International Tourism, Tourism Management, Leisure Management, Computing. A modular framework also offers joint honours degrees in Law, French, German, Operations Management, Tourism Studies, Leisure Studies, Organisation Studies, Business Economics. Also available is a one-year top up programme leading to

BA(Hons) Business Administration and HNDs in Business, Business Information Technology and Computing.

Facilities:

The Centre for Sports and Leisure management, located within the School, provides a comprehensive service to support student sports activities. A large sports hall, incorporating a fitness suite, playing fields and active collaboration with the Students Union provide ample opportunity to engage in both competitive sports and general exercise. Bolton has excellent water sports facilities and a range of accessible in-door facilities. The Students Union occupies its own building and provides a wide range of social activities.

Departments/Faculties:

The School houses the Centre for Enterprise and Management, the Centre for Sport and leisure management, the Social Organisations Research Group and subject groups in accountancy, computing, business information systems, leisure, tourism, languages, marketing, human resource management, operations management, organisation studies, economics, strategic management,

Links with Academic Institutions:

The School collaborates with other UK universities in the development of its research work - most notably in the fields of management development, organisational psychology and risk and hazard management. There are established exchange programmes with universities in the USA, France, Germany, Spain, Portugal and Finland. European exchange programmes are supported through Erasmus. There are links with Italy, Portugal. Belgium and France focusing on telematics development and with China, focusing on research in financial information systems.

Links with Industry:

The School's Advisory Council consists of senior business people from the local business community. There are strong working links with TECs in the region, Business Link and the Chamber of Commerce. The School provides in-house management development programmes for the Fire Service and an international print company. With over 850 part-time students, the School provides education and training to over 400 local businesses. Short courses and NVQ programmes provide further links with local businesses. The School's strong international presence brings it into touch with a wide range of organisations in different parts of the world.

Student Testimonials:

Craig Burrell, BA (Hons) Business Administration, "Bolton has impressive facilities, especially the computing ones which are constantly updated and expanded."

Lisa Adams BA (Hons) Combined Studies, "Excellent tuition from lecturers who are always willing to give time to the individual. A very positive learning environment. The beer's good too."

Lindsey Depledge, BA (Hons) Business Administration, "Bolton has some great facilities and my time here has been great fun, and the lecturers are really friendly."

General Undergraduate Courses

BA (Hons) Business Studies

A modular programme offering a wide range of option choices, a short period of work experience with core modules in Business Environment, Business Organisation and Business Finance, with Business Policy and a project in the third year.

Modular Course?	Yes
Qualifications:	BA
Application Deadline:	UCAS deadline
Commencement Date:	September
Entry Requirement:	C and D at A level; GNVQ Advanced
Applications to Places:	
Registered:	350
Awards:	

	Duration	EC Fees	Non-EC Fees
Full time	3 years	£1000	£5500 or £6200
Part time	4.5 years	£1000	£5500 or £6200
Sandwich			

BA (Hons) Business Administration

A one year top up programme designed specifically for HND Business award holders.

Modular Course?	No
Qualifications:	BA Hons
Application Deadline:	UCAS deadline
Commencement Date:	September
Entry Requirement:	HND in Business Studies - credit profile
Applications to Places:	
Registered:	40
Awards:	n/a

	Duration	EC Fees	Non-EC Fees
Full time	1 year	£1000	£5500 or £6200
Part time			
Sandwich			

Modular degree

Modular Course?	Yes
Qualifications:	BA Hons; BSc Hons; Joint Honours; HNC; HND
Categories:	Human Resources; Finance; Marketing

Modular degree

Modular Course?	Yes
Qualifications:	BA Hons; BSc Hons
Categories:	International Business; Production; Leisure

The Business School

Bournemouth University Business School

Address:	Talbot Campus
	Fernbarrow
	Poole
	BH12 5BB
Area:	South West England
Phone:	01202 524 111
Fax:	01202 595 151
Email:	**business@bournemouth.ac.uk**
Website:	**www.bournemouth.ac.uk**

Email Application Available?	No
How to apply by email:	
Total Number of Teaching Staff:	90
Staff Teaching Undergraduate Courses	
Research Rating:	2
Teaching Rating:	Satisfactory
Additional Rating Information	
Male:Female Student Ratio	50:50
Head of Business School	Professor David Jones
Head of Undergraduate Studies	Ms Chris Shiel
Admissions Contact	Susan Egan

About the School:

The School provides a broad range of undergraduate programmes and services which are well-founded in terms of vocational significance, quality and student appeal. The School has an academic staff of around 50 and they are able to call on specialised resources throughout the University, as well as a register of associates.

About Undergraduate Studies:

All courses aim to develop the practical skills and personal qualities which employers value. Areas of particular strength include problem solving, decision making, enterprise, communication, teamwork, computer literacy and basic business awareness. The courses are based at the main campus which has comprehensive library and computer facilities. All students have the opportunity to learn a language and the University has links with partner institutions in several European countries.

Facilities:

Bournemouth itself is a lively and active place. The Fire Station, the Student Union bar, offers a fantastic social facility for students with a night club, bar and bistro all in one building. There are many clubs and societies founded by the Union covering a wide range of interests.

BA (Hons) Business Studies

This programme is available in two different formats: 4-year sandwich and 5-year part-time. This well-established course gives students the opportunity to specialise while acquiring a general business degree. The first year introduces students to core business activities, while the second year develops students ability to manage a range of activities. The sandwich programme features a year's work placement, while the final year encourages integrative and strategic thinking.

Students who wish to pursue their language skills may select optional routes eventually leading to the award BA (Hons) Business Studies with French/German/Languages.

Modular Course?	No
Qualifications:	BA Hons
Application Deadline:	June then through clearing
Commencement Date:	
Entry Requirement:	As standard for degree courses (see University prospectus). Suitable candidates with relevant experience will be invited for an interview.
Applications to Places:	11:1
Registered:	393
Awards:	

	Duration	EC Fees	Non-EC Fees
Full time	1 year	On request	On request
Part time	5 years	On request	On request
Sandwich	4 years	On request	On request

BSc (Hons) Business Information Systems Management

This course aims to provide an opportunity for students to acquire understanding and skills in both business management and computer-based information systems. Technical and management aspects of information systems are covered to enable graduates to contribute effectively to the development and management of the essential IT resources which affect the way individuals work and companies do business, grow and compete.

Modular Course?	No
Qualifications:	BSc Hons
Application Deadline:	June then through clearing
Commencement Date:	
Entry Requirement:	As standard for degree courses (see University prospectus).
Applications to Places:	11:1
Registered:	315
Awards:	

	Duration	EC Fees	Non-EC Fees
Full time	4 years	On request	On request
Part time			
Sandwich			

BSc (Hons) Business Decision Information Systems

A contemporary degree designed to equip the new generation of managers with the skills to succeed in the rapidly changing world of business and technology. The course enables students to formulate and implement effective solutions to business problems and specific career fields include management consultancy, business analyst, information systems, strategic operations planning and management business logistics and operations management.

Modular Course?	No
Qualifications:	BSc Hons
Application Deadline:	June then through clearing
Commencement Date:	September
Entry Requirement:	As standard for degree courses, with 12 points at A level.
Applications to Places:	
Registered:	
Awards:	

	Duration	EC Fees	Non-EC Fees
Sandwich	4 years		

BSc (Hons) Business Information Systems

This course enables students who have achieved a high standard in an HND Business Studies, Business Information Technology or similar, and have acquired an interest and ability in Information Technology (IT), to continue their studies to Honours Degree level.

The course emphasises the development of business information systems using contemporary network and data management technologies. Course content and teaching/learning methods are directed towards a practical application of theory in conjunction with consideration of strategic and organisational issues facing companies that wish to exploit IT.

Modular Course?	No
Qualifications:	BSc Hons
Application Deadline:	July
Commencement Date:	September
Entry Requirement:	Post HND students with three distinctions on final year greades
Applications to Places:	
Registered:	25
Awards:	

	Duration	EC Fees	Non-EC Fees
Full time	1 year	On request	On request

BA (Hons) International Business Administration

This course leads to an international recognised degree with a high profile. Adaptable and resourceful business men and women are developed who have the versatility and personal qualities to manage a range of business activities. Previous career destinations have been in a wide variety of specialist areas, which have included opportunities in tourism, publishing, banking, retail, information systems and the public.

Modular Course?	No
Qualifications:	BA Hons
Application Deadline:	July
Commencement Date:	September
Entry Requirement:	Post HND students with three distinctions on final year grades
Applications to Places:	
Registered:	25
Awards:	

	Duration	EC Fees	Non-EC Fees
Full time	1 year	On request	On request

Bradford Management Centre

Bradford Management Centre

Address:	Emm Lane
	Bradford
	BD9 4JL
Area:	North East England
Phone:	01274 234393
Fax:	01274 546866
Email:	**ubmc@bradford.ac.uk**
Website:	**www.brad.ac.uk/acad/mancen/**
Email Application Available?	No
How to apply by email:	
Total Number of Teaching Staff:	110
Staff Teaching Undergraduate Courses	70
Research Rating:	4
Teaching Rating:	Satisfactory
Additional Rating Information	
Male:Female Student Ratio	52:48
Head of Business School	Professor Arthur Francis
Head of Undergraduate Studies	Dr Bryan Lowes
Admissions Contact	Dr Tom Wesley

About the School:

Bradford Management Centre, established in 1963, is one of Europe's largest and longest-established business schools. It provides comprehensive and innovative programmes of management education at the undergraduate, postgraduate, doctoral and executive levels. Research is given a high priority to ensure that the Centre's teaching is based on the best possible understanding of the organisations and systems our students will have to face. The Centre is self-contained for learning, with modern fully-equipped lecture theatres and seminar/tutorial rooms, management library, bookshop, computer facilities, language unit, career service, restaurant/bar facilities and accommodation.

About Undergraduate Studies:

The Management Centre's undergraduate courses offer over 80 taught modules spanning a wide range of management subjects from which students study 36 over 3 years. This offers students a wide choice of subjects and they can use this choice to tailor their studies to their developing interests and management career plans.

Facilities:

The Management Centre is attractively located in thirteen acres of parkland on the north-west side of Bradford, about three miles from the city centre and the main University campus. Postgraduate students have access to the full range of social and sports facilities at the Centre and on the main campus. Attractions include the Theatre on the Mill, a flexible studio theatre, the Tasmin Little Music Centre, a modern fully-equipped Sports Centre and a Nautilus health and fitness suite. Bradford offers all the social and cultural amenities expected of a thriving city; high on its list of attractions is the National Museum of Photography, Film and Television and the Hockney Gallery at Saltaire.

Departments/Faculties:

Bradford Management Centre is a large department within the Faculty of Social Sciences and Humanities of the University of Bradford.

Links with Academic Institutions:

The Management Centre has a strong international reputation through its world-wide links and partnerships with academic institutions for teaching and research. Management programmes are delivered through institutions in India, Malaysia, Singapore, Dubai and Israel. Students participate in joint programmes with leading schools in the Netherlands, France, Spain, Germany, Austria, Denmark and North America.

Links with Industry:

Links with local, national and international companies contribute to the relevance and practicality of our programmes. Directors and senior managers from leading companies make regular contributions, companies provide 'real' projects for MBA students and Bradford has an excellent record in placing graduates in challenging and rewarding management positions.

Student Testimonials:

Clare Lowther took A levels in History, French and English Literature at school in Newcastle. ' I knew from the outset I wanted a business studies course, and with opening up of the European Union, I thought the combination with a language I enjoyed would be useful. I saw the Bradford video, came and had a look around the campus and the city, and decided that this was where I wanted to be. The Management centre had a good reputation too; both in the UK and Europe. I am very pleased I chose to come here and do this course. Gareth Jones took A levels in Economics, French, Spanish and General Studies at school in Birmingham. 'I chose the Bradford course for several reasons. The Management Centre had a good reputation, and I liked the fact that there was two-thirds business and one-third language, rather than half-and-half as at many places. The language is all practical too, no literature or theory. I've enjoyed the course, especially the taught aspects and the tutorials. There's a good friendly atmosphere.

BSc Business and Management Studies

The course is modular and based on semesters, with six courses completed each semester. First year courses provide foundation modules in Accounting and Finance, Business Economics, Business Law, Organisational Behaviour, Information Management, a Language (French, German, Spanish or Japanese), Marketing and Production/Operations Management. In the second and final years, students design an individual programme of study by selecting a total of 24 modules from a list of over 50. These modules include functional subjects such as Accounting and Finance, Marketing, Information Management, Human Resource Management and Production/Operations Management. In addition there are international modules such as International Business, International Finance and International Marketing plus modules integrating knowledge from different areas such as Strategic Management and International Tourism Management. Students can add an international dimension to their course of studies by spending one semester or the whole of their second year in Australia, Canada, USA or Europe on a credit transfer basis. Those students on the four year programme spend their third year in a work placement which also provides an opportunity to acquire a diploma in professional training.

Modular Course?	Yes
Qualifications:	BSc
Application Deadline:	UCAS deadline
Commencement Date:	September
Entry Requirement:	All candidates must satisfy the general entry requirement for the University. Students must hold a GCSE grade C or above (or equivalent) in Mathematics. The normal offer to applicants taking three A levels is 20 points with no requirements for any particular subjects (General Studies is acceptable). Alternative qualifications equivalent to A level will be willingly considered.
Applications to Places:	7:1
Registered:	130
Awards:	147

	Duration	EC Fees	Non-EC Fees
Full time	3 years	£1000	£6296
Part time			
Sandwich	4 years	£1000	£6296

BA International Management and French/German/Spanish

These courses provide an understanding of the disciplines or business together with a high standard of oral and written fluency in languages (French, German or Spanish). Students spend their first, second and final years at the Management Centre, while the third year is spent studying or working in a French, German or Spanish speaking environment.

The courses are modular and semester based, with six courses completed each semester including the language courses. First year courses provide foundation modules in Accounting and Finance, Business Economics, Business Law, Organisational Behaviour, Information Management, Marketing, Production/Operations Management in addition to one's chosen language. In the second and final years, students design an individual programme of study for their business/management component by selecting from a wide range of modules, whilst continuing their core language studies. During their second year, students can add a wider international dimension by opting to spend a semester or the whole of the academic year in Australia, Canada, USA or Europe on a credit transfer basis. Throughout their studies, students are encouraged to develop their interpersonal, presentation and teamwork skills to enhance their own personal effectiveness.

Modular Course?	Yes
Qualifications:	BA
Application Deadline:	UCAS deadline
Commencement Date:	September
Entry Requirement:	All candidates must satisfy the general entry requirement for the University. Students must hold a GCSE Grade C or above (or equivalent) in Mathematics and an A level in French, German or Spanish at Grade C or equivalent. The normal offer to applicants taking three A levels is 20 points (General Studies is acceptable). Alternative qualifications equivalent to A level will be
Applications to Places:	7:1
Registered:	40
Awards:	37

	Duration	EC Fees	Non-EC Fees
Full time	4 years	£1000	£6296
Part time			
Sandwich			

Bradford Business School

Bradford Business School

Address:	Great Horton Road
	Bradford, West Yorks
	BD7 1AY
Area:	North West England
Phone:	01274 753274
Fax:	01274 741060

Email:

Website:

Email Application Available?	No
How to apply by email:	
Total Number of Teaching Staff:	136
Staff Teaching Undergraduate Courses:	80
Research Rating:	n/a
Teaching Rating:	Satisfactory
Additional Rating Information	
Male:Female Student Ratio	
Head of Business School	Maurice Aske
Head of Undergraduate Studies	
Admissions Contact	Michael Ainsworth

About the School:

Bradford Business School is part of the School of Business and Professional Studies which is the largest provider of commercial training in the area with 6000 students and 136 full time lecturing staff. The Higher Education portfolio encompasses 2 Masters programmes, 12 degree programmes and HNDs, as well as a Certificate in Management and a Diploma in Management Studies.

Facilities:

The Business School is located in the centre of Bradford, close to the commercial and cultural heart of the city. It has good working relationships with an extensive network of employers who send students on courses and provide a wide range of placement experiences for undergraduates. The Business School is located next to Bradford University's main campus and shares much of its social and cultural activities.

General Undergraduate Courses

BA (Hons) Organisation Studies

This social science-based course offers a unique blend of theoretical and practical studies for a wide range of professional and managerial careers in the public and private sectors. Students can follow the degree pathway or pursue a specialism in the areas of Human Resources Management, Equal Opportunities, Public Sector Management, or Race and Ethnicity. All students complete an 8-week professional placement in semester 4 in an organisation of their choice.

Modular Course?	Yes
Qualifications:	BA
Application Deadline:	On request
Commencement Date:	
Entry Requirement:	On request
Applications to Places:	
Registered:	92
Awards:	

	Duration	EC Fees	Non-EC Fees
Full time	3 years	On request	On request
Part time			
Sandwich			

BA (Hons) Business Administration

This degree offers strands in Accounting, European Studies, Law and Marketing. The aim of the programme is to produce graduates with all-round business enterprise and problem-solving skills. Through counselling and guidance, students are given the opportunity to develop specialist skills in selected business functions.

Modular Course?	Yes
Qualifications:	BA
Application Deadline:	On request
Commencement Date:	
Entry Requirement:	On request
Applications to Places:	
Registered:	187
Awards:	

	Duration	EC Fees	Non-EC Fees
Full time	3 years	On request	On request
Part time			
Sandwich			

BA (Hons) Law and European Business

The degree is an integrated programme that combines a knowledge of business law with a broad understanding of European business. The degree lays a solid foundation on which to build a professional or managerial career based on personal, legal and business skills. Graduates would be equipped for careers in European marketing, imports and exports, legal administration, European sales management, consumer affairs, and general careers in law and business.

Modular Course?	Yes
Qualifications:	BA
Application Deadline:	On request
Commencement Date:	
Entry Requirement:	On request
Applications to Places:	
Registered:	90
Awards:	

	Duration	EC Fees	Non-EC Fees
Full time	3 years	On request	On request
Part time			
Sandwich			

BA (Hons) Psychology and Management

Focuses on the application of psychological theories and techniques in the practice of management. Modules include interpersonal relations in organisations, experimental psychology, and students can also choose electives from a wide range of psychology modules within the CAT Scheme.

Modular Course?	Yes
Qualifications:	BA
Application Deadline:	On request
Commencement Date:	
Entry Requirement:	On request
Applications to Places:	
Registered:	24
Awards:	

	Duration	EC Fees	Non-EC Fees
Full time	3 years	On request	On request
Part time			
Sandwich			

BA (Hons) Human Resource Management

This programme is aimed at people who wish to develop their people management skills and understand the external processes that influence HRM theory.

Modular Course?	Yes
Qualifications:	BA

Application Deadline:	On request
Commencement Date:	
Entry Requirement:	On request
Applications to Places:	
Registered:	20
Awards:	

	Duration	EC Fees	Non-EC Fees
Full time	3 years	On request	On request
Part time			
Sandwich			

BA (Hons) Public Sector Management

A social science based degree course that offers a blend of theoretical and practical studies for a wide range of managerial careers in the public sector. An eight week placement in a public sector organisation is included in semester 4.

Modular Course?	Yes
Qualifications:	BA
Application Deadline:	On request
Commencement Date:	
Entry Requirement:	On request
Applications to Places:	
Registered:	10
Awards:	

	Duration	EC Fees	Non-EC Fees
Full time	3 years	On request	On request
Part time			
Sandwich			

BA (Hons) Management and Organisations

A general grounding in management, coupled with the opportunity to follow specialist pathways: HRM, Travel and Tourism Management, Information Resource Management, Managing Diversity, Public Sector Management.

Modular Course?	Yes
Qualifications:	BA
Application Deadline:	On request
Commencement Date:	
Entry Requirement:	On request
Applications to Places:	
Registered:	90
Awards:	

	Duration	EC Fees	Non-EC Fees
Full time	3 years	On request	On request
Part time			
Sandwich			

LLB

The course is recognised as a qualifying degree by the Law Society. It covers all seven of the Law Society's required subjects but also has an emphasis on business law.

Modular Course?	Yes
Qualifications:	LLB
Application Deadline:	On request
Commencement Date:	
Entry Requirement:	On request
Applications to Places:	
Registered:	100

	Duration	EC Fees	Non-EC Fees
Full time	3 years	On request	On request
Part time			
Sandwich			

BA (Hons) Accountancy and Law

The course combines the study of accountancy and law and explores the links between these professional areas. Exemptions from accounting bodies are being sought.

Modular Course?	Yes
Qualifications:	BA
Application Deadline:	On request
Commencement Date:	
Entry Requirement:	On request
Applications to Places:	
Registered:	20

	Duration	EC Fees	Non-EC Fees
Full time	3 years	On request	On request
Part time			
Sandwich			

BA (Hons) Marketing and Law

The course gives a strong foundation in marketing and law with a stress on the needs of marketeers.

Modular Course?	Yes
Qualifications:	BA
Application Deadline:	On request
Commencement Date:	
Entry Requirement:	On request
Applications to Places:	
Registered:	20
Awards:	

	Duration	EC Fees	Non-EC Fees
Full time	3 years	On request	On request
Part time			
Sandwich			

BA (Hons) Financial Services

The course covers the institutions involved in finance – banks, building societies, insurance companies and new players such as Marks and Spencer. It looks at the scope of financial services, the markets and the regulation of the industry.

Modular Course?	Yes
Qualifications:	BA
Application Deadline:	On request
Commencement Date:	
Entry Requirement:	On request
Applications to Places:	
Registered:	36
Awards:	

	Duration	EC Fees	Non-EC Fees
Full time	3 years	On request	On request
Part time			
Sandwich			

BA (Hons) Office Systems Management

The degree provides a marketable combination of personal skills, a knowledge of computing systems, financial control, behavioural science, quantitative methods and business awareness.

Modular Course?	Yes
Qualifications:	BA
Application Deadline:	On request
Commencement Date:	
Entry Requirement:	On request
Applications to Places:	
Registered:	18
Awards:	

	Duration	EC Fees	Non-EC Fees
Full time	3 years	On request	On request
Part time			
Sandwich			

HND Business and Finance

This course is designed to develop the skills essential to being an effective manager, equipping the students for a successful career in commerce, manufacturing and the service industries. A choice of options allows students to specialise in the following areas; Marketing, Financial and Systems Management and Business Management.

Modular Course?	No
Qualifications:	HND
Application Deadline:	On request
Commencement Date:	
Entry Requirement:	On request
Applications to Places:	
Registered:	30
Awards:	

	Duration	EC Fees	Non-EC Fees
Full time	2 years	On request	On request
Part time			
Sandwich			

HND Travel and Tourism Management

This course is a practical preparation for management in travel, tourism, or related industries such as hotels, catering or internal transportation. The course is run in conjunction with HND programmes in Leisure and Hotel and Catering Management and there are opportunities to draw on the experience of staff from all three courses. Option modules can be taken across the programme, including: Transportation Operations; Human Resource Management; Conference and Exhibitions; Hospitality, Arts and Entertainment.

Modular Course?	No
Qualifications:	HND
Application Deadline:	On request
Commencement Date:	
Entry Requirement:	On request
Applications to Places:	
Registered:	40
Awards:	

	Duration	EC Fees	Non-EC Fees
Full time	2 years	On request	On request
Part time			
Sandwich			

HND Leisure Studies

This course covers the theoretical and practical aspects of supervisory management in leisure across three vocational streams: Sport and Physical Recreation, Arts and Entertainment or Countryside Recreation. The course includes two periods of work experience that provide first hand practical experience of working in the leisure industry. The course allows progression to the School's own honours degrees in Business Administration and Organisation Studies.

Modular Course?	No
Qualifications:	HND
Application Deadline:	On request
Commencement Date:	
Entry Requirement:	On request
Applications to Places:	
Registered:	40
Awards:	

	Duration	EC Fees	Non-EC Fees
Full time	2 years	On request	On request
Part time			
Sandwich			

HND Hotel, Catering and Institutional Management

This course is a practical preparation for management in hospitality, catering and leisure. It covers the theoretical and practical aspects of supervisory management and includes a 26-week period of work experience that provides first hand practical experience of working in the industry. The course allows progression to the School's own honours degrees in Business Administration and Organisation Studies and should lead to employment in a range of first-line management positions including hotel and accommodation services and restaurant and catering management.

Modular Course?	No
Qualifications:	HND
Application Deadline:	On request
Commencement Date:	
Entry Requirement:	On request
Applications to Places:	
Registered:	24
Awards:	

	Duration	EC Fees	Non-EC Fees
Full time	2 years	On request	On request
Part time			
Sandwich			

HND Business Information Techology

The course is designed for those who wish to work at a senior level as computing practitioners. The course focuses on the latest developments in Information Technology and develops the knowledge and skills needed for a wide range of computing and business careers.

Modular Course?	No
Qualifications:	HND
Application Deadline:	On request
Commencement Date:	
Entry Requirement:	On request
Applications to Places:	
Registered:	16
Awards:	

	Duration	EC Fees	Non-EC Fees
Full time	2 years	On request	On request
Part time			
Sandwich			

HND Business and Marketing

The course covers the broad range of business activities but also gives opportunities to specialise in marketing.

Modular Course?	No
Qualifications:	HND
Application Deadline:	On request
Commencement Date:	

Entry Requirement:		On request
Applications to Places:		
Registered:		30
Awards:		

	Duration	EC Fees	Non-EC Fees
Full time	2 years	On request	On request
Part time			
Sandwich			

HND Business and Personnel

The course covers the broad range of business activities but also gives opportunities to specialise in personnel.

Modular Course?		No
Qualifications:		HND
Application Deadline:		On request
Commencement Date:		
Entry Requirement:		On request
Applications to Places:		
Registered:		25
Awards:		

	Duration	EC Fees	Non-EC Fees
Full time	2 years	On request	On request
Part time			
Sandwich			

Faculty of Business

University of Brighton
Faculty of Business

Address:	Mithras House
	Lewes Road
	Brighton
	BN2 4AT
Area:	London and South East England
Phone:	01273 600 900
Fax:	01273 642 160
Email:	**admissions@bton.ac.uk**
Website:	**www.bus.bton.ac.uk**
Email Application Available?	No
How to apply by email:	
Academic staff:	100
Non academic staff:	50
Research Rating:	3a
Teaching Rating:	Satisfactory - Business
Dean of Faculty:	Professor Jon Bareham
Head of Undergraduate Programmes:	
Business & Finance:	Dr Robert Griffith Jones
Service Management:	Dr Paul Frost
Contact for admissions:	
Business & Finance:	Mr Steve Hogan
Service Management:	Mr Chris Dutton
Full Time Equivalents:	2213
Undergraduates:	1804
Ratio of females and males - undergraduate	53:47
Ratio of applicants to places:	5:1 to 26:1

About the Faculty:

The faculty has offered business and management education for over 30 years. The international orientation of our courses provides students with the opportunity to work in a multi-cultural environment. Two of our courses have won prestigious national prizes - the Partnership Awards - sponsored by industry, in recognition of our innovative teaching methods. A new centre of excellence - funded by ESRC - has been set up to further support our research and consultancy in innovation management.

As one of the closest universities to mainland Europe, we have active links throughout the EU. Gatwick Airport is 30 minutes by road, London one hour by road and northern France two hours by high-speed ferry. The lecturing staff at the university have extensive industrial and commercial experience which is regularly updated through applied research and consultancy.

Brighton's heritage as a fashionable 19th century resort lives on. The town is known for its artistic and cultural life, stately seafront terraces and piers. The university provides a wide variety of accommodation, careers advice and language support. A new library with modern study facilities was opened on the main site of the faculty in 1996.

General Undergraduate Courses

Food Retail Management, BA(Hons)

Food retailing in the UK is recognised as being at the leading edge of industry development world-wide. This course is relevant not only to the major supermarket chains, but also to multiple retailing, delicatessens and other specialist outlets. Managers are needed with enterprise, people skills and industry knowledge. This course will develop these skills, and graduates typically join large multinational firms' management training programmes.

Registered: 31

	Duration	EC Fees	Non-EC Fees
Full-time	3 years		
Sandwich	4 years		

Hospitality Management, BA(Hons)

Please see also BA(Hons) International Hospitality Management. These courses develop knowledge in the hotel and food-service sectors - Hospitality. One of the most rapidly growing industries throughout the world - managers with interpersonal skills, technical knowledge and commitment are in great demand. Industrial Placements are based throughout the UK and abroad, and International Hospitality students must spent at least half of their placement outside of their native country.

Registered: 122

	Duration	EC Fees	Non-EC Fees
Full-time	3 years		
Sandwich	4 years		

International Hospitality Management, BA(Hons)

Please see also BA(Hons) Hospitality Management. These courses develop knowledge in the hotel and food-service sectors - Hospitality. One of the most rapidly growing industries throughout the world - managers with interpersonal skills, technical knowledge and commitment are in great demand. Industrial Placements are based throughout the UK and abroad, and International Hospitality students must spent at least half of their placement outside of their native country.

Registered: 52

	Duration	EC Fees	Non-EC Fees
Full-time	3 years		
Sandwich	4 years		

International Tourism Management, BA(Hons)

Please see also BA(Hons) Tourism Management. The tourism courses focus on the management of tourism in terms of visitor attractions, heritage and cultural aspects, and destinations. Managers in this field are needed with technical knowledge, business acumen and entrepreneurial skills. The Industrial Placements (compulsory for International Tourism students) are usually spent with tourism operators in the UK and beyond.

Registered: 85

	Duration	EC Fees	Non-EC Fees
Full-time	3 years		
Sandwich	4 years		

Tourism Management BA(Hons)

Please see also BA(Hons) International Tourism Management. The tourism courses focus on the management of tourism in terms of visitor attractions, heritage and cultural aspects, and destinations. Managers in this field are needed with technical knowledge, business acumen and entrepreneurial skills. The Industrial Placements (optional for Tourism students) are usually spent with tourism operators in the UK and beyond.

Registered: 311

	Duration	EC Fees	Non-EC Fees
Full-time	3 years		
Sandwich	4 years		

Travel Management, BA(Hons)

The travel industry comprises or airlines, cruise (and ferry) operators and railways. This course shares teaching with the tourism courses, and also looks at the travel agency, financial services and travel consultancy industries. There is a wide range of careers available to graduates of this course throughout the industry in management support and customer service roles.

Registered: 92

	Duration	EC Fees	Non-EC Fees
Full-time	3 years		
Sandwich	4 years		

BA (Hons) Accounting and Finance

Provides a sound academic base for issues that arise in the professional accountancy world. The course gained a "Partnership Award" for "Innovation in Teaching and Learning in Higher Education". Students can pursue their individual interests through a choice of specialist options in both the second and final years.

Modular Course?	Yes
Qualifications:	BA Hons
Application Deadline:	UCAS
Commencement Date:	27 September 1999
Entry Requirement:	On request
Applications to Places:	5:1 to 26:1
Registered:	205
Awards:	

	Duration	EC Fees	Non-EC Fees
Full time	3 years	£1000	£6600
Sandwich	4 years	£1000	£6600

HND Business and Finance/ Marketing/Personnel

These three courses provide an opportunity to combine an academic foundation in a wide range of administrative and management careers, with the opportunity to specialise in certain career paths. They offer the intellectual challenge and opportunity to progress studies, the chance to learn practical business skills, and an optional foreign language. All students cover Market Relations, Operating Environment, Managing Finance & Information, Managing People &. Activities, Organisational Structures & Processes, and finally planning & Decision Making.

Modular Course?	Yes
Qualifications:	HND
Application Deadline:	UCAS
Commencement Date:	27 September 1999
Entry Requirement:	On request
Registered:	81
Awards:	

	Duration	EC Fees	Non-EC Fees
Full time	2 years	£1000	£6600

BA (Hons) Business Administration (Overseas only); BA (Hons) Business Administration (Post HND); BA (Hons) Business Administration with Law; BA (Hons) Business Administration with Marketing

These courses are the HND graduate and overseas student equivalents to a full-time Business Studies degree. The overseas option can be completed inside of three years, and HND graduates within eighteen months. As with BA (Hons) Business Studies graduates, students may carry exemption from various professional bodies including the Chartered Institute of Marketing and the Institute of Chartered Accountants.

Modular Course?	Yes
Qualifications:	BA Hons
Application Deadline:	UCAS
Commencement Date:	27 September 1999
Entry Requirement:	On request
Applications to Places:	5:1 to 26:1
Registered:	133
Awards:	

	Duration	EC Fees	Non-EC Fees
Full time	1.5 to 3 years	£1000	£6600
Part time			
Sandwich			

BA (Hons) Business Studies; BA (Hons) Business Studies with Law; BA (Hons) Business Studies with Marketing

These courses provide a detailed insight into the overall business environment, whilst giving the chance to specialise in one of the many functional areas of business. It develops creative and analytical thinking, awareness of international and environmental factors alongside a host of academic skills. Students are also supported in their third-year choice of Industrial Placement opportunities, and can opt to study for a university "Diploma in Languages".

Modular Course?	Yes
Qualifications:	BA Hons
Application Deadline:	UCAS
Commencement Date:	27 September 1999
Entry Requirement:	On request
Applications to Places:	5:1 to 26:1
Registered:	487
Awards:	

	Duration	EC Fees	Non-EC Fees
Part time	5 years	£1000	£6600
Sandwich	4 years	£1000	£6600

BA (Hons) International Business

This course combines Business Studies with foreign languages and a year abroad. The third year is often spent in an affiliated business school in France, Germany, Greece, Italy, the Netherlands or Sweden. This study or an overseas Industrial Placement will provide a good insight into other business cultures and enough language proficiency to enable a career in foreign countries. The final year allows specialisation, and the chance to apply previous expericene from the first three years.

Modular Course?	Yes
Qualifications:	BA Hons
Application Deadline:	UCAS
Commencement Date:	27 September 1999
Entry Requirement:	On request
Applications to Places:	5:1 to 26:1
Registered:	122
Awards:	

	Duration	EC Fees	Non-EC Fees
Sandwich	4 years	£1000	£6600

Specialist Undergraduate Course

Accountancy, Foundation

This course develops an understanding of the subjects that are fundamental to accountancy. It provides an educational foundation for careers in professional employment or further studies. Assessment is a combination of examinations and continuously assessed coursework. The course is recognised by the major professional bodies, and successful completion may allow entry to Certificate or Professional programmes, or exemptions.

Modular Course?	Yes
Qualifications:	
Application Deadline:	UCAS
Commencement Date:	27 September 1999
Entry Requirement:	On request
Applications to Places:	5:1 to 26:1
Registered:	8
Awards:	

	Duration	EC Fees	Non-EC Fees
Full time	1 year	£1000	£6600

BA (Hons) Accountancy with Law

Please also see the BA(Hons) Law and Accountancy course. Both degrees provide the opportunity to study two disciplines that increasingly interact in such areas as; corporate sales and acquisitions, taxation, employment and insolvency. The completion of all law modules gains exemption from the Council of Legal Education's Common Professional Examination.

Modular Course?	Yes
Qualifications:	BA Hons
Application Deadline:	UCAS
Commencement Date:	27 September
Entry Requirement:	On request
Applications to Places:	5:1 to 26:1
Registered:	61
Awards:	

	Duration	EC Fees	Non-EC Fees
Full time	3 years	£1000	£6600
Sandwich	4 years	£1000	£6600

Association of Chartered Certified Accountants (ACCA)

The course is taught in three one-year phases; Foundation, Certificate and Professional. Upon completion of the three phases students need only sit four of the fourteen ACCA papers to gain ACA status, in addition to a formal academic qualification. Excellent career opportunities exist public practice, industry, commerce, banking government and education.

Modular Course?	Yes
Qualifications:	BA Hons; ACCA
Application Deadline:	UCAS
Commencement Date:	27 September 1999
Entry Requirement:	On request
Applications to Places:	5:1 to 26:1
Registered:	73
Awards:	

	Duration	EC Fees	Non-EC Fees
Full time	1-3 years	£1000	£6600

BA (Hons) International Finance and Capital Markets

This degree is directly relevant to careers in stockbroking, portfolio management, corporate finance and corporate treasury management. It is appropriate for researching and trading in bonds, currency, futures, options and swaps. Also highly recommended the course for those interested in becoming management consultants or financial market regulators. The optional one-year Industrial Placement may be undertaken in financial institutions in the UK or overseas.

Modular Course?	Yes

Qualifications:	BA Hons
Application Deadline:	UCAS
Commencement Date:	27 September 1999
Entry Requirement:	On request
Applications to Places:	5:1 to 26:1
Registered:	New
Awards:	

	Duration	EC Fees	Non-EC Fees
Full time	3 years	£1000	£6600
Sandwich	4 years	£1000	£6600

BA (Hons) Law and Accountancy

Please also see the BA(Hons) Accountancy with Law course. Both degrees provide the opportunity to study two disciplines that increasingly interact in such areas as; corporate sales and acquisitions, taxation, employment and insolvency. The completion of all law modules gains exemption from the Council of Legal Education's Common Professional Examination.

Modular Course?	Yes
Qualifications:	BA Hons
Application Deadline:	UCAS
Commencement Date:	27 September 1999
Entry Requirement:	On request
Applications to Places:	5:1 to 26:1
Registered:	New
Awards:	

	Duration	EC Fees	Non-EC Fees
Full time	3 years	£1000	£6600
Sandwich	4 years	£1000	£6600

Bristol Business School

Bristol Business School

Address:	Bristol Business School
	University of the West of England
	Frenchay Campus
	Coldharbour Lane
	Bristol
	BS16 1QY
Area:	South West England
Phone:	0117 976 3848
Fax:	0117 976 2718
Email:	**Business@uwe.ac.uk**
Website:	**http://www.uwe.ac.uk**
Email Application Available?	No
How to apply by email:	Please email your name and address, course title or subject area/level at which you wish to study to: Business@uwe.ac.uk and our Admissions Office will send you more information and an application form.
Total Number of Teaching Staff:	143
Staff Teaching Undergraduate Courses	100
Research Rating:	2
	AMBA accredited MBA
Teaching Rating:	Excellent
Additional Rating Information	
Male:Female Student Ratio	50:50
Head of Business School	Professor Mike Rees BSc (Eng) MSc ACGI Ceng MIEE FIMgt FRSA
Head of Undergraduate Studies	Peter Milford BSc (Hons) ACA
Admissions Contact	Sharon Bohin

About the School:

Bristol Business School is one of the largest faculties of the University of the West of England. The school was established in 1987 and is now the major provider of business and management education in the west of England and one of the country's leading business schools with more than 3000 students, around half of whom are part-time, and 150 academic staff. It offers an extensive portfolio of flexible programmes at undergraduate, postgraduate and professional levels, providing for a wide cross-section of organisations and employers, from junior managers to directors. The School also offers a major source of expertise in management education, training and development. Bristol Business School has a twin-track commitment to high quality and wider access. The quality of education in business and management studies has been rated excellent by HEFCE and the School has built successful partnerships with local colleges and employers in the area. It has also established an extensive network of relationships with business schools in Europe and North America to sustain its international exchange programmes.

About Undergraduate Studies:

Bristol Business School's degree and HND programmes combine high quality, focused and relevant awards with a wide range of choice. There is a strong international dimension and use of information technology throughout the programme. Named degrees are BA (Hons) Business Studies/Business Administration, BA (Hons) International Business Studies, BA (Hons) Marketing, BA (Hons) Finance, BA (Hons) Accounting and Finance, BA (Hons) Business/Business Administration/International Business Studies with Tourism. HND Business Administration and HND Business Studies (Marketing) complete the undergraduate portfolio.

Departments/Faculties:

Six subject based schools within Bristol Business School offer expertise in Accounting and Finance, Human Resource Management, Marketing, Operations Management, Organisational Behaviour and Strategic Management.

Links with Academic Institutions:

Bristol Business School has international links with business schools, particularly strong in Europe and North America. Our MBA European route is offered in partnership with The Graduate School of Business, University of Nancy 2, France; and George-Simon-Ohm Fachhochschule, Nürnberg, Germany.

Links with Industry:

Bristol Business School's partnership programmes link in-house training and development to formal management qualifications. Consultancy services and management development can help to improve both individual and corporate management performance. All of our services are tailor-made to meet the specific needs of each client.

Employers find they benefit from our undergraduate placement programme as much as the students do: placement students have a high level of commitment, enthusiasm and overall performance.

Programmes are supported by a range of facilities, including information technology laboratories, closed-circuit television studios with video cameras and editing facilities, an extensive library and access to language laboratories. The University has excellent student facilities which include the sports, social and cultural activities organised by the Students' Union, and is located on a purpose-built campus close to an excellent motorway and rail network with easy access to the city centre and the West Country. Excellent computing and library facilities encourage you to carry out research and develop analytical skills.

Student Testimonials:

"As a mature student it has been nice to return to studying in a friendly and supportive environment. A good choice of modules enables you to opt for those most relevant to your career." (BA (Hons) Business Administration student)

"Bristol Business School has a good reputation for offering high standard business programmes. The course was very demanding but very rewarding" (BA (Hons) Accounting and Finance student)

"The course provides excellent career grounding. Academic staff are very approachable, and provide good support throughout the degree." (BA (Hons) International Business Studies student)

General Undergraduate Courses

BA Degree Programme

Within its degree programme, the School offers a range of honours degrees. The modular structure allows students to benefit from the flexibility provided by a range of modules, together with the opportunity, in some cases, to transfer between named awards at the end of the first year of study. All students may study a language if they wish and an optional placement year is a feature of several of the full-time award routes. Within the curriculum, there is a strong focus on both the international dimension and the use of information technology. The third year of both the International Business Studies and International Business Studies with Tourism degrees is spent abroad. The development of skills is integrated within taught modules, with emphasis on critical analysis, problem solving, presentational and teamworking skills. Students with appropriate qualifications such as an HND may be admitted direct to Stage 2 or 3.

Modular Course?	No
Qualifications:	BA
Application Deadline:	UCAS deadline (for part-time apply to University)
Commencement Date:	September
Entry Requirement:	GCSE grade C in Maths and English language, plus 16 points at A Level, or BTEC National Diploma with merits and distinctions or Advanced GNVQ at Merit plus additional units or an A Level.
Applications to Places:	10:1

	Duration	EC Fees	Non-EC Fees
Registered:			
Awards:			

	Duration	EC Fees	Non-EC Fees
Full time	3-4 years	Up to £1000 pa	£6,150 pa
Part time	Up to 7 years	£126 per module	
Sandwich	4 years	Up to £1000 pa	£6,150 pa

BTEC HND Programme

The School offers full-time HND Business Administration and HND Business Studies with Marketing programmes. These programmes aim to supply the knowledge, understanding and skills necessary for a successful career in business or finance, and the content of the programme is both integrated and practical to ensure that students obtain, not just knowledge, but also skills and competencies in their chosen field. All students study core modules representing 50% of study time, and then select a number of free choice modules from a range which includes languages. A significant number of students progress onto degree programmes on completion of their HND.

Modular Course?	No
Qualifications:	HND
Application Deadline:	UCAS deadline
Commencement Date:	September
Applications to Places:	10:1
Registered:	
Awards:	

	Duration	EC Fees	Non-EC Fees
Full time	2 years	Up to £1000 pa	£6,150 pa

Buckinghamshire Business School

Buckinghamshire Business School

Address:	Newland Park
	Gorelands Lane
	Chalfont St. Giles
	HP8 4AD
Area:	London and South East England
Phone:	01494 603 192
Fax:	01494 874 230
Email:	buckscol.ac.uk
Website:	http://www.buckscol.ac.uk/business

Email Application Available?	Yes
How to apply by email:	
Total Number of Teaching Staff:	57
Staff Teaching Undergraduate Courses	36
Research Rating:	2
Teaching Rating:	Satisfactory
Additional Rating Information	
Male:Female Student Ratio	60:40
Dean of Business School	Nigel V Cox
Senior Tutor and Admissions Contact:	George Rippon

About the School:

The College was founded in 1892. The Business Faculty was formed in 1970 and became a separate Business School in 1990. It is located in an idyllic setting in beautiful countryside near the village of Chalfont St. Giles.

There are some 2500 registered students, 57 members of Faculty and 25 part-time visiting lecturers. It offers a wide range of business studies/management degrees and diplomas, at undergraduate, professional and vocational and post-graduate levels.

About Undergraduate Studies:

The undergraduate programme is modular and the Business School is a member of ECTIS. Credit points gained are interchangeable. There are six single honours degrees, a varied programme of combined honours, both joint and major/minor. A full list of major/minor and joint honours is available on our webpages.

Facilities:

The Newland Park Campus is twenty-five miles from Central London with easy access to the M25 (junction 17) and the London Underground (Chalfont and Latimer). It is set in 250 acres of countryside offering accommodation (700 study bedrooms 400 of which were new for 97/98) and leisure facilities. There is a modern Social Centre with shop, bar, catering and entertainment facilities, together with a range of sports and recreation facilities. Special weekend trips are organised for outdoor pursuits. The Students' Union organises a wide variety of clubs and societies.

Links with Academic Institutions:

More than 25 years ago the Business School foresaw the value of linking business/management studies to modern languages. This has made it pre-eminent in the fields of European and International Business Studies. Links and exchanges flourish with universities and businesses in France, Germany, Norway, Sweden, Italy, Spain, Czech Republic, Poland, Holland, Denmark, Belgium, Romania, Russia, USA, South Africa, Finland, Portugal and Mexico.

General Undergraduate Courses

BA (Hons) Business Administration

This three year full-time course provides a relevant academic foundation for careers in business and for further specialist academic or professional study. It is designed for students wishing to develop all round business skills in preparation for future management positions within industry and commerce in the UK and abroad. In Year One the core modules develop skills appropriate to the course and careers in business and enhance understanding of important elements of the business environment. In Year Two the emphasis of the core moves towards business functions, includes core modules in Marketing, Management Accounting, Human Resources Management, Logistics and Information Systems and Technology. Through credit transfer arrangements it is possible for suitable students to replace part of the Year Two study with an equivalent study period in an international partner university. In the final year the core consists of Strategic Management and a Dissertation. In addition, students specialise in one of the following areas: Marketing, Human Resources Management, Accounting and Finance, Operations Management, Computer Business Modeling. There is a wide choice of electives available throughout the course, including the study of languages, international aspects of business or other modules of relevance to career and academic interests. The final year of this course is available to suitably qualified diploma students in full-time, part-time and distance learning modes.

Modular Course?	Yes
Qualifications:	BA Hons
Application Deadline:	UCAS deadlines
Commencement Date:	September
Entry Requirement:	The minimum requirements for

admission are: a minimum
of 2 Advanced Level passes or
equivalent and at least 5
GCSE/GCE subjects, including
passes in Mathematics
and English or equivalent.
Applications are welcomed
from mature students without
formal qualifications but
with proven ability.

Applications to Places:		6:1
Registered:		425
Awards:		

	Duration	EC Fees	Non-EC Fees
Full time	3 years	£1000 pa	£5750 pa
Part time			
Sandwich			

BA (Hons) Business Studies

This four year sandwich course is identical in content and structure on the BA (Hons) Business Administration except that students undertake a placement in Year Three of the course. The placement period provides the opportunity for students to gain relevant practical experience of business activity and organisation. It aims to assist the student in integrating theory and practice in the final year of the course and to assist the development of skills relevant to a future career in the business world. The Business School has a placements office and extensive international links with academic institutions. Although it is the responsibility of the student to arrange a suitable placement, the placements office will provide active help and international contacts can be used for those students seeking an overseas placement. The course aims to provide a relevant academic foundation for a career in business and for further specialist academic or professional study. It is designed for those students wishing to develop all round business skills in preparation for future managerial positions within industry and commerce in the UK or abroad.

Modular Course?	Yes
Qualifications:	
Application Deadline:	UCAS deadlines
Commencement Date:	September
Entry Requirement:	The minimum requirements for admission are: a minimum of 2 Advanced Level passes or equivalent and at least 5 GCSE/GCE subjects, including passes in Mathematics
Applications to Places:	6:1
Registered:	192
Awards:	

	Duration	EC Fees	Non-EC Fees
Full time			
Part time			
Sandwich	4 years	£1000 pa	£5750 pa

BA (Hons) European Business Studies

This four year degree is a well established course operating within a successful network of partner institutions across Europe. It is designed for those who wish to combine the study of business disciplines with languages, to produce a qualification which is relevant to the Europe of the 21st century. Over Years One and Two the main European Language is studied in preparation for the overseas study and placement semesters in Year Three. Students should apply to the course featuring this first language. In the final year the core consists of Strategic Management and a Dissertation. In addition, students specialise in one of the following areas: Marketing, Human Resources Management, Accounting and Finance, Operations Management, Computer Business Modeling. They also study a second foreign language and choose from a comprehensive list of options. By the end of the course students will have specialised in one of the major functional areas of business, acquired fluency in one and a good working knowledge of another European language, and have benefited from study and work experience in another European country.

Modular Course?	Yes
Qualifications:	BA Hons
Application Deadline:	UCAS deadlines
Commencement Date:	September
Entry Requirement:	The minimum requirements for admission are: a minimum of 2 Advanced Level passes or equivalent and at least 5 GCSE/GCE subjects, including passes in Mathematics and English or equivalent. Qualifications in Languages appropriate to the main language you wish to study and to the level chosen. Applications are welcomed from mature students without formal qualifications but with proven ability and with interests in European business issues.
Applications to Places:	6:1
Registered:	113
Awards:	

	Duration	EC Fees	Non-EC Fees
Full time	4 years	£1000 pa	£5750 pa
Part time			
Sandwich			

BA (Hons) International Business Studies

The four year BA (Hons) in International Business Studies provides a relevant academic foundation for careers in international business and for further specialist academic or professional study. It combines the study of core and specialist business modules, modules in aspects of the international business environment, and study of a major European language (French, German, Spanish or Italian). Students should apply to the course featuring this language. In the final year, students specialise in one of the following areas: Marketing, Human Resources Management, Accounting and Finance, Operations Management, Computer Business Modeling. They may also elect to study a second language in the final year of the course. Year Three of the programme consists of a study semester in a partner institution in the United States or Europe and a work placement. Where the study semester is in Europe it will normally be in an institution where the medium of instruction on the course is English.

Modular Course?	Yes
Qualifications:	BA Hons
Application Deadline:	UCAS deadlines
Commencement Date:	September
Entry Requirement:	The minimum requirements for admission are: a minimum of 2 Advanced Level passes or equivalent and at least 5 GCSE/GCE subjects, including passes in Mathematics and English or equivalent. Qualifications in Languages appropriate to the main language you wish to study and to the level chosen. Applications are welcomed from mature students without formal qualifications but with proven ability and with interests in international business issues.
Applications to Places:	6:1
Registered:	113
Awards:	

	Duration	EC Fees	Non-EC Fees
Full time	4 years	£1000 pa	£5750 pa
Part time			
Sandwich			

BA (Hons) International Marketing

This three year degree course provides relevant a academic foundation for careers in international marketing and for further specialist academic or professional study. It is designed for those who wish to combine the study of international marketing and business with a language, to provide a qualification which will meet the needs of business in the increasingly global business environment. Over Years One and Two students take modules in relevant aspects of business and international marketing studies and in a European language (French, German, Italian or Spanish). In the final year of the course students continue to develop the international marketing focus of the course and are able to continue with a second language as an elective. Other electives are offered and all students write a dissertation on an international marketing theme. Through credit transfer it is possible for suitable students to replace part of the year two study with an equivalent study period in an international partner university.

Modular Course?	Yes
Qualifications:	BA Hons
Application Deadline:	UCAS deadlines
Commencement Date:	September
Entry Requirement:	The minimum requirements for admission are: a minimum of 2 Advanced Level passes or equivalent and at least 5 GCSE/GCE subjects, including passes in Mathematics and English or equivalent. Qualifications in Languages appropriate to the main language you wish to study and to the level chosen. Applications are welcomed from mature students without formal qualifications but with proven ability and with interests in international business issues.
Applications to Places:	6:1
Registered:	20
Awards:	

	Duration	EC Fees	Non-EC Fees
Full time	3 years	£1000 pa	£5750 pa
Part time			
Sandwich			

BA International Business and Marketing Logistics

This is a new four year course which has been developed jointly with a partner institution in Finland. Students will spend the first three years studying at Buckinghamshire Business School and the final year at Rauma, Finland, and will be awarded both the British and the Finnish degrees after successfully completing the course. The course will be taught in English throughout but students will have the opportunity to gain an understanding of Finnish in the fourth year. The first year of the course is identical in structure and content to the BA (Hons) Business Administration, and gives students the chance to transfer to the BA International Business and Marketing Logistics at the end of the first year. Year Two follows the common business core and begins to focus on marketing logistics, which will be expanded in Year Three. Studies in Finland will prove practical insights into International Marketing Logistics within the setting of the Nordic/Baltic region, as well as giving students the opportunity to experience cultural diversity and marketing.

Modular Course?	Yes
Qualifications:	BA
Application Deadline:	UCAS deadlines
Commencement Date:	September
Entry Requirement:	The minimum requirements for admission are: a minimum of 2 Advanced Level passes or equivalent and at least 5 GCSE/GCE subjects, including passes in Mathematics and English or equivalent. Applications are welcomed from mature students without formal qualifications but with proven ability.
Applications to Places:	6:1
Registered:	n/a
Awards:	

	Duration	EC Fees	Non-EC Fees
Full time	4 years	£1000 pa	£5750 pa
Part time			
Sandwich			

BA (Hons) Human Resource Management

This three year course provides an excellent foundation in business studies and the opportunity to specialise. It is also an excellent route into further academic study. The first year provides the foundation in business studies from which students can chose to specialise in years two and three. Students can pursue interests in employee relations, resourcing and development areas.

Modular Course?	Yes
Qualifications:	BA Hons
Application Deadline:	UCAS deadlines
Commencement Date:	September
Entry Requirement:	The minimum requirements for admission are: a minimum of 2 Advanced Level passes or equivalent and at least 5 GCSE/GCE subjects, including passes in Mathematics and English or equivalent. Applications are welcomed from mature students without formal qualifications but with proven ability.
Applications to Places:	6:1

Registered:	n/a
Awards:	

	Duration	EC Fees	Non-EC Fees
Full time	3 years	£1000 pa	£5750 pa
Part time			
Sandwich			

BA Small Business Management

This course prepares students for careers in small businesses or gives them the knowledge to start their own businesses. The first year is a business studies foundation and is followed by specialist study on the characteristics, opportunities and needs of small firms. In Year Three students write a dissertation on issues related to small business.

Modular Course?	No
Qualifications:	BA
Application Deadline:	UCAS deadlines
Commencement Date:	September
Entry Requirement:	The minimum requirements for admission are: a minimum of 2 Advanced Level passes or equivalent and at least 5 GCSE/GCE subjects, including passes in Mathematics and English or equivalent. Applications are welcomed from mature students without formal qualifications but with proven ability.
Applications to Places:	6:1
Registered:	n/a
Awards:	

	Duration	EC Fees	Non-EC Fees
Full time	3 years	£1000 pa	£5750 pa
Part time			
Sandwich			

Higher National Diploma: Business Studies/Equine Studies with Management

A two year full-time course, providing a broad-based and practical foundation to careers in business management. On completion of the course students may be admitted to the final stage of an appropriate degree course. In Year One, all students follow core modules in Business Environment, Information Analysis, Law, Marketing, Financial Analysis and Organisational Analysis. In Year Two there are core modules in Business Planning and Development, Human Resource Development and Financial Management. In addition to core studies, students have a wide choice of option modules, enabling specialisation in Marketing, Finance,

Personnel, and Languages as a foundation for future career development. HND Equine Studies with Management is new for 1998 and HND Animal Management will be available in 1999. Both are in collaboration with Berkshire College of Agriculture.

Modular Course?	No
Qualifications:	HND
Application Deadline:	UCAS deadlines
Commencement Date:	September
Entry Requirement:	The minimum requirements for admission are: a minimum of 2 Advanced Level passes or equivalent and at least 5 GCSE/GCE subjects, including passes in Mathematics and English or equivalent. Applications are welcomed from mature students without formal qualifications but with proven ability.
Applications to Places:	6:1
Registered:	149
Awards:	

	Duration	EC Fees	Non-EC Fees
Full time	2 years	£1000 pa	£5750 pa
Part time			
Sandwich			

Administration or Distribution Management Principles. Mature students (over 21) may be accepted without formal qualifications.

Applications to Places:	6:1
Registered:	31
Awards:	

	Duration	EC Fees	Non-EC Fees
Full time			
Part time	2 years	Year One: £390; Year Two: £105	
Sandwich			

Higher National Certificate (Part-time) Business and Finance

This two year part-time course is designed to provide vocational education for those aspiring to or engaged in a career in industry or commerce. The course takes place on either two evenings or one afternoon and one evening each week and is located at the High Wycombe site of the College. Students will study a broad spectrum of business related topics and will choose one of three specialisms which will be covered in more detail during Year Two. The specialist streams offered on the course are: Marketing Management; Personnel Studies; Finance. Assessment is based on a series of assignments of the core and option modules, plus end of year examinations. The HNC is recognised as an entry qualification to further advanced courses, including conversion courses to a degree.

Modular Course?	No
Qualifications:	HNC
Application Deadline:	On request
Commencement Date:	
Entry Requirement:	Aged 18 and above, three GCSEs at A,B or C grade, plus at least one A-level or BTEC award of Diploma/Certificate in Business Studies or a Certificate in Public

The Judge Institute of Management Studies

University of Cambridge

Address:	University of Cambridge
	Trumpington Street
	Cambridge
	CB2 1AG
Area:	London and South East England
Phone:	+44 (0)1223 337051/2/3
Fax:	+44 (0)1223 339581
Email:	**jims-enquiries@lists.cam.ac.uk**
Website:	**http://www.jims.cam.ac.uk**

Email Application Available?	No
How to apply by email:	
Total Number of Teaching Staff:	65
Staff Teaching Undergraduate Courses	16
Research Rating:	4
Teaching Rating:	Satisfactory
Additional Rating Information	
Male:Female Student Ratio	3:1
Head of Business School	Professor Sandra Dawson
Head of Undergraduate Studies	Dr Chris Hope
Admissions Contact	Kay Fieldhouse

About the School:

The Judge Institute of Management Studies was founded in 1990 to act as a focus for management teaching and research in the University, which until then had been mainly conducted in the Faculties of Engineering and Economics. The Institute is named after Sir Paul and Lady Judge, its major benefactors. It is located in the centre of the University in a dramatic complex of purpose-designed buildings, opened by Her Majesty The Queen in 1996. Its first class facilities include a library, computer facility, teaching rooms and common rooms.

About Undergraduate Studies:

The Management Studies Tripos is available to Cambridge undergraduates as an option for their final year, having studied another subject for the first two or three years of their degree. Details of general undergraduate admission to the University are set out in the University Admissions prospectus, available from: Cambridge Intercollegiate Applications Office:
Tel: + 44 (0) 1223 333308
Fax: + 44 (0) 1223 366383

E- mail: ucam-undergraduate-admissions@lists.cam.ac.uk
Institute staff also teach on the Manufacturing Engineering Tripos and Engineering Tripos as part of undergraduate engineering degrees.
Contact: Dr Chris Hope

Facilities:

All students are members of a Cambridge University College. Most Colleges have a full programme of social and recreational events as well as many clubs and societies. Sport features strongly in Cambridge life, with most Colleges having their own sports grounds and facilities. Each year a number of students find time to represent their Colleges and, on occasion, the University, in competitive fixtures.

Departments/Faculties:

Academic staff are members of six subject groups: business and management economics, human resources and organisations, operations and information systems, finance and accounting, management science, strategy and marketing. The academic staff aim to advance theory, develop methodology and produce work of practical relevance within each subject group.

Links with Academic Institutions:

Teaching and research benefit greatly from a wide network of associate faculty in universities throughout the world. For example, the Institute's FAST (Financial Analysis & Securities Trading) programme is being run in association with Carnegie Mellon University.

Links with Industry:

The Institute's corporate relations are handled formally by its Advisory Board, the majority of whom are Chairmen or CEOs of major organisations. Informal advice is received through an international network of consulting connections and research collaborations. The guest speaker programme, formal events and practical projects also introduce businesses to the Institute.

Student Testimonials:

"Having completed my Part I in Natural Sciences, I decided to change to Management Studies as I thought it would be of greater use to me in my career. The course has definitely met this expectation, providing me with a broad based business knowledge, which has helped me with my career choice and given me greater confidence in pursuing it." Katherine Pearson, UK, MST class of 97; now with Arthur Anderson as a Tax Consultant.

Management Studies Tripos

Open to all third and fourth-year Cambridge undergraduates. The course provides an opportunity for students to develop a thorough understanding of management in an intellectually rigorous fashion.

Modular Course?	No
Qualifications:	BA Hons
Application Deadline:	Beginning of May
Commencement Date:	October
Entry Requirement:	Open to all 3rd & 4th year Cambridge undergraduates.
Applications to Places:	
Registered:	45
Awards:	Best Student Project, Best Performance Overall

	Duration	EC Fees	Non-EC Fees
Full time	9 months	£4,270	£10,932
Part time			
Sandwich			

Canterbury Business School

Canterbury Business School

Address:	Canterbury Business School
	The University
	Canterbury
	Kent
	Canterbury
	CT2 7PE
Area:	London and South East England
Phone:	(01227) 827726
Fax:	(01227) 761187
Email:	CBS_Admissions@ukc.ac.uk
Website:	http://www.ukc.ac.uk/CBS/

Email Application Available?	Yes
How to apply by email:	Via CBS Web-site: http://www.ukc.ac.uk/CBS/
Total Number of Teaching Staff:	50
Staff Teaching Undergraduate Courses	35
Research Rating:	3a
Teaching Rating:	Satisfactory
Additional Rating Information	
Male:Female Student Ratio	50:50
Head of Business School	Professor Brian Rutherford
Head of Undergraduate Studies	Mr Gerald Crompton
Admissions Contact	Mr Robert Jupe (all progs save Man Sci - Mr John Lamb)

About the School:
Canterbury Business School (CBS) is the business and management department of the University of Kent at Canterbury. The School offers a wide range of undergraduate, postgraduate and corporate programmes. The Business School has close links with private and public sector organisations, both nationally and internationally, which enables it to combine up-to-date management theory with experience.

About Undergraduate Studies:
CBS is the largest of the social science departments at Kent. The School offers undergraduate degrees in Accounting and Finance, Business Administration, Industrial Relations and Human Resource Management and Management Science. We have an expanding range of international programmes, with a year abroad taken between your second and final year. Undergraduate study at Kent is divided into Part I (first year) and Part II (second and third years). Although the results obtained in Part I do not count towards the overall class of your degree, you must pass Part I to proceed to Part II.

Facilities:
Campus accommodation, available either in college or on a self-catering basis, is guaranteed to all first-year undergraduates provided our offer of a place has been firmly accepted before 10 September of the year of entry and all postgraduates who firmly accept an offer of a place before 31 July in the year of entry. The 300 acre parkland campus is a self-contained community with its own shops, restaurants, cafeterias, bars, a theatre, cinema, careers service, medical centre and sports centre. The sports centre has a huge range of indoor and outdoor facilities to suit all tastes. Most forms of campus entertainment are provided by the Students' Union, having nearly 100 societies. The SU also runs a shops and travel service.

Departments/Faculties:
Canterbury Business School is the management and business department of the University of Kent at Canterbury.

Links with Academic Institutions:
Canterbury Business School is a member of the Association of Business Schools. The School has links with a number of overseas institutions, enabling it to provide opportunities for overseas study within its programmes. At undergraduate level students taking Accounting or Business Administration can study in France (Lyon), or Germany (Marburg). Management Science students can study in France (Lyon), Germany (Jena or Marburg), Italy (Turin), Spain (Oviedo or Granada) or the US (Bloomington, Indiana).

Links with Industry:
Canterbury Business School plays an important role in local and national business affairs as a provider of research, consultancy and training, and is a recognised centre of expertise in management disciplines. Recent corporate clients include, Hammersmith Hospitals NHS Trust, Kent Chamber of Commerce and Industry, Dover Harbour Board, Price Waterhouse (European Firms) and National Westminster Bank.

Student Testimonials:
"Industrial Relations is an extremely enjoyable degree and demands a lot of you. For anyone who has an interest in people and in business then the IR degree at Kent is an excellent choice". Barbara Masser BA (Hons) Industrial Relations (Social Psychology).

"I spent a year in industry as a Personnel Officer with Kent and Canterbury Hospitals NHS Trust. This gave me invaluable experience before my present job with Prudential Insurance." Tracy Packer - Management Science.

"I was happy to come to Canterbury because of the location. It is near to London, which offers many facilities including a good night life, whilst also being near to France". David Atibol British and France Accounting.

Accounting & Finance

Modular Course?   No
Qualifications: BA Hons
Categories: Finance

Bachelor of Business Administration (BBA)

Modular Course?   No
Qualifications: BBA
Categories: Business Administration

Industrial Relations and Human Resource Management

Modular Course?   No
Qualifications: BA Hons
Categories: Human Resources

Management Science

Modular Course?   No
Qualifications: BSc Hons
Categories:

Cardiff Business School

Cardiff Business School

Address:	Aberconway Building
	Collum Drive
	Cardiff
	CF1 3EU
Area:	Wales
Phone:	01222 874417
Fax:	01222 874419
Email:	**harbourG@cardiff.ac.uk**
Website:	**http://www.cf.ac.uk/uwcc/carbs/ carbs.html**

Email Application Available?	No
How to apply by email:	
Total Number of Teaching Staff:	124
Staff Teaching Undergraduate Courses	108
Research Rating:	5
Teaching Rating:	Excellent
Additional Rating Information	
Male:Female Student Ratio	55:45
Head of Business School	Professor Roger Mansfield
Head of Undergraduate Studies	Professor Maurice Pendlebury
Admissions Contact	Dr Phillip Worsfold

About the School:

Cardiff Business School was created in its present form in 1987 at the time of the merger of the two Cardiff colleges. Undergraduate courses in business and related subjects have been taught in Cardiff since the latter part of the 19th century in a number of departments which were finally merged in 1987. Since 1987, Cardiff has developed into one of the larger university business schools in the United Kingdom providing undergraduate and postgraduate courses in business administration.

About Undergraduate Studies:

Cardiff Business School offers a range of courses including accounting, business administration and economics. The undergraduate school is fully integrated with the postgraduate school with a very strong research-based faculty. All courses provide a mixture of theory and practice to equip people for a career in commerce, industry or the professions.

Cardiff Business School is part of the University of Wales College of Cardiff which provides via its student union a wide variety of social, cultural and sporting facilities comparable to the best in the United Kingdom. In addition to the general facilities available, there are a number of societies relating specifically to the Business School which provide educational, social, cultural and sporting facilities. The School offers easy access to all the facilities of the city of Cardiff.

Departments/Faculties:

The Business School has four sections: Accounting; Economics; Human Resource Management;

Links with Academic Institutions:

The Business School is part of the University of Wales College of Cardiff.

Links with Industry:

The Business School has major links with many local, national and international companies.

General Undergraduate Courses

Business Administration

A broad-based rigorous programme in management.

Modular Course?	Yes
Qualifications:	BSc; BSc Hons
Application Deadline:	31 January 1999
Commencement Date:	25 September 1999
Entry Requirement:	BBC at A-level
Applications to Places:	9:1
Registered:	184
Awards:	192

	Duration	EC Fees	Non-EC Fees
Full time	3 years	£1000	£6510
Part time			

BSc Accounting

A rigorous course in accounting

Modular Course?	Yes
Qualifications:	BSc; BSc Hons
Application Deadline:	31 January 1999
Commencement Date:	25 September 1999
Entry Requirement:	BBC at A-level
Applications to Places:	8:1
Registered:	141
Awards:	139

	Duration	EC Fees	Non-EC Fees
Full time	3 years	£1000	£6510
Part time			
Sandwich			

Banking and Finance

A broad economics-based approach to banking and finance

Modular Course?	Yes
Qualifications:	BSc; BSc Hons

Application Deadline:		31 January 1999	
Commencement Date:		25 September 1999	
Entry Requirement:		BBC at A-level	
Applications to Places:		5:1	
Registered:		52	
Awards:		44	

	Duration	EC Fees	Non-EC Fees
Full time	3 years	£1000	£6510
Part time			
Sandwich			

Marketing and Strategy.

Business School

Business School

Address:	Perry Barr
	Birmingham
	B42 2SU
Area:	Midlands
Phone:	0121 331 5200
Fax:	0121 331 6366
Email:	**E-mail business.school@uce.ac.uk**
Website:	**www.uce.ac.uk**
Email Application Available?	Yes
How to apply by email:	E-mail
	business.school@uce.ac.uk
Total Number of Teaching Staff:	107
Staff Teaching Undergraduate Courses	103
Research Rating:	2
Teaching Rating:	Highly Satisfactory
Additional Rating Information	
Male:Female Student Ratio	50:50
Head of Business School	Professor Upkar Pardesi
Head of Undergraduate Studies	Professor Brian Anderton
Admissions Contact	Cicely Sangha, 0121 331 6349

About the School:

The University of Central England Business School is a
major regional, national and international centre for
business and managerial education. It is one of the
largest business schools in the UK and has a substantial
proportion of part-time students. The School which has
around 4,400 students is organised into 6 departments:
Accountancy; Business; Economics; Finance; Marketing
and Languages; Management. It also has a
Management and Training Centre to facilitate and foster
links with educational and business organisations in the
UK and overseas.

The School aims to provide high quality vocational
education that meets the needs of individuals and
business through a portfolio of courses from
undergraduate to doctoral level. Most courses are
offered on a flexible part-time basis to meet the needs
of students with work and personal commitments. A
number of programmes are also tailored to the needs
of individual organisations, while professional
programmes can also be tailored or delivered in-house.
Business School students have access to the full range of
cultural and social facilities provided by the University.
The School is situated 2 to 3 miles from the centre of
Birmingham with its excellent range of social and
cultural amenities.

About Undergraduate Studies:

The Business School has an extensive portfolio of
vocationally orientated undergraduate full- and part-
time courses that have been designed and developed to
meet the changing needs of our students and
employers. All our courses provide a broad awareness
of the discipline and help to develop the students
intellectually, whilst focusing on their competencies and
skills required to quickly move into the world of work.
The courses also aim to develop the students analytical
and problem solving skills and encourage them to
become more self reliant in managing their own
development and learning.

Facilities:

The Union of Students at UCE provides students with
the opportunity to have an excellent social life. It also
gives support, advice and information on a wide variety
of issues and represents students throughout the
university.

The Union of Students has two bars of its own at the
moment. These are at the Perry Barr Campus and the
Edgbaston Campus. Each bar exists to provide a safe
and friendly student environment for all student social
needs.

The Union runs a range of over 30 clubs covering the
whole spectrum of sport, including non-competitive
activities, and gives you the opportunity to represent
both the Union of Students and national teams.

Departments/Faculties:

Within the Business School:
Department of Accountancy
Department of Business
Department of Finance
Department of Economics,
Department of Marketing & Languages
Department of Management

Links with Academic Institutions:

We work in partnership with six local FE colleges,
Birmingham College of Food and Worcester College of
Technology in the delivery of our undergraduate and
postgraduate courses. The Business School offers
student exchange opportunities with four partner
universities in the USA, and 23 partner universities
across Europe.

We deliver our undergraduate and MBA programmes in
partnership with Business Schools in India, Singapore
and Hong Kong.

Links with Industry:

The Business School works with a large number of
private and public sector organisations. Organisations to
whom the Business School delivers in-company
programmes, or that sponsor or fund research, training
and consultancy activity include: Barclays Bank, Lucas,
Midland Bank, Price Waterhouse, Rover Group, and the
West Midlands Fire Service.

Student Testimonials:

'I chose the UCE Business School because it is nationally renowned up and down the country. I didn't want to go too far away from home. Birmingham has so much to offer as well so I didn't have the need to leave home.'
'Birmingham has many things compared to London. It has really good bars and shopping centres. Even though it is not London. it comes across as a smaller scale to London....it is very similar...'
'For me, Birmingham was a brilliant opportunity to study, basically because it is England's second city. Student life is probably second to none because there are so many colleges and universities. There are bars and clubs that cater for students...... I would consider Birmingham to be principally a student type of city.'
'I came to Birmingham because the I like the city life....the fact that there is lots going on. '

General Undergraduate Courses

BA (Hons) Business Studies (Sandwich)

Since 1973 this course has proved one of the most popular undergraduate programmes in the university. It provides a well rounded business education and many of its graduates are in senior management positions. Building on the experience gained since its inception, and on feedback gained form industry, the programme has been continuously evaluated and updated to reflect the changing requirements of national and international business today and tomorrow.

Modular Course?	Yes
Qualifications:	BA Hons;
Application Deadline:	UCAS deadline
Commencement Date:	September
Entry Requirement:	3 A-levels (C,C,D), BTEC National 3 Distinctions plus Merit passes, GNVQ 12 units Distinction plus A-level grade C, 18 units Distinction/ Merit. GCSE grade C in Mathematics, English Language.
Applications to Places:	10:1
Registered:	330
Awards:	110

	Duration	EC Fees	Non-EC Fees
Full time			
Sandwich	4 Years	£1000	£6000

BA (Hons) Business Administration with Minors

This programme offers a range of vocationally-relevant minor subjects, including French, German, Spanish, Marketing, Accounting, Finance, Human Resource Management, Business Information Systems, Law, and Enterprise. The Business Administration Core develops students' ability to make employment choices and manage their own careers, while the minor subject enables students to concentrate on a key functional area of business. During the final year, students undertake an action learning project related to a specific business problem.

Modular Course?	No
Qualifications:	BA Hons; Joint Honours
Application Deadline:	UCAS deadline
Commencement Date:	September
Entry Requirement:	14 points at A-level, GNVQ Merit/ Distinction, GCSE grade C in Mathematics, English Language.
Applications to Places:	10:1
Registered:	400
Awards:	110

	Duration	EC Fees	Non-EC Fees
Full time	3 years	£1000	£6000
Part time	5 years	On request	On request
Sandwich			

BA (Hons) Economics

This programme includes core modules in key areas such as Economic Analysis, Economics and Society, Quantitative Methods, Macro- and Micro-Economics, and Political Economy, as well as a wide range of options. Students have the opportunity to spend one semester in the second year studying at linked universities in Europe or North America.

Modular Course?	No
Qualifications:	BA Hons
Application Deadline:	UCAS deadline
Commencement Date:	September
Entry Requirement:	12 points at A-level. GCSE grade C in Mathematics, English Language. GNVQ Merit/ Distinction
Applications to Places:	10:1
Registered:	120
Awards:	

	Duration	EC Fees	Non-EC Fees
Full time	3 years	£1000	£6000
Part time			
Sandwich			

BA (Hons) Finance

This programme includes core modules in key areas such as Economics, Financial Accounting, Quantitative Methods, Organisational Behaviour, Decision Techniques, Marketing Techniques, Management in Financial Services, Corporate Finance and Personal Portfolio Planning, as well as a wide range of options, including Banking, Insurance, Securities and Investment and International Finance streams. Students have the opportunity to spend one semester in the second year studying at linked universities in Europe or North America.

Modular Course?	No
Qualifications:	BA Hons
Application Deadline:	UCAS deadline
Commencement Date:	September
Entry Requirement:	12 points at A-level. GCSE grade C in Mathematics, English Language. GNVQ Merit/Distinction
Applications to Places:	10:1
Registered:	120
Awards:	

	Duration	EC Fees	Non-EC Fees
Full time	3 years	£1000	£6000
Part time			
Sandwich			

BA (Hons) Hospitality Management

This course sets out to prepare students for a career in management within the hospitality industry. The degree is based on a solid core of business and management studies, together with specialist hospitality studies. Practical elements of the programme are carried out in conjunction with Birmingham College of Food and Tourism.

Modular Course?	No
Qualifications:	BA Hons
Application Deadline:	UCAS deadline
Commencement Date:	September
Entry Requirement:	10 points in two A-levels. GNVQ Merit/Distinction. GCSE grade C in Mathematics, English Language, BTEC Merits.
Applications to Places:	10:1
Registered:	100
Awards:	

	Duration	EC Fees	Non-EC Fees
Full time	3 years	£1000	£6000
Part time			
Sandwich			

BA (Hons) Accountancy (full-time)

This programme develops students academically through the study of Accountancy, with a wide range of options. The programme enhances students' skills and contributes to the achievement of professional qualifications, providing a high level of professional exemptions.

Modular Course?	No
Qualifications:	BA Hons
Application Deadline:	UCAS deadline
Commencement Date:	September
Entry Requirement:	12 points at A-level. BTEC National 3 Distinctions (including Accounts plus Merits). GNVQ Merit/Distinction. GCSE grade C in Mathematics, English Language.
Applications to Places:	10:1
Registered:	250
Awards:	

	Duration	EC Fees	Non-EC Fees
Full time	3 years	£1000	£6000
Part time			
Sandwich			

BA (Hons) Marketing (full-time) & BA (Hons) Marketing with French or German or Spanish (full-time)

This programme is designed to provide a foundation of business knowledge and personal transferable skills, together with the in-depth study of aspects of marketing. Core studies include marker research, the marketing mix and marketing strategy, while there are themed electives including international marketing, marketing communications and services marketing. Students taking a languages minor spend the second semester of year 2 studying at a partner university in mainland Europe.

Modular Course?	No
Qualifications:	BA Hons
Application Deadline:	UCAS deadline
Commencement Date:	September
Entry Requirement:	14 points at A level, GCSE Grade C in Mathematics, English Language and, for languages minors, French, German or Latin as appropriate: GNVQ Distinction/Merit.
Applications to Places:	10:1
Registered:	230
Awards:	

	Duration	EC Fees	Non-EC Fees
Full time	3 years	£1000	£6000
Part time			
Sandwich			

BA (Hons) Entrepreneurship

This programme is particularly designed to meet the needs of students who have aspirations to start their own businesses, or to make a direct input to the running of family businesses or other medium/small sized businesses. This programme is based around an action-learning framework which is informed by the Small Firms Lead Body's National Standards for the development of competencies required to work in small firms and to create new businesses. (Subject to validation in 1998/99).

Modular Course?	No
Qualifications:	BA Hons
Application Deadline:	UCAS deadline
Commencement Date:	September
Entry Requirement:	12 points at A Level, GCSE Grade C in mathematics and English language, GNVQ Merit/ Distinction.
Applications to Places:	10:1
Registered:	
Awards:	

	Duration	EC Fees	Non-EC Fees
Full time	3 years	£1000	£6000
Part time			
Sandwich			

BA (Hons) Business Economics (full-time)

This programme provides a sound grounding in the principles of economics, and applies economics to the real world problems of business in the UK and international economy. Within the framework of economic principles, students develop an understanding of business problems, business policy, strategy and decision making. Numeracy and IT skills development are also an integral part of the programme.

Opportunities exist for one semester in the second year to be studies at linked universities in Europe and North America.

Modular Course?	No
Qualifications:	BA Hons
Application Deadline:	UCAS deadline
Commencement Date:	September
Entry Requirement:	12 points at A Level, GCSE Grade C in Mathematics and English Language, GNVQ Merit/ Distinction.
Applications to Places:	10:1
Registered:	
Awards:	

	Duration	EC Fees	Non-EC Fees
Full time	3 years	£1000	£6000
Part time			
Sandwich			

BA (Hons) European Business and Languages (full-time)

This programme is designed to prepare students for employment in European and multi-national corporations, by developing knowledge and understanding of business, generic business expertise, and foreign language skills. Two foreign languages are studied throughout the course, though not necessarily at the same level. The second year of the programme is spent at a partner institution in mainland Europe, and consists of further study of business subjects and foreign languages, followed by a period of structured and assessed work experience.

Modular Course?	No
Qualifications:	BA Hons
Application Deadline:	UCAS deadline
Commencement Date:	September
Entry Requirement:	14 points at A level including one foreign language, GCSE Grade C in Mathematics and English Language, GNVQ Merit/Distinction.
Applications to Places:	10:1
Registered:	50
Awards:	

	Duration	EC Fees	Non-EC Fees
Full time	3 years	£1000	£6000
Part time			
Sandwich			

BA (Hons) Accountancy and Finance (full-time)

This joint honours programme is designed to provide a sound understanding of the principles and concepts of Accountancy, and key issues in the area of Finance such as the structure and operation of financial institutions and markets, raising finance, investment, financial management and financial analysis. (Programme subject to validation during 1988/99).

Modular Course?	No
Qualifications:	BA Hons
Application Deadline:	UCAS deadline
Commencement Date:	September
Entry Requirement:	12 points at A level, GCSE Grade C Mathematics and English; GNVQ Merit/Distinction.
Applications to Places:	10:1
Registered:	
Awards:	

	Duration	EC Fees	Non-EC Fees
Full time	3 years	£1000	£6000
Part time			
Sandwich			

BSc (Hons) Management (full-time)

This programme has a highly distinctive approach to the study of management and management competencies at undergraduate level. The course content has been structured around the Management Standards, and students work in small action-learning sets. The programme is very applied, seeking to develop key skills and competencies, and students work with mentors who are practising managers in industry, commerce and public sector organisations. The model of teaching, learning and assessment has been designed with the needs of Advanced GNVQ students particularly in mind.

Modular Course?	No
Qualifications:	BSc Hons
Application Deadline:	UCAS deadline
Commencement Date:	September
Entry Requirement:	GNVQ Merit/Distinction, Grade C English Language and Mathematics; 12 points at A level.
Applications to Places:	10:1
Registered:	110
Awards:	

	Duration	EC Fees	Non-EC Fees
Full time	3 years	£1000	£6000
Part time			
Sandwich			

HND Business & Finance

This programme enables students to build up a coherent programme of study leading to employment, further study or professional qualifications. The first year covers business principles and practice including Business Environment, Quantitative and Accounting Techniques, Business Analysis, and People and Decision-Making. The second year allows students to develop specialist interests through a wide range of options, while competence modules throughout the course focus on developing individual personal and business skills. The final integrative Business Project encourages students to relate theory to practice.

Modular Course?	No
Qualifications:	HND
Application Deadline:	UCAS deadline
Commencement Date:	September
Entry Requirement:	8 points in 2 A-levels or AS-levels, 2 Distinctions plus Merit in a relevant BTEC National Diploma, GNVQ Merit,

	GCSE grade C in Mathematics, English Language.
Applications to Places:	10:1
Registered:	110
Awards:	

	Duration	EC Fees	Non-EC Fees
Full time	2 years	£1000	£6000
		+ BTEC registration	+ BTEC registration
Part time	1-2 years	On request	On request
Sandwich			

Specialist Undergraduate Course

B.A. Hons. Finance

Modular Course?	Yes
Qualifications:	BA Hons
Categories:	Finance

B.A. Hons. Marketing/ B.A. Hons. Marketing with French/German/Spanish

Modular Course?	Yes
Qualifications:	BA Hons
Categories:	Marketing; International Business; Retailing

B.A. Hons. Accountancy

Modular Course?	Yes
Qualifications:	BA Hons
Categories:	Finance

B.A. Hons. European Business & Languages

Modular Course?	Yes
Qualifications:	BA Hons
Categories:	International Business

B.A. Hons. Economics/ B.A. Hons. Economics with Minors/B.A. Hons. Business Economics

Modular Course?	Yes
Qualifications:	BA
Categories:	Finance; Small Business; Public Sector

Faculty of Business and Social Studies

Cheltenham and Gloucester Faculty of Business and Social Studies

Address:	The Park
	Cheltenham
	GL50 2QF
Area:	South West England
Phone:	01242 543 253
Fax:	01242 543 208

Email:

Website:

Email Application Available?	No
How to apply by email:	
Total Number of Teaching Staff:	80
Staff Teaching Undergraduate Courses	60
Research Rating:	2
Teaching Rating:	Satisfactory
Additional Rating Information	
Male:Female Student Ratio	50:50
Head of Business School	Paul Taylor
Head of Undergraduate Studies	Sue Davis
Admissions Contact	Pat Willey

About the School:
The School offers a range of programmes in the areas of business, finance, management, marketing, financial services, human resource management, information technology and modern languages. There are approximately 80 full-time staff, 1300 full-time equivalent students and 1300 part-time students. Courses are run mainly through a modular scheme at undergraduate and postgraduate level. There is also an extensive range of professional and national vocational qualifications and research degree programmes are offered to PhD level.

About Undergraduate Studies:
All of the programmes offer a high degree of flexibility and choice, with part-time and full-time courses and the benefits of a modular programme. Students have the opportunity to take responsibility for their own learning and have a significant input into the design of their individual awards. For example, they can select modules outside their main area of study and defer their choice of specialism if necessary.

Facilities:
The College is located in the historic picturesque town of Cheltenham, renowned for its architecture and its spa, and host to the Cheltenham Festival of Literature and Cheltenham International Festival of Music. The town and the College offer an extensive range of social, cultural, sporting and leisure facilities and Cheltenham is situated at the foot of the Cotswolds in some of the finest countryside in England.

General Undergraduate Courses

Business Management

This programme equips students with transferable business, educational and personal skills. The first year focuses on an understanding of business management, introducing analytical and technological tools. In the second and third years, students study modules that provide a full understanding of management as well as specialist activities such as human resource management, marketing, and finance. There is a work placement between the second and third years.

Modular Course?	Yes
Qualifications:	Cert HE/Dip HE/Degree
Application Deadline:	UCAS deadline
Commencement Date:	October
Entry Requirement:	On request
Applications to Places:	15:1
Registered:	300
Awards:	BA (Hons)

	Duration	EC Fees	Non-EC Fees
Full time	4 years	On request	On request
Part time	5 years	On request	On request
Sandwich	4 years	On request	On request

Financial Management

This course provides a broad foundation in management theory and practice and develops the specialist skills needed for financial management. The second and third years involve an increasing level of specialisation while retaining a core of operational and strategic modules. There is a work placement between the second and third years.

Modular Course?	Yes
Qualifications:	Cert HE/Dip HE/Degree
Application Deadline:	UCAS deadline
Commencement Date:	October
Entry Requirement:	On request
Applications to Places:	8:1
Registered:	50
Awards:	BA (Hons)

	Duration	EC Fees	Non-EC Fees
Full time	4 years	On request	On request
Part time	5 years	On request	On request
Sandwich			

Financial Services Management

This programme will help students gain an understanding of the financial services business and prepare for a management position. Students are encouraged to develop a critical and analytical view of the industry and build specialist knowledge. After a basic grounding during the first year, the second level introduces the fundamentals of resource management and provides an insight into the regulatory framework. The second and third year programmes allow students to arrange the programme to include a specialist route such as risk management, investment management or financial services marketing. There is a work placement between the second and third years.

Modular Course?	Yes
Qualifications:	Cert HE/Dip HE/Degree
Application Deadline:	UCAS deadline
Commencement Date:	October
Entry Requirement:	On request
Applications to Places:	5:1
Registered:	30
Awards:	BA (Hons)

	Duration	EC Fees	Non-EC Fees
Full time	4 years	On request	On request
Part time	5 years	On request	On request
Sandwich	4 years	On request	On request

Human Resource Management

This programme will help students gain a broad understanding of management theory and practice while developing specialist skills for a career in Human Resource Management. During the first year, students develop the knowledge and skills needed to address more complex human resource issues. The second and third years involve an increasing level of specialisation while retaining a core of operational and strategic modules. There is a work placement between the second and third years.

Modular Course?	Yes
Qualifications:	Cert HE/Dip HE/Degree
Application Deadline:	UCAS deadline
Commencement Date:	October
Entry Requirement:	On request
Applications to Places:	10:1
Registered:	100
Awards:	BA (Hons)

	Duration	EC Fees	Non-EC Fees
Full time	4 years	On request	On request
Part time	5 years	On request	On request
Sandwich	4 years	On request	On request

Marketing Management

This programme will help students gain a broad understanding of management theory and practice while developing specialist skills for a career in marketing. During the first year, students develop the knowledge and skills needed to address more complex marketing. The second and third years involve an increasing level of specialisation in marketing management and the investigation of strategic and marketing management issues. There is a work placement between the second and third years.

Modular Course?	Yes
Qualifications:	Cert HE/Dip HE/Degree
Application Deadline:	UCAS deadline
Commencement Date:	October
Entry Requirement:	On request
Applications to Places:	10:1
Registered:	170
Awards:	BA (Hons)

	Duration	EC Fees	Non-EC Fees
Full time	4 years	On request	On request
Part time	5 years	On request	On request
Sandwich	4 years	On request	On request

International Business Management/International Marketing Management

These new programmes will be introduced in 1998-99 to enable students to prepare for careers in an increasingly global business environment.

Modular Course?	Yes
Qualifications:	Cert HE/Dip HE/Degree
Application Deadline:	UCAS deadline
Commencement Date:	October
Entry Requirement:	On request
Applications to Places:	
Registered:	
Awards:	BA (Hons)

	Duration	EC Fees	Non-EC Fees
Full time	4 years	On request	On request
Part time	5 years	On request	On request
Sandwich	4 years	On request	On request

Programmes in Computing and Information Technology

The School offers a choice of undergraduate courses to equip students with the professional and academic skills needed to develop and implement solutions to business problems. There are opportunities for work placement during the courses. Courses are available in the following areas: Business Computer Systems; Business Information Technology; Computing; Multimedia.

Modular Course?	Yes

Qualifications: Cert HE/Dep HE/Degree
Application Deadline: UCAS deadline
Commencement Date: October
Entry Requirement: On request
Applications to Places: 7:1
Registered: 385
Awards: BSc (Hons)

	Duration	EC Fees	Non-EC Fees
Full time	3-4 years	On request	On request
Part time	5 years	On request	On request
Sandwich	4 years	On request	On request

City University Business School

City University Business School

Address:	Frobisher Crescent
	Barbican Centre
	London
	EC2Y 8HB
Area:	London and South East England
Phone:	0171 477 8600
Fax:	0171 477 8880

Email: cubs-postgrad@city.ac.uk

Website: http://www.city.ac.uk/cubs

Email Application Available?	No
How to apply by email:	
Total Number of Teaching Staff:	81
Staff Teaching Undergraduate Courses	81
Research Rating:	4
Teaching Rating:	Excellent
Additional Rating Information	
Male:Female Student Ratio	2:1
Head of Business School	Professor Leslie Hannah, Dean
Head of Undergraduate Studies	Professor Allan Williams, Deputy Dean
Admissions Contact	Registry

About the School:

City University Business School is based in the heart of the City of London, the world's top international financial centre, and is a leading provider of business and management education at undergraduate, postgraduate and post-experience levels.

In 1994 the Higher Education Funding Council of England awarded the Business School's business and management teaching the top rating of 'excellent'. It rated as excellent both of the undergraduate courses that it then assessed: the BSc course in Business Studies and the BSc course in Management Systems. You can be confident that the teaching you receive is of the highest quality. Importantly for a business school, you can also be sure that the course is up to date.

Our location offers students unrivalled opportunities to develop contacts within the City of London. The School can currently boast over 1700 students across its portfolio of management programmes.

About Undergraduate Studies:

The School offers six undergraduate programmes in banking & international finance, business studies, insurance & investment, investment & financial risk management, management & systems and property

valuation & finance. All programmes are taught over three years, however students can spend an additional year, either on a professional placement or studying abroad.

Departments/Faculties:

The Business School is situated in one of the UK's leading arts complexes - the Barbican Centre- and is within easy reach of a wealth of cinemas, theatres, art galleries and museums. London landmarks such as St Paul's Cathedral and the Tower of London are close by. Students can also access a wide range of recreational facilities provided by the University, including regular public lectures, concerts, chamber recitals, opera, orchestral and jazz events. The University playing fields cater for most sports and the nearby Saddlers Sports Centre provides a comprehensive programme of indoor recreation and sport.

Links with Academic Institutions:

As a member of AMSEC students have the opportunity for overseas study in Berlin (Technische Universität), Brussels (Ecôle de Commerce Solvay, Université Libre), Madrid (Universidad Complutense), Oslo (Norwegian School of Management), Paris (Ecôle Supérieure de Commerce de Paris), Rome (Libera Universita Internationale Degli Studi Sociali) and Vienna (Universität Wien).

Links with Industry:

Through its close proximity to the City of London, and its links with City companies and institutions, the School regularly draws on active City practitioners to enhance teaching and learning. Close contact with City-based firms is further enhanced through a series of prestigious events and public lectures.

Student Testimonials:

"The academic and market knowledge provided by the course helped secure my first position after graduating, convincing my employer I had the background to do the job".
Huzefa Vora, BSc Investment & Financial Risk Management, 1995

"Successful marketing is dependent on creative flair based on sound analytical foundation. City University Business School provides that solid base on which to build a successful career"
Stephen Factor, BSc in Business Studies

"This course provides an excellent foundation for a career in the City, both from an academic and a practical point of view"
Karen Mason, BSc in Banking & International Finance

BSc Banking and International Finance

This course produces graduates who will be future leaders of the financial community. Students will be capable of analysing and solving complex problems in banking and finance, and will have developed a full understanding of the financial sector as well as IT and communications skills. Modules include Banking and Financial Management, Economics, Accounting, Law, Quantitative Methods, as well as an optional foreign language. Students may, for specific modules, be exempted from the Chartered Institute of Bankers ACIB examinations.

Modular Course?	No
Qualifications:	BSc
Application Deadline:	UCAS deadline
Commencement Date:	October
Entry Requirement:	A/AS-level BBB preferably in maths based subjects. Advanced GNVQ Distinction in business plus 1 A-level, BTEC distinction overall, IB 30, SCE (H) AAABB
Applications to Places:	4:1
Registered:	154
Awards:	

	Duration	EC Fees	Non-EC Fees
Full time	3 years	£1000	£6250
Part time			
Sandwich	4 years	£1000	£6250

BSc Business Studies

This course provides a sound basis for rapid progression in a professional or managerial career. Core subjects include essential management skills Ñ Marketing, Accounting, Economics, Management and Quantitative Methods. These are integrated into further strategic modules to give students 'the bigger picture'. Options allow students to specialise in the final year, providing the best career advantage. A foreign language is a further option.

Modular Course?	No
Qualifications:	BSc
Application Deadline:	UCAS deadline
Commencement Date:	October
Entry Requirement:	A/AS-level BBB. Advanced GNVQ Distinction in business plus 6 add units/1 A-

level grade B, BTEC distinction overall, IB 31, SCE (H) AAABB

Applications to Places:	4:1
Registered:	239
Awards:	

	Duration	EC Fees	Non-EC Fees
Full time	3 years	£1000	£6250
Part time			
Sandwich	4 years	£1000	£6250

BSc Insurance and Investment

This course will give you a sound understanding of the concept of risk and its application to the business of insurance and investment. Modules cover Business and Finance, Economics, Accounting, Law, Quantitative Methods, Securities and Investment, Corporate Finance, Financial Analysis, General and Life Assurance. A European language and further third year options help students to position themselves in the most attractive way for career opportunities.

Modular Course?	No
Qualifications:	BSc
Application Deadline:	UCAS deadline
Commencement Date:	October
Entry Requirement:	A/AS-level BBC. Advanced GNVQ Distinction in business plus 6 add units/1 A-level grade B, BTEC distinction overall, IB 31, SCE (H) AAABB
Applications to Places:	4:1
Registered:	146
Awards:	

	Duration	EC Fees	Non-EC Fees
Full time	3 years	£1000	£6250
Part time			
Sandwich	4 years	£1000	£6250

BSc Investment and Financial Risk Management

This course provides a solid grounding in the instruments available for investment and financial risk management. Modules include Economics, Accountancy, Law, Quantitative Methods, Financial Markets and Institutions, Financial Analysis and Securities and Investment. European language and business courses are available as an option.

Modular Course?	No
Qualifications:	BSc
Application Deadline:	UCAS deadline
Commencement Date:	October
Entry Requirement:	A/AS-level BBC. Advanced GNVQ Distinction in business plus 6 add units/1 A-level grade B, BTEC

distinction overall, IB 31, SCE
(H) AAABB

Applications to Places:	4:1
Registered:	146
Awards:	

	Duration	EC Fees	Non-EC Fees
Full time	3 years	£1000	£6250
Part time			
Sandwich	4 years	£1000	£6250

BSc Property Valuation and Finance

This course is highly regarded by property employers in London and gives a broad understanding of property's role in investment, business and industry. Course modules include Economics, Corporate Finance, Investment, Marketing. Accounting, Quantitative Methods, Building Design and Construction, Law, Investment, Property Development Appraisal, Property Investment Analysis and Funding. IT and language skills are also developed as an essential part of the degree.

Modular Course?	No
Qualifications:	BSc
Application Deadline:	UCAS deadline
Commencement Date:	October
Entry Requirement:	A/AS-level BBC. Advanced GNVQ Distinction in business plus 6 add units/I A-level grade B, BTEC distinction overall, IB 31, SCE (H) AAABB
Applications to Places:	4:1
Registered:	146
Awards:	

	Duration	EC Fees	Non-EC Fees
Full time	3 years	£1000	£6250
Part time			
Sandwich	4 years	£1000	£6250

BSc Management and Systems

This course will give you a sound interdisciplinary education that is particularly suitable for a career in management and also prepares you for a career in the financial world. Modules cover Management and Systems Science, Organisational Behaviour and Personnel Management, Management of Technology, International Relations, Economics, Marketing, Quantitative Methods and Integrating Studies. Students will also have the opportunity to study a European language.

Modular Course?	No
Qualifications:	BSc
Application Deadline:	UCAS deadline
Commencement Date:	October
Entry Requirement:	A/AS-level BBB. Advanced GNVQ

Distinction in
business, BTEC 3 merits and 4
distinctions, IB 28, SCE
(H) AAABB

Applications to Places:	4:1
Registered:	162
Awards:	

	Duration	EC Fees	Non-EC Fees
Full time	3 years	£1000	£6250
Part time			
Sandwich	4 years	£1000	£6250

Coventry Business School

Coventry Business School

Address:	Priory Street
	Coventry
	CVI 5FB
Area:	Midlands
Phone:	(01203) 838410
Fax:	(01203) 838400
Email:	**info.cbs@coventry.ac.uk**
Website:	**http://www.coventry.ac.uk**
Email Application Available?	No
How to apply by email:	
Total Number of Teaching Staff:	80
Staff Teaching Undergraduate Courses	65
Research Rating:	2
Teaching Rating:	Satisfactory
Additional Rating Information	School ratings are due to come up for appraisal in 2000.
Male:Female Student Ratio	55:45
Head of Business School	Dr David Morris (Dean of School)
Head of Undergraduate Studies	Chris Gore (Mrs) (Associate Dean of Undergraduate Programmes)
Admissions Contact	Undergraduate Course Support Teams for: Business Studies, Leisure, Tourism, Sport Management, Marketing Management, Equine Studies; Economics, Planning; Business Administration, Joint Degree Programme, Business Enterprise

About the School:
Coventry Business School (CBS) has over 4,000 students studying on a wide range of courses, from Higher National Diploma level to PhD. Study within the school takes place on a central campus in the William Morris Building. This building incorporates state of the art computer facilities, lecture theatres and student facilities such as a bistro. The Business School has five computer laboratories equipped with high performance networked PCs providing a wide variety of business software including access to the Internet and CD-ROMs for research purposes. The School also incorporates an Audio-Visual Suite, which is available for developing presentation skills and analysing group interaction.

About Undergraduate Studies:
The size of the Business School means that it is able to offer a wide variety of courses, with options which can be drawn from the full range of specialist skills, allowing students to tailor their studies to their skills. Many of the undergraduate courses provide the opportunity to specialise in a variety of subject areas.

Most courses have employer panels associated with them and are designed to provide a good base for future employment. Past graduates have been extremely successful, not only in obtaining employment, but in reaching the top levels of their chosen professions.

Facilities:
The university has 37 acres of sports grounds for soccer, rugby, hockey and tennis as well as a golf course. On campus there are badminton courts, a multi-gym, and rooms for volleyball, basketball, judo, karate and table tennis. In addition the City's main sports centre is adjoining the University campus. Special arrangements for students are provided for the use of its facilities, which include an Olympic-size swimming pool. The recently opened 'Planet' club is a major extension of the Student's Union facilities, offering bars and live entertainment, including bands and comedians, seven days a week. The City itself also offers pubs, clubs, theatres and a wide variety of restaurants.

Departments/Faculties:
Within the business school there are five faculties; business, economics, management, marketing and planning. These areas include the study of leisure, tourism and sport, equine studies, human resource management, supply chain management, business policy, and local economic development.

Links with Academic Institutions:
CBS's network of academic institutions currently numbers over 30 with a widening network in Europe and beyond. Within the UK we offer our equine courses with Warwickshire college, as well as business courses in conjunction with colleges around the country. Overseas educational links include German, Spanish, French, Finnish, Italian, Canadian, Malaysian and Japanese Universities such as the Fachhochschule Aachen, Valencia University, Caen University in France, Windsor in Canada and Reitaku in Tokyo.

Links with Industry:
CBS has extensive links with British and multinational companies such as BMW/Rover, Ford/Jaguar, Peugeot, Rank Xerox, Lucas, TNT, British Telecom and GEC, as well as other leading regional organisations such as the South Warwickshire Health Authority. CBS also looks towards Eastern Europe and courses in management education are organised for professional managers from Poland and other Eastern countries on a regular basis.

Student Testimonials:

Dianne Kaye graduated with an Honours degree in Leisure Management and is now the Manager of the Corporate Department at Holmes Place, Barbican.

"The sport, fitness and excercise modules I studied in years one and two of the programme helped me secure employment in a health club environment. The modules in business and management helped me progress quickly to a managerial position within the organisation."

Gurbaksh Sidhu carried out her placement in the Pricing Department of Massey Ferguson as part of the BA Business Studies degree.

"I work with the sub-manager for Functional Pricing, dealing with everyday pricing enquiries. There are some routine tasks - but there's also a lot of ad-hoc work. You have to think on your feet. Massey Ferguson is a very customer-orientated company - it always aims to serve the best interests of its customers. That's been a good learning point. I have increased my computing skills, and also improved my communication skills. I've learnt how to plan my own day - I've grown in confidence."

General Undergraduate Courses

BA (Hons) Business Studies

The course aims to provide a broad-based business education, containing both academic and vocational elements, which prepare students for a wide range of career opportunities in business. Students will gain basic knowledge and relevant techniques of all the main business functions and develop the ability to apply the relevant functional knowledge and techniques to the business decision-making process.

Modular Course?	Yes
Qualifications:	BA Hons
Application Deadline:	No application deadline unless courses are oversubscribed.
Commencement Date:	October
Entry Requirement:	16 points or a similar qualification at GNVQ, BTEQ or an equivalent level
Applications to Places:	10:1
Registered:	111
Awards:	93

	Duration	EC Fees	Non-EC Fees
Full time			
Part time			
Sandwich	4 years		

BA Leisure Management / BA Leisure Management with European Study

The Leisure Management degree is a course which is designed to study the management within, and of the leisure industry in all its forms. The study of business and management are thus central to the understanding and practise of leisure management, but are combined with a quality programme of study which embraces the planning of leisure provision and the resourcing of leisure activities. The Leisure Management degree can include a year work placement. It can be taken with a language, and involves an overseas placement year.

Modular Course?	Yes
Qualifications:	BA Hons
Application Deadline:	No application deadline unless course oversubscribed
Commencement Date:	October
Entry Requirement:	14 - 16 points or a similar qualification at BTEC, GNVQ or an equivalent level
Applications to Places:	
Registered:	
Awards:	42

	Duration	EC Fees	Non-EC Fees
Full time	3 years		
Part time			
Sandwich	4 years		

BA Economics / Business Economics / Financial Economics / International Economics

The economics courses provide students with a sound economics knowledge and understanding of economic theory enabling you to understanding of economic theory enabling you to analyse and interpret current economic issues in a general, international, financial and business context.

Modular Course?	Yes
Qualifications:	BA Hons
Application Deadline:	No application deadline unless courses oversubscribed
Commencement Date:	October
Entry Requirement:	12 - 18 points or a similar qualification at an equivalent level
Applications to Places:	7:1
Registered:	79
Awards:	57

	Duration	EC Fees	Non-EC Fees
Full time	3 years		
Part time			
Sandwich			

BA Business Enterprise / HND Business Enterprise

It is a learning programme which will develop graduates who can manage business-related tasks in a proactive way, solve business problems, and influence the business environment in which they work. This programme allows students to complete the HND after two years, or the degree in three years.

Modular Course?	Yes
Qualifications:	BA Hons; HND
Application Deadline:	No application deadline unless course oversubscribed
Commencement Date:	October
Entry Requirement:	8 points or a similar qualification at an equivalent level
Applications to Places:	6:1
Registered:	Course starting from 1998/99
Awards:	Course not previously run

	Duration	EC Fees	Non-EC Fees
Full time	2 / 3 years		
Part time			
Sandwich			

BA Urban and Regional Planning / with Local Economic Development / with Recreation

The planning courses will provide you with the necessary skills and knowledge to work in town and country planning, local economic development and recreation planning in a wide range of public and private sector organisations and businesses.

Modular Course?	Yes
Qualifications:	BA Hons
Application Deadline:	No application deadline unless course oversubscribed
Commencement Date:	October
Entry Requirement:	12 points or a similar qualification at GNVQ, BTEC or an equivalent level
Applications to Places:	3:1
Registered:	34
Awards:	32

	Duration	EC Fees	Non-EC Fees
Full time	3 years		
Part time			
Sandwich	4 years		

Additional Courses

Business Administration, American and European Business
Administration, American and European Economics, Economics
with Planning, Economics and French,
Economics and German, Economics and Law,
Joint Degree Programme offering 32 different business combinations.

Modular Course?	Yes
Qualifications:	BA
Application Deadline:	
Commencement Date:	
Applications to Places:	
Registered:	
Awards:	

	Duration	EC Fees	Non-EC Fees
Full time			
Part time			
Sandwich			

Specialist Undergraduate Course

Marketing Management

Modular Course?	Yes
Qualifications:	BA Hons
Categories:	Marketing

Tourism Management

Modular Course?	Yes
Qualifications:	BA Hons
Categories:	Leisure

Sport Management

Modular Course?	Yes
Qualifications:	BA Hons
Categories:	Leisure

Equine Studies

Modular Course?	Yes
Qualifications:	BA Hons
Categories:	Equine Industry/Management of horse-related businesses

Horse Studies

Modular Course?	Yes
Qualifications:	HND
Categories:	Equine Industry/Management of horse-related businesses

Croydon Higher Education Centre

Croydon Higher Education Centre

Address:	Fairfield,
	Croydon,
	CR9 1DX
Area:	London and South East England
Phone:	0181 686 5700
Fax:	0181 760 5821
Email:	**info@ croydon. ac.uk.**
Website:	**www. croydon. ac. uk**

Email Application Available?	No
How to apply by email:	
Total Number of Teaching Staff:	50
Staff Teaching Undergraduate Courses	35
Research Rating:	n/a
Teaching Rating:	Satisfactory
Additional Rating Information	FEFC Teaching and Learning -
	Grade 2
Male:Female Student Ratio	40:60
Head of Centre	John Last
Head of Undergraduate Studies	Sue Crowley
Admissions Contact	Kim Sadler

About the School:
The work builds on a strong tradition of education, development and training in business, management and related professional programmes in Croydon. The Centre has more than 3000 students on over 30 different programmes. About 80% of these attend on a part-time basis, however the School has also developed popular full-time degrees in Business and Law.

About Undergraduate Studies:
Croydon College is at the forefront of developments in the support of student learning. In 1994, it was awarded the Queen's Prize for Higher and Further Education in recognition of the quality of its Flexible Learning Workshop programme. This programme offers a large range of self-study material to support our programmes as well as tutors to advise on all aspects of learning, including research and study skills.

Facilities:
The Student's Association arranges a wide variety of social and sporting events, and runs the College bar and shop. Croydon has its own theatre, cinemas and art gallery, yet is only 20 minutes by train from London.

Links with Academic Institutions:
Affilated with the University of Sussex.

Links with Industry:
Well-established links with local industry within a number of professional areas including retail and purchasing.

BA (Hons) Business Studies
Options for this course are: BA (Hons) Business with Accounting and Finance; BA (Hons) Business with Law; BA (Hons) Business with Human Resource Management; BA (Hons) Business with Marketing; BA (Hons) Business; BA (Hons) Business with Legal Studies. This can be studied as a one year programme for qualifying HND students, or as a 3 year degree programme.

Modular Course?	No
Qualifications:	BA Hons
Application Deadline:	UCAS deadline
Commencement Date:	September/October
Entry Requirement:	HND Business with merit in 75%
	of year 2 modules,
	advanced GNVQ Business/
	Management at merit or pass
	with two additional units, APL for
	HND graduates.
Applications to Places:	4:1
Registered:	
Awards:	

	Duration	EC Fees	Non-EC Fees
Full time	1 or 3 years	On request	On request
Part time	2 or 4 years	On request	On request
Sandwich			

LLB Law (University of London)

This is an external degree awarded by the University of London, with examinations set and assessed by the University. Teaching takes the form of formal lectures, supported by class discussion, group work and guidance in additional reading.

Modular Course?	No
Qualifications:	LLB
Application Deadline:	UCAS deadline
Commencement Date:	September/October
Entry Requirement:	2 A levels grade C or above plus
	3 GCSE or GCE O levels
	grade C or above
	3 A levels grade C or above, plus
	one GCSE or GCE O
	level grade C or above
	2 A levels and 2 AS levels grade
	C or above
Applications to Places:	4:1
Registered:	
Awards:	

	Duration	EC Fees	Non-EC Fees
Full time	3	On request	On request
Part time	4		
Sandwich	n/a		

Leicester Business School

Faculty of Business and Law

Address:	The Gateway
	Leicester
	LE1 9BH
Area:	Midlands
Phone:	Postgrad: 0116 257 7230; U'grad 0116 250 6135
Fax:	Postgrad: 0116 250 6329; U'grad 0116 251 7548

Email:

Postgrad: stadm@dmu.ac.uk;

Undergrad   koadm@dmu.ac.

Website: http://www.dmu.ac.uk

Email Application Available?	No
How to apply by email:	
Total Number of Teaching Staff:	130
Staff Teaching Undergraduate Courses	130
Research Rating:	3b
Teaching Rating:	Excellent
Additional Rating Information	
Male:Female Student Ratio	50:50
Head of Business School	Dean, Professor John Coyne
Head of Undergraduate Studies	Andy Rees
Admissions Contact	Karen O'Brien

About the School:

The School of Business at De Montford University is one of the ten largest providers of business education in the country with approximately 6000 students registered on to its range of undergraduate, postgraduate and professional programmes. The quality of the teaching and educational experience was recognised by the awarding of an 'Excellent' rating by the Higher Education Funding Council and the 1996 RAE exercise confirmed the School's position as a well respected research centre.

The School enjoys the highest possible status with the professional bodies with which it works - it is an IPD Centre of Excellence, an educational centre of excellence for the Market Research Society, a centre of excellence for CIMA and boasts the highest level of exemptions from both accounting bodies for its BA Accounting and Finance programme. The School's commercial arm, Business Solutions, which oversees many consultancy and research projects, has an annual turnover of £5m.

About Undergraduate Studies:

Graduates are will prepared to enter a wide variety of business-related areas of work in both the public and private sectors. Alternatively, there are opportunities to undertake further study at postgraduate level.

Departments/Faculties:

Department of Accounting and Finance
Department of Business and Management Studies
Department of Corporate Strategy
Department of Human Resource Management
Department of Marketing
Department of Public Policy and Managerial Studies

Links with Academic Institutions:

The School has links with a large number of European institutions via the Socrates Exchange Programme. An exchange programme also operates on the full-time MBA programme with a group of European partners which allows students to spend one semester of the programme abroad.

Student Testimonials:

"While I was at DMU I enjoyed the study format and the diverse range of subjects within the course. The staff were always helpful and considerate, with excellent back-up facilities."

General Undergraduate Courses

BA/BA (Hons) Business Studies

Aims to provide advanced general education for business combined with practical work experience and a measure of specialisation.

Modular Course?	Yes
Qualifications:	BA; BA Hons
Application Deadline:	UCAS deadline
Commencement Date:	September
Entry Requirement:	18 points
Applications to Places:	14:1
Registered:	160
Awards:	152

	Duration	EC Fees	Non-EC Fees
Full time		£1000	
Part time		£125 per module	
Sandwich		£500	

BA/BA (Hons) Business Administration

Grounds students with a sound understanding of business analysis and practice and gives them the opportunity to specialise in key areas.

Modular Course?	Yes

Qualifications:	BA; BA Hons
Application Deadline:	UCAS deadline
Commencement Date:	September
Entry Requirement:	14 points
Applications to Places:	6:1
Registered:	70
Awards:	74

	Duration	EC Fees	Non-EC Fees
Full time	£1000		
Part time			
Sandwich			

HND Business and Finance

Provides a vocational business education which is relevant to those people working in both the public and private sectors.

Modular Course?	Yes
Qualifications:	HND
Application Deadline:	UCAS deadline
Commencement Date:	September
Entry Requirement:	6 points
Applications to Places:	7:1
Registered:	40
Awards:	38
Full time	£1000
Part time	£125 per module
Sandwich	

BA/BA (Hons) Joint Honours Programme

Provides a sound grounding in basic business concepts, ideas and methodologies and combines an excellent general education in business with an opportunity to specialise in areas of interest. Students can select two from: Accounting; Business; Human Resource Management; Management; Marketing; Finance; Public Policy.

Modular Course?	No
Qualifications:	BA; BA Hons
Application Deadline:	UCAS deadline
Commencement Date:	September
Entry Requirement:	14 points
Applications to Places:	6:1
Registered:	New course
Awards:	n/a

	Duration	EC Fees	Non-EC Fees
Full time	£1000		
Part time			
Sandwich			

Specialist Undergraduate Course

BA/BA (Hons) Marketing

Modular Course?	Yes
Qualifications:	BA; BA Hons
Categories:	Marketing; Retailing

BA/BA (Hons) Human Resource Management

Modular Course?	Yes
Qualifications:	BA Hons
Categories:	Human Resources; Management

BA/BA (Hons) Accounting and Finance

Modular Course?	Yes
Qualifications:	BA; BA Hons
Categories:	Finance

BA/BA (Hons) Public Administration and Managerial Studies

Modular Course?	Yes
Qualifications:	BA; BA Hons
Categories:	Public Sector

HND Public Administration

Modular Course?	Yes
Qualifications:	HND
Categories:	Public Sector

BA/BA (Hons) Public Policy and Management

Modular Course?	Yes
Qualifications:	BA; BA Hons
Categories:	Public Sector

Dearne Valley Business School

Dearne Valley Business School

Address:	Doncaster College
	High Melton
	Doncaster
	DN5 7SZ
Area:	North East England
Phone:	01302 553666
Fax:	01302 553644 or 01302 553776
Email:	joanne.layhe@don.ac.uk
Website:	www.don.ac.uk/DVBS/index.htm
Email Application Available?	Yes
How to apply by email:	Prospective student to detail programme of interest and give address details and brochures and application forms will be sent via the external mail system.
Total Number of Teaching Staff:	30
Staff Teaching Undergraduate Courses	30
Research Rating:	n/a
Teaching Rating:	n/a
Additional Rating Information	
Male:Female Student Ratio	
Head of Business School	David Fell
Head of Undergraduate Studies	David Chesley
Admissions Contact	David Chesley or The Administrator

About the School:
The School was founded in 1992 as a result of £1million of City Challenge funding. In 1997 / 98 it has recruited 2500 students on to its programmes that range from NVQ 3 through HND and Undergraduate programmes to Postgraduate and Doctoral programmes. The School currently employs 30 full time teaching staff who all possess an appropriate mix of academic qualifications and business experience at senior management levels. The School has extensive links with UK businesses and 30% of its work is customised and delivered in-company. The School has also developed international links within USA, Asia and Europe.

About Undergraduate Studies:
The School offers a range of Undergraduate programmes with the opportunity to specialise in Marketing, Finance, Personnel, Operations, Administration, International Business and Management Information Systems. The innovative design of the programmes enables students to acquire practical skills and the appropriate professional qualification in addition to the Bachelors Degree. The subsequent career placement records of our students are impressive. Opportunities to study in the USA are available.

Facilities:
There is a full range of sporting facilities including a nine hole golf course within the School grounds.
Gymnasium
Multi -gym weight lifting, rowing machine etc.
Student Bar
Full range of conference facilities
There is accommodation on site for 250 students.

Departments/Faculties:
The School has five operational areas.
Postgraduate and Professional Programmes
Undergraduate Programmes
Training and Consultancy
Research and Development
Administration

Links with Academic Institutions:
The School's undergraduate and postgraduate degrees are validated by the University of Hull. The School has developed student exchange links with Georgetown College Kentucky, USA and the University of North Carolina at Wilmington, USA.

Links with Industry:
The School has extensive business links and its corporate client list includes:
British Aerospace, ICI, Du Pont, National Power, Yorkshire Chemicals, Avesta Sheffield, Bridon, JI Case, Denso Marston, Kvaerner Boving, Community Health Sheffield, Barnsley MBC, Rotherham MBC, Wakefield MDC, Lifetime Careers, Brook Crompton, Asda, Nokia, Royal Mail Rolls Royce Motor Cars and Halifax Property Services.
The School also works with a growing number of SMEs.

Student Testimonials:
"Dearne Valley has much to be proud of in respect of its business and management studies programmes" The Higher Education Funding Council for England.
"As an international student, I have found this to be a good learning environment and a quality programme which has increased by career opportunities". Donald Sweeting, Undergraduate Student

HND in Business / Marketing / Personnel /

Two year full time programme

Modular Course?	No
Qualifications:	HND
Application Deadline:	
Commencement Date:	Sept 1999
Entry Requirement:	A level or GNVQ
Applications to Places:	
Registered:	
Awards:	

	Duration	EC Fees	Non-EC Fees
Full time	Two years	£1000.	approx £6000 p.a.
Part time	n/a	n/a	n/a
Sandwich	n/a	n/a	n/a

BA (Hons) Business/ Marketing/Administration/ Personnel/International Bus.

Full time BA (Hons) programmes specialising in the above

Modular Course?	No
Qualifications:	BA Hons; IPD, CIM, IAM
Application Deadline:	
Commencement Date:	
Entry Requirement:	A levels HND Experience
Applications to Places:	
Registered:	
Awards:	

	Duration	EC Fees	Non-EC Fees
Full time	3 - 4 years	£1000	Approx £6000
Part time	3 - 6 years	£950	
Sandwich	3 - 4 years	£1000	Approx £6000

HND Top Up to BA (Hons) Business - Studies, Personnel, Admin, Marketing, International Business

Top up programme to a degree

Modular Course?	No
Qualifications:	BA Hons; IPD, CIM, IAM
Application Deadline:	
Commencement Date:	Sept 99
Entry Requirement:	HND/HNC 240 CATS points for one year top up
Applications to Places:	
Registered:	
Awards:	

	Duration	EC Fees	Non-EC Fees
Part time	1 - 3 years	£1000	n/a
Sandwich	1- 2 years	£1000.	Approx £6000

Dundee Business School

Dundee Business School

Address:	Bell Street
	Dundee
	DD1 1HG
Area:	Scotland
Phone:	01382 308401
Fax:	01382 308400

Email:

Website: **www.tay.ac.uk**

Email Application Available?	**No**
How to apply by email:	
Total Number of Teaching Staff:	**60**
Staff Teaching Undergraduate Courses	**60**
Research Rating:	**1**
Teaching Rating:	**Satisfactory**
Additional Rating Information	
Male:Female Student Ratio	**51:49**
Head of Business School	**Graeme Martin**
Head of Undergraduate Studies	**Robert Jelly MA MBA CA**
Admissions Contact	**Maggie McCann BA (Hons)**

About the School:

Dundee Business School is an intregal part of the University of Abertay Dundee, one of Scotland's foremost centres of higher technological education that has been producing high quality graduates for more than a century. The Business School was set up in 1993, and its mission is to provide high quality postgraduate and post-experience education, applied research and commercial services to a range of local and international clients and students. The School is constantly expanding its role in the overseas marketplace and currently operates taught MBA programmes in Malaysia, Hong Kong, Cyprus and Greece in conjunction with local institutions.

The Business School is housed in Dundee's historic Dudhope Castle, just ten minutes walk from the city centre and the facilities offered by the University's main campus. Teaching rooms and a computer suite are sited at the Castle and there is dedicated car parking on site.

About Undergraduate Studies:

Virtually all of the University's courses are taught by modules, each of which is taught over one semester, i.e. one half of an academic year. One of the significant advantages of the Modular Scheme is that it provides greater flexibility of course content as, depending on the chosen course, in addition to core modules, it is possible to choose optional and elective modules from a wide range of subjects. This allows the course to be tailored to suit individual interests and career aspirations.

Facilities:

Dundee has a wealth of sporting and leisure facilities, particularly golf, and its proximity to mountains and glens makes it an ideal centre for hill-walking and skiing. There are also plenty of less energetic pursuits, including cinemas, theatres, concerts and museums. The Students' Association provides recreational facilities within the University. Overseas students are well served by an International Students' Society within the University who organise social events to make students welcome.

Student Testimonials:

'The BA in Law course has not only improved my knowledge of Scotland's legal system but it has taught me how to apply it; especially in the areas of conveyancing and executry law. During my course I was fortunate to gain a summer job with a solicitor's office in Edinburgh and I was delighted to find that the BA in Law course had provided me with excellent training for the job. My employer even commented that I required no formal training as my course at University had already done that.'
Saphena Hassan, Graduate in BA Law

'I look forward to the Marketing course every week. The staff are helpful... I had problems with changing an elective and the tutor helped me all day. They are really approachable and there is mutual respect, that's really good.'
Jane Grandison BA (Hons) Marketing and Retail Management 1st year.

'Last year I graduated from the University of Abertay Dundee with an Honours degree in European Business Management with Languages. Four years of lectures, coursework and trips around Europe has finally come to an end. I was honestly sad to see that part of my life come to an end, students on our course had become very close, and now it was time for us all to go our own ways. Most went back to their respective homes, however, I chose to stay on in Dundee.'
Karen Batley, BA (Hons) European Business Management with Languages

General Undergraduate Courses

BA (Hons) in European Business Law

The key feature of this course is that it combines a theoretical and applied study of business law of the UK, the law of one other member state and European Community law. The programme of study aims to equip graduates for careers in business, commerce or public administration in a European context particularly within regulatory or advisory bodies. A variety of teaching methods is used on the course with an emphasis on student participation. In the third year of the course the students live abroad studying at an institution of higher education in another EU Member State.

Modular Course?	Yes	
Qualifications:	BA; BA Hons	
Application Deadline:	UCAS deadline	
Commencement Date:	September	
Entry Requirement:	SCE - BBC including English	
	GCE - CD including English at	
	GCSE level	
	Irish Leaving Cert (H) - BBCC	
	including English.	
Applications to Places:	3:1	
Registered:	29	
Awards:	10	

	Duration	EC Fees	Non-EC Fees
Full time	4 years	£1000	£5750
Part time			
Sandwich			

BA (Hons) in Travel Law

The travel industry is one of the world's largest industries, and represents a major human activity. This degree built upon the School's internationally recognised work in Travel Law, operates within a suite of Law courses which have significant commonality of curriculum in their early years, enabling students to specialise in travel Law or transfer to other Law specialisms should they change their career aspirations once enrolled.

Modular Course?	Yes	
Qualifications:	BA; BA Hons	
Application Deadline:	UCAS deadline	
Commencement Date:	September	
Entry Requirement:	SCE - BBC including English GCE	
	- CD including English at GCSE	
	level Irish Leaving Cert (H) -	
	BBCC including English	
Applications to Places:		
Registered:		
Awards:		

	Duration	EC Fees	Non-EC Fees
Full time	4 years	£1000	£5750
Part time			
Sandwich			

BA (Hons) in Business Administration

This course is designed to provide holders of an HND in Business Administration with the opportunity to gain a degree by successfully completing one year of study and an honours degree after two years of study. In the degree year students will consider aspects of organisation and management, business law, human resource management, marketing, accounting, information systems and quantitative management.

Modular Course?	Yes	
Qualifications:	BA; BA Hons	
Application Deadline:	UCAS deadline	
Commencement Date:	September	
Entry Requirement:	An appropriate HND (direct from	
	HND into Year 3 only)	
Applications to Places:	4:1	
Registered:	52	
Awards:	62	

	Duration	EC Fees	Non-EC Fees
Full time	2 years	£1000	£5750
Part time			
Sandwich			

BA (Hons) in Business Studies

This course prepares graduates for a wide range of careers in industry and the public sector. Its 'thin sandwich' structure (i.e.: it has two six-month periods of paid supervised work placement) provides opportunities to spend periods in Europe or farther afield experiencing different types of employment and working in different functional management areas.

Modular Course?	Yes	
Qualifications:	BA; BA Hons	
Application Deadline:	UCAS deadline	
Commencement Date:	September	
Entry Requirement:	SCE - BBCC	
	GCE - CC or DDD	
	Irish Leaving Cert. (H) - BBCCC	
	An appropriate HNC/HND	
Applications to Places:	8:1	
Registered:	75	
Awards:	64	

	Duration	EC Fees	Non-EC Fees
Full time	4 years	£1000	£5750
Part time			
Sandwich			

BA (Hons) in European Business Management with Languages

and who wish to give their study a European orientation. The language modules have a management focus, with emphasis on interactive and team work. The year abroad - the third year of the course - is a fully integrated period of study which offers students the opportunity to develop their linguistic skills as well as their understanding of other European business cultures.

Modular Course?	Yes
Qualifications:	BA; BA Hons
Application Deadline:	UCAS deadline
Commencement Date:	September
Entry Requirement:	SCE - BBCCC, including English and French, German or Spanish GCE - CC or DDD, including English and French, German or Spanish Irish Leaving Cert. (H) - BBCCC, including English and French, German or Spanish
Applications to Places:	3:1
Registered:	23
Awards:	15

	Duration	EC Fees	Non-EC Fees
Full time	4 years	£1000	£5750
Part time			
Sandwich			

BA (Hons) in Marketing; BA (Hons) in Marketing with Languages; BA (Hons) in Marketing with Retail Management

All students on this programme of marketing courses study a foundation year comprising marketing modules and modules from supporting disciplines such as information technology, economics and behavioural sciences. In years two, three and four there is a progressive specialisation in each degree pathway but, in order to ensure that all students acquire a high level of general marketing skills, a core set of marketing modules is studied by all students of the programme. At the beginning of year three, students studying one of the more specialised degrees i.e.: Marketing with Retail Management, Marketing with Languages, may change to the Marketing degree. In year four there is a range of option subjects available for each degree pathway.

Modular Course?	Yes
Qualifications:	BA; BA Hons
Application Deadline:	UCAS deadline
Commencement Date:	September
Applications to Places:	3:1
Registered:	37
Awards:	

	Duration	EC Fees	Non-EC Fees
Full time	4 years	£1000	£5750
Part time			
Sandwich			

BA (Hons) in Management

The programme has been designed to provide both a broadly-based preparation for a career in management and to enable students to tailor their studies to suit the specific requirements of different types of organisational environment, for example, service organisations, international corporate business, small and medium sized businesses, not-for-profit organisations, and emerging sectors such as leisure and recreation management. The programme emphasises the acquisition by students of interpersonal, informational and decisional skills, their development of knowledge and understanding of the operating context of contemporary organisations and of the purposes and processes of modern management.

Modular Course?	Yes
Qualifications:	BA; BA Hons
Application Deadline:	UCAS deadline
Commencement Date:	September
Entry Requirement:	SCE - BBCC GCE - CC or DDD Irish Leaving Cert (H) - BBCCC An appropriate HNC/HND
Applications to Places:	
Registered:	
Awards:	

	Duration	EC Fees	Non-EC Fees
Full time	4 years	£1000	£5750
Part time			
Sandwich			

BA (Hons) in Marketing and Design

The course will provide a vocational marketing route for design skilled HND students who have demonstrated their ability to progress into degree studies. This course seeks to bridge the gap between design and marketing through the provision of the extension of HND studies in art and design to level 3 undergraduate study. Marketing modules will deliver the knowledge and skills required to conceptualise and manage the integration of design and marketing. A level 4 programme is also provided to further develop these skills. This will be achieved through a combination of more advanced study, as well as an applied project at level 4. The teaching programme seeks to accommodate the differences between the educational backgrounds of UAD students and those with an HND background through the tutorial

Modular Course? programmes for each module.	Yes
Qualifications:	BA; BA Hons
Application Deadline:	UCAS deadline
Commencement Date:	September
Entry Requirement:	An appropriate HND (direct from HND into Year 3 only)
Applications to Places:	1:1
Registered:	11
Awards:	

	Duration	EC Fees	Non-EC Fees
Full time	2 years	£1000	£5750

BA (Hons) in Accounting

The course is recognised by all of the principal accountancy bodies. The Board of Accreditation of Educational courses, on behalf of the Institute of Chartered Accountants in England and Wales; the Chartered Institute of Management Accountants and the Chartered Institute of Public Finance & Accountancy, grants exemption from the foundation or level 1 course of these bodies and in certain circumstances from other subjects in their professional level examinations. This course is also fully accredited by the Institute of Chartered Accountants of Scotland. The University's degree course in accounting is. Therefore, an appropriate qualification for students who wish to develop a professional career in accountancy.

Modular Course?	Yes
Qualifications:	BA; BA Hons/HND/HNC
Application Deadline:	UCAS deadline
Commencement Date:	September
Entry Requirement:	SCE - BBBC, including English
	GCE - BC Irish leaving Cert (H) -
	BBCCC, including English
Applications to Places:	5:1
Registered:	38
Awards:	65

	Duration	EC Fees	Non-EC Fees
Full time	4 years	£1000	£5750
Part time			
Sandwich			

BA (Hons) in Accountancy and Finance

The course is recognised by all of the principal accountancy bodies. The Board of Accreditation of Educational Courses, on behalf of the Institute of Chartered Accountants in England and Wales; the Chartered Institute of Management Accountants and the Chartered Institute of Public Finance and Accountancy, grants exemption from the foundation or level 1 course of these bodies and in certain circumstances from other subjects in their professional level examinations. The Chartered Association of Certified Accountants also grants similar exemptions. This course is also fully accredited by the Institute of Chartered Accountants of Scotland. The University's degree course in accounting is, therefore, an appropriate qualification for students who wish to develop a professional career in the industry.

Modular Course?	Yes
Qualifications:	BA; BA Hons
Application Deadline:	UCAS deadline
Commencement Date:	September
Entry Requirement:	SCE - BBC, including English GCE

	- CD Irish Leaving Cert (H) -
	BBCC An appropriate HNC/HND
Applications to Places:	2:1
Registered:	8
Awards:	

	Duration	EC Fees	Non-EC Fees
Full time	4 years	£1000	£5750
Part time			
Sandwich			

BA (Hons) in Taxation and Revenue Law

This is the first taxation degree to be offered by a Scottish University. It is being introduced to meet the growing requirement for taxation specialists with the necessary intellectual and practical skills to work in a wide range of jobs. The course builds on the School's expertise in taxation and revenue law in order to provide a specialist vocationally relevant degree in taxation which is underpinned by a thorough background in accounting, law, information systems and information technology.

Modular Course?	Yes
Qualifications:	BA; BA Hons
Application Deadline:	UCAS deadline
Commencement Date:	September
Entry Requirement:	SCE - BBC
	GCE - CD
	Irish Leaving Cert (H) - BBCC
	An appropriate HND/HNC
Applications to Places:	2:1
Registered:	3
Awards:	

	Duration	EC Fees	Non-EC Fees
Full time	4 years	£1000	£5750
Part time			
Sandwich			

BA (Hons) in Financial Servies

This course aims to provide students with a vocationally relevant qualification which incorporates a high level of information technology relevant to the financial services industry. A feature of the course design allows holders of an HND in Financial Services or a similar HND to continue their studies to an honours degree in two years. The course is interdisciplinary and students who wish to study a European language will have the option to do so in all years of the programme. The degree can lead to a wide range of careers in banking, insurance, building societies, investment management, stock-broking, management consultancy and accountancy.

Modular Course?	Yes
Qualifications:	BA; BA Hons
Application Deadline:	UCAS deadline

Commencement Date:	September	
Entry Requirement:	SCE - BBC	
	GCE - CD	
	Irish leaving Cert (H) - BBCC	
	An appropriate HNC/HND	
Applications to Places:	2:1	
Registered:	3	
Awards:	1	

	Duration	EC Fees	Non-EC Fees
Full time	4 years	£1000	£5750
Part time			
Sandwich			

BA (Hons) in Law (including Diploma in Conveyancing & Executry Law)

The course provides a range of subjects which form part of the Scottish Legal System, including detailed study of the theory and practice of conveyancing and executry administration. On successful completion of the third year of the course students obtain a BA in Law. If they choose to study conveyancing and wills, trusts and succession in the third year, they will also be awarded the Diploma in Conveyancing and Executry Law. This will enable them after a period of postgraduate training to become a licensed conveyancer and executry practitioner, authorised by the Scottish Conveyancing and Executry Services Board.

Modular Course?	Yes
Qualifications:	BA; BA Hons; Diploma HE
Application Deadline:	UCAS deadline
Commencement Date:	September
Entry Requirement:	SCE - BBC including English
Applications to Places:	4:1
Registered:	35
Awards:	30

	Duration	EC Fees	Non-EC Fees
Full time	4 years	£1000	£5750
Part time			
Sandwich			

Durham University Business School

Durham University Business School

Address:	Mill Hill Lane
	Durham
	DH1 3LB
Area:	North East England
Phone:	0191 374 2211
Fax:	0191 374 3748
Email:	**mso.dubs@durham.ac.uk**
Website:	**http://www.dur.ac.uk/dubs**
Email Application Available?	No
How to apply by email:	
Total Number of Teaching Staff:	58
Staff Teaching Undergraduate Courses	8
Research Rating:	3a
Teaching Rating:	Satisfactory
Additional Rating Information	
Male:Female Student Ratio	25:75
Head of Business School	Professor Tony Cockerill
Head of Undergraduate Studies	John Ritchie
Admissions Contact	Lynn Young/Alison Fairlamb

About the School:

Durham University Business School is an integral part of the University of Durham, one of the oldest and most respected universitites in the UK. The School was established in 1965 and has developed an international reputation for its innovative approach to management education and enterprise development. More than 100 academic and administrative staff offer three MBA programmes and a wide range of other graduate and executive programmes, together with research and consultancy, all at regional, national and international level.

About Undergraduate Studies:

Management is a subject which can be approached from many different perspectives. At Durham this is reflected by the opportunity to study Management in conjunction with other disciplines rather than as a single honours course. You can choose to take Management as a major element of your overall degree from a wide range of degree courses:

Modern Chinese and Management Studies
Japanese and Management Studies
Combined Honours in Arts
Combined Honours in Social Sciences
Business Economics
Business Finance

Facilities:

As part of the University of Durham, the School has access to a wide range of social and cultural facilities including a major sports centre, fourteen colleges and societies, fifty-six sports clubs and a Students Union. The School has its own coffee lounge, bar and residential lounge. The City of Durham, with its cathedral and castle is heralded as one of UNESCO's World Heritage Sites.

Departments/Faculties:

Small Business Centre
Centre for Executive Education
Centre for Risk and Crisis Management
Study of Supply Chain Strategy
Foresight Research Centre
Public Sector Management Research
Sports in the Community

Links with Academic Institutions:

Acadia University, Nova Scotia, Canada
The Academy of National Economy, Moscow
Chinese Europe International Business School, China
UNIDO, Austria
Curtin Business School, Perth, Australia
National Economic University, Hanoi
Narsi Monjee Institute for Management Studies, Mumbai, India

Links with Industry:

Amec
Barclays Bank
Black & Decker
Institute of Directors
National Westminster Bank
North East Water
Samsung
Schlumberger
TWR

General Undergraduate Courses

BA (Hons) Undergraduate Programme

Although the Business School does not offer a single honours degree in management, it contributes to undergraduate programmes run by other departments, leading to a BA (Hons). Management can be chosen as a major element of a wide range of degree courses including: Modern Chinese and Management; Japanese and Management; Engineering and Management. A variety of modules within Arts and Social Science degrees are offered, including combined honours. In the first year, the core module Introduction to Management offers a broad perspective on modern management and the key issues facing managers.

Participants may also take the Management Project and Methods module which allows them to research and write a report on a specific management topic. The second and third years concentrate on studying particular management areas in much greater depth and participants may also write a dissertation. Teaching and learning are via lectures, seminars, tutorials, case-study workshops, and project work with individual supervision for the dissertation.

Modular Course?	No
Qualifications:	BA Hons
Application Deadline:	UCAS deadlines
Commencement Date:	October
Entry Requirement:	A-level scores ABC/BBC.
Applications to Places:	
Registered:	
Awards:	

	Duration	EC Fees	Non-EC Fees
Full time	3 years	£1000	£6600
Part time			
Sandwich			

School of Management

School of Management

Address:	Norwich
	NR4 7TJ
Area:	North East England
Phone:	01603 593 209
Fax:	01603 593 715
Email:	**mgt.admiss@uea.ac.uk**
Website:	**http://www.mgt.uea.ac.uk/**

Email Application Available?	Yes
How to apply by email:	ug.mgt@uea.ac.uk
	pg.mgt@uea.ac.uk
Total Number of Teaching Staff:	16
Staff Teaching Undergraduate Courses	16
Research Rating:	n/a
Teaching Rating:	n/a
Additional Rating Information	As the school was only recently founded in 1995, it is inappropriate to apply research and teaching ratings at this time. The University, however, has a reputation for, and a commitment to, excellence in both teaching and research.
Male:Female Student Ratio	55:45
Head of Business School	Professor Keith Fletcher
Head of Undergraduate Studies	
Admissions Contact	Undergraduate Admissions Secretary

About the School:
The School of Management was formed in 1995 as a collective, interdisciplinary school. The structure of the school allows it to draw upon the additional strengths of the Schools of Economics, Education and Professional Development, Information Systems, and Law. Its fundamental ethos is global, strategic and reflective. The school aims to provide high quality teaching provision which is informed by the innovative nature and excellence of its research.

About Undergraduate Studies:
We expect our graduates will have developed an interest and understanding of a range of business and management issues. Courses are intended to be academically satisfying and at the same time to facilitate integration into chosen careers or provide the necessary

foundation for those who wish to go into business for themselves. About two-thirds of our accounting graduates take up training with accountancy firms. Our management graduates enter a wide range of positions in business, commerce and the public sector.

Facilities:
The students' union at UEA has a reputation for innovation and excellence which has placed it as one of the most popular and highly regarded student unions in the UK. UEA is a major concert venue and attracts many of the leading groups. It also hosts the acclaimed Sainsbury Centre for Visual Art. In addition to the activities on campus, Norwich provides a rich variety of entertainments and activities, with major theatres, cinemas, concert halls and art centres as well as clubs and discos. On campus there are tennis courts, an all-weather athletics track and facilities for most sports. The University has also been awarded substantial grant funding for a new sports complex on campus.

Links with Academic Institutions:
The international students at UEA come from more than 100 different countries world-wide. The University has formal exchange agreements with 43 universities in the USA and Canada, is one of fifteen UK universities that make up the British Universities India Consortium, and has collaborative agreements with four Japanese and two Korean universities, allowing the exchange of staff and students.

Links with Industry:
Faculty in the School of Management have close and fruitful links with firms, both regionally and nationally, and these links enhance the quality of our courses. Norfolk is currently attracting interest from a number of major firms as a vibrant and attractive place to locate, and the University is actively building links with firms through its business liaison office. In addition, we are host to the Computers in Teaching Initiative in Accounting and Management, and the Hoshin Kanri Network which include some of the leading companies in the UK.

Student Testimonials:
"UEA was one of only a few universities that offered Accounting with Law and I'm really enjoying it. You benefit from expertise throughout the University - I have lectures in economics, maths, statistics and computing, as well as law. And in my third year, I might even take a unit in music, as I love singing. That's what I like about UEA - it's got a really modern outlook and you can gear your course towards what you need." Rachel Smith, first year Accounting with Law student.
"My time at UEA was thoroughly enjoyable. The course prepared me well for my career in business, and I am now a trainee management accountant for Lloyds Bank. The staff in the School of Management are very approachable and the support given is excellent. There

are a full range of courses which allows you to acquire as broad or as specialised an education in business as you desire. When considering various universities, this wide choice appealed to me very much and was the main reason I chose UEA and the School of Management. It was a decision that I have not regretted." Andrew Myson, Accounting and Finance, 1997

General Undergraduate Courses

Accounting and Finance

The course is particularly appropriate if you are planning to enter the accountancy profession and obtain a professional accountancy qualification after graduation.

Modular Course?	No
Qualifications:	BSc Hons
Application Deadline:	August
Commencement Date:	September
Entry Requirement:	A levels BBB/BBC, with at least a grade B in GCSE mathematics, but A-level mathematics would be an advantage.
Applications to Places:	6 to 1
Registered:	42
Awards:	46

	Duration	EC Fees	Non-EC Fees
Full time	3 years	£750	£6980
Part time			
Sandwich			

Accounting Information Systems

This course places a greater emphasis on the role of accounting as the provider of information to management. You will gain specialised knowledge of computer and information systems, and on enhanced ability to communicate effectively with information specialists in the design and operation of modern accounting systems.

Modular Course?	No
Qualifications:	BSc Hons
Application Deadline:	August
Commencement Date:	September
Entry Requirement:	A levels of BBB/BBC. A grade B at GCSE mathematics is required, but A level mathematics may be an advantage.
Applications to Places:	5 to 1
Registered:	11
Awards:	12

	Duration	EC Fees	Non-EC Fees
Full time	3 years	£750	£6980
Part time			
Sandwich			

Accounting with Law

This course is offered in conjunction with the School of Law and will be of particular interest if you are aiming to pursue a career in management or the financial sector.

Modular Course?	No
Qualifications:	BSc Hons
Application Deadline:	August
Commencement Date:	September
Entry Requirement:	A levels at BBB/BBC, with Grade B in GCSE mathematics.
Applications to Places:	5.5 to 1
Registered:	14
Awards:	4

	Duration	EC Fees	Non-EC Fees
Full time	3 years	£750	£6980
Part time			
Sandwich			

Business Finance and Economics

This course is offered in conjunction with the School of Economics and is built around the core disciplines of accounting, finance and economics.

Modular Course?	No
Qualifications:	BSc Hons
Application Deadline:	August
Commencement Date:	September
Entry Requirement:	A level of BBB/BBC. An A level in mathematics is preferred, but a grade B at GCSE is required.
Applications to Places:	
Registered:	8
Awards:	17

	Duration	EC Fees	Non-EC Fees
Full time	3 years	£750	£6980
Part time			
Sandwich			

Accounting with Management

This course is designed for students who wish to study for a professionally accredited degree but at the same time have the opportunity to broaden their interests into general management subjects.

Modular Course?	No
Qualifications:	BSc Hons
Application Deadline:	August
Commencement Date:	September

Entry Requirement:			A levels BBB/BBC. We prefer A level mathematics, but a grade B at GCSE is required.
Applications to Places:			6 to 1
Registered:			3
Awards:			NA
Full time	3 years	£750	£6980
Part time			
Sandwich			

Business Management

This course gives you a general and critically based understanding of business management, and offers the opportunity to develop particular specialisms.

Modular Course?	No
Qualifications:	BSc Hons
Application Deadline:	August
Commencement Date:	September
Entry Requirement:	A levels BBB/BBC with at least a C in GCSE Mathematics.
Applications to Places:	12 to 1
Registered:	81
Awards:	NA

	Duration	EC Fees	Non-EC Fees
Full time	3 years	£750	£6980
Part time			
Sandwich			

Business Information Systems

This course is offered in conjunction with the School of Information Systems and is designed for students who either envisage a career designing and implementing computerised wytems in a business environment, or who wish to become managers with a full knowledge of what IT can do for them.

Modular Course?	No
Qualifications:	BSc Hons
Application Deadline:	August
Commencement Date:	September
Entry Requirement:	A level BBB/BBC, with at least a grade B in GCSE Mathematics.
Applications to Places:	
Registered:	
Awards:	

	Duration	EC Fees	Non-EC Fees
Full time	3 years	£750	£6980
Part time			
Sandwich			

The East London Business School

Undergraduate Programme Area

Address:	Longbridge Road
	Dagenham
	Essex
	RM8 2AS
Area:	London and South East England
Phone:	0181 590 7000
Fax:	0181 849 3451
Email:	ugselbs@uel.ac.uk
Website:	http://www.elbs.uel.ac.uk

Email Application Available?	Yes
How to apply by email:	ugselbs@uel.ac.uk
Total Number of Teaching Staff:	140
Staff Teaching Undergraduate Courses	60
Research Rating:	2
Teaching Rating:	Satisfactory
Additional Rating Information	
Male:Female Student Ratio	60:40
Head of Business School	Philip Knowles
Head of Undergraduate Studies	Graham Curtis
Admissions Contact	Sue Carrette

About the School:

The East London Business School is part of the University of East London. It has 140 visiting and full-time staff belonging to four subject groups - Acccounting and Finance, Business Information Systems, Strategic & International Management and Human Resource Management. 2,500 students read full-time, sandwich and part-time degrees and diplomas. The School has a strong international dimension both in its staff and students, and in the teaching on research programmes. All postgradute and post-experience courses are taught at Duncan House close to Stratford and close to London Docklands which also houses its SME orientated Business Development Centre which is part ERDF-funded.

About Undergraduate Studies:

The Business School participates in the University-wide modular degree scheme. Undergraduates can read Accounting, Business Studies and Business Information as single, joint honours or minor pathways. Highlights of the programme include the Ford programmes, links with the Far East and flexible undergraduate courses.

Facilities:

The University has a self-contained sports centre, incorporating a swimming pool and gym at the Barking campus. There are over 60 societies flourishing within the University covering a very wide range of interests and activities.

Departments/Faculties:

The School operates a matrix management structure. It is divided into three programme areas, Undergraduate, Postgraduate and Corporate Programmes while staff are distributed across its four subject areas.

Links with Academic Institutions:

ELBS has a wide range of European Socrates partners and is in partnership with Institutions in Singapore, Malaysia, China and India. The Business School carries out undergraduate business education for Queen Mary and Westfield College.

Links with Industry:

ELBS has an Industrial Partnership Programme with Ford, UK, Ford, Europe and Jaguar, currently, over 200 employees of these companies study on ELBS courses at their work place. Over 100 SMEs are full partners of our Business Development Centre and the School is running an innovative IT training programmes for Logica.

Student Testimonials:

"I enjoy the course because it is challenging and provides a wide range of topics for study. It also gives a thorough grounding in professional practice which is what I want to pursue." (Student, BA (Hons) Accounting and Finance.)

"The syllabus is up-to-date and reflects the current state of technology in industry. Issues raised on the course have helped me to identify solutions and pitfalls which I come across in my work." (First Class Honours student, BSc (Hons) Distributed Information Systems.)

General Undergraduate Courses

BA (Hons) Accounting and Finance

A three-year specialist course designed to provide a thorough understanding of the theory and practice of accounting and finance and subjects related to it, evaluate and resolve problems. The degree is accredited by all the major accountancy bodies and offers exemption from foundation and professional stage examinations

Modular Course?	Yes
Qualifications:	BA Hons; Joint Honours; Diploma HE; Certificate HE
Application Deadline:	UCAS deadline

	Duration	EC Fees	Non-EC Fees
Commencement Date:			September and February each year
Entry Requirement:			Two good GCE A level passes supported by passes in at least three GCSE subjects, including English Language and Mathematics at grade C or above.
Applications to Places:			10:1
Registered:			90
Awards:			96

	Duration	EC Fees	Non-EC Fees
Full time	3 years	£1000	£6200
Part time	Min 4.5 years	£145 per subject	£1030 per subject
Sandwich			

BA (Hons) Business Studies (with sandwich) BA (Hons) Business Administration (non-sandwich)

The course not only introduces students to the latest business concepts and management techniques but also enables students to respond critically to the latest 'fads and fashions' in management. The watchword is critical evaluation not blank acceptance of received wisdom. The Business Studies courses include major contributions from a number of subject areas within the Business School, namely Accounting, Strategic and International Management, Business Information Systems, Human Resource Management and Marketing. In addition, students can combine their studies with languages and other subjects and can include a work placement in UK or abroad

Modular Course?	Yes
Qualifications:	BA Hons; Joint Honours; Diploma HE; Certificate HE
Application Deadline:	UCAS deadline
Commencement Date:	September and February each year
Entry Requirement:	Two good A levels plus GCSE grade C or above in Mathematics and English Language or equivalent. OR A good pass in BTEC National Diploma (including 3 or 4 distinctions in 2nd Year units) plus GCSE grade C or above in Mathematics and English Language or equivalent. OR Advanced GNVQ passes in Business (Distinction) plus GCSE grade C or above in Mathematics and English Language
Applications to Places:	20:1

Registered:	180
Awards:	169

	Duration	EC Fees	Non-EC Fees
Full time	3 years	£1000	£6200
Part time	Min 4.5 years	£145 per subject	£1030 per subject
Sandwich			

BSc Business Information Systems

The Computing and Business Information Systems (CBS) Subject Area provides a range of courses which enable students to develop skills in systems analysis, design, programming, distributed systems and the management of technology. There are several named pathways within the subject area each leading to a differently named degree. Under the modular scheme it is possible to take CBS units solely leading to a Single Honours degree or to combine a programme of CBS units with other subjects in the University's Undergraduate Degree Scheme leading to a Combined Honours degree.

Modular Course?	Yes
Qualifications:	BSc Hons; Joint Honours; Diploma HE; Certificate HE
Application Deadline:	UCAS deadline
Commencement Date:	September and February each year
Entry Requirement:	Two good A level passes OR Advanced GNVQ (Merit) OR BTEC National Diploma (majority Merits in Year 2) OR A pass in a recognised Access course.
Applications to Places:	8:1
Registered:	110
Awards:	70

	Duration	EC Fees	Non-EC Fees
Full time	3 years	£1000	£6200
Part time	Min 4.5 years	£145 per subject	£1030 per subject
Sandwich			

Specialist Undergraduate Course

BA (Hons) Business Studies

Modular Course?	Yes
Qualifications:	Joint Honours; Diploma HE; Certificate HE
Categories:	Human Resources; Finance; Marketing

BA (Hons) Business Studies (Marketing)

Modular Course?	Yes

| Qualifications: | BA Hons; Joint Honours; Diploma HE; Certificate HE |
| Categories: | Marketing; Management; International Marketing |

BA (Hons) Business Studies (Human Resource Management)

Modular Course?	Yes
Qualifications:	BA Hons; Joint Honours; Diploma HE; Certificate HE
Categories:	Human Resources; Finance; Industrial Relations

BA (Hons) Business Studies (Business Finance)

Modular Course?	Yes
Qualifications:	BA Hons; Joint Honours; Diploma HE; Certificate HE
Categories:	Finance

BA (Hons) International Business

Modular Course?	No
Qualifications:	BA Hons; Joint Honours; Diploma HE; Certificate HE
Categories:	Management; International Business

University Certificate Fundamentals of Accounting

Modular Course?	No
Qualifications:	Certificate Level I
Categories:	Finance; Management

BA (Hons) Accounting and Finance

Modular Course?	Yes
Qualifications:	BA Hons
Categories:	Finance

BSc (Hons) Distributed Information Systems

Modular Course?	Yes
Qualifications:	BSc Hons; Joint Honours; Diploma HE; Certificate HE
Categories:	Management; Transport

BSc (Hons) Information Systems

Modular Course?	Yes
Qualifications:	BSc Hons; Joint Honours; Diploma HE; Certificate HE
Categories:	IT Systems

BSc (Hons) Software Engineering

Modular Course?	Yes
Qualifications:	BSc Hons; Joint Honours; Diploma HE; Certificate HE
Categories:	IT Systems

BSc Business Information Systems

Modular Course?	Yes
Qualifications:	BSc Hons; Joint Honours; Diploma HE; Certificate HE
Categories:	Management; IT Systems

BSc (Hons) Computing

Modular Course?	Yes
Qualifications:	BSc Hons; Joint Honours; Diploma HE; Certificate HE
Categories:	IT Systems

Edinburgh University Management School

Edinburgh University Management School

Address:	7 Bristo Square
	Edinburgh
	EH8 9AL
Area:	Scotland
Phone:	0131 650 3826
Fax:	0131 650 3053
Email:	**Management.School@ed.ac.uk**
Website:	**http://www.ems.ed.ac.uk**

Email Application Available?	Yes
How to apply by email:	Via website (see above)
Total Number of Teaching Staff:	70
Staff Teaching Undergraduate Courses	36
Research Rating:	5
Teaching Rating:	Excellent
Additional Rating Information	RAE 5a Dept of Accounting &
	Business Method -
	teaching rating Excellent
	RAE 4a Dept of Business Studies -
	teaching rating
	Highly Satisfactory
	Highly Satisfactory on SHEFC
	maps to Excellent on
	HEFC
Male:Female Student Ratio	50:50
Head of Department of Business Studies	Professor Paul Thompson
Director of Management School	Professor James Fleck
Admissions Contact	Dr JI Ansell

About the School:

The Department of Business Studies was one of the pioneers of business education in Britain. The first Bachelor of Commerce degrees were awarded in 1920, and we remain in the forefront of business teaching. Over its history, the Department has been a leading innovator with the introduction of core disciplines in Business Studies. The Department now has nine professors leading the full range of business competencies. Over the last few years, the Department has expanded to 46 members of staff.

About Undergraduate Studies:

The breadth of teaching allows a student to study a very general business studies degree or to specialise within specific disciplines such as Finance, Human Resource Management, Marketing and Management Science. Allied with the opportunity to take a wide range of options outside the Department, the degree programme has great flexibility. For example, joint degrees with Psychology, Law, Economics, Sociology, and Mathematics may be taken. Teaching facilities are excellent, including two fully-equipped computing laboratories. The Department has strong links with the financial and banking sectors and our students are sought after by employers. Through ERASMUS and other exchange programmes, students can study in a wide range of other countries.

Facilities:

The department is close to the city centre and the halls of residence. Edinburgh is one of the most attractive cities in Europe with a wide range of facilities, including several theatres, concert halls, cinemas and night clubs. A full range of sporting venues exist within Scotland's capital including Murrayfield and Meadowbank stadiums. There is easy access to the Scottish highlands and to the sea. A thriving Student Association provides a wide range of social and sporting facilities, and the University's sports hall and sports grounds are excellent.

Departments/Faculties:

The Department of Business Studies
The Department of Accounting & Business Method

Links with Industry:

The CONNECT programme, initiated by and based in The University of Edinburgh is now a Scotland-wide programme supported by other Scottish higher education institutions, and is based in The Management School. It aims to link high-tec entrepreneurs with the financial, technical and managerial resources that they need for success. The Teaching Company Scheme - a partnership with local businesses - is proving mutually beneficial. Four companies are currently taking advantage of the Scheme's benefits.

The Management School also provides a number of executive programmes for various firms, including a world-wide training course for Schlumberger Field Engineers on general management concepts.

General Undergraduate Courses

Bachelor of Commerce Degree

The Bachelor of Commerce Honours Degree is taken in four years. The degree starts with a general introduction to Business Studies in which students take the full range of disciplines within the Department.

Students will also take two other subjects from a wide range of offerings across the Faculty of Social Sciences. Students usually select Accounting and Economics, though Psychology is currently popular. Second and third year students will be allowed to select from a wide range of options and again will take some courses outside the Department. In the second year, students take a course in Quantitative Methods and, in the third year, General Management and Strategy. In the final year, students take six courses selected from an extensive range of subjects which include: Corporate Finance; Business Economics; Advertising, Retailing; International Business; Risk Management; Management of Innovation; Organisational Behaviour; Business Ethics.

Students may study abroad for a year in the third year as part of a degree and there are a range of exchange programmes to the USA, Sweden, Germany, Spain, Belgium and France. In some of the exchange institutions, classes are taught in English. Given the flexibility of the degree, each student is assigned to a Director of Study who helps the student make option choices. There are a range of Joint Degrees with Business Studies. These include: Accounting; Economics; French; German; Law; Mathematics; Spanish; Statistics. Each of these courses follow a similar pattern to the single Honours degree, though students will also spend their time on other disciplines, usually taking a course a year. In the final year, Joint Honours students will usually spend half their time taking Business Studies options and the remaining time studying other disciplines.

Modular Course?	No
Qualifications:	Bachelor of Commerce
Application Deadline:	15 December
Commencement Date:	
Entry Requirement:	BBB at A level, BBBB at Higher. Other qualifications considered. Requirements for Joint degrees on request.
Applications to Places:	14:1
Registered:	
Awards:	

	Duration	EC Fees	Non-EC Fees
Full time	4 years	On request	On request
Part time			
Sandwich			

Entry Requirement:		On request
Applications to Places:		
Registered:		
Awards:		
Full time	On request On request	On request
Part time		
Sandwich		

MA International Business

This degree aims to meet the needs of the market for Business Studies students with an international orientation. It is not specifically language-orientated.

Modular Course?	No —
Qualifications:	MA
Application Deadline:	On request
Commencement Date:	

European Business School London

European Business School London

Address:	Inner Circle
	Regent's Park
	London
	NW1 4NS, UK
Area:	London and South East England
Phone:	+44(0)171 487 7507
Fax:	+44(0)171 487 7425
Email:	**ebs@regents.ac.uk**
Website:	**http://www.regents.ac.uk**
Email Application Available?	No
How to apply by email:	
Total Number of Teaching Staff:	200
Staff Teaching Undergraduate Courses	200
Research Rating:	n/a
Teaching Rating:	n/a
Additional Rating Information	
Male:Female Student Ratio	60:40
Head of Business School	Professor E. De La Croix
Head of Undergraduate Studies	Professor E De La Croix
Admissions Contact	External Relations

About the School:

Situated in the heart of one of the most important financial centres in the world, the European Business School London was established in 1979 and has become a centre of excellence in international business and management education. Our graduates are skilful, experienced and confident; they approach business issues with a dynamic mix of academic and practical response.

About Undergraduate Studies:

The European Business School London was established in 1979 and has become a centre for excellence in international business and management education. EBS London works closely with the business world to ensure that its graduates match the requirements of companies and multinationals looking to recruit future managers.

Facilities:

EBS London has teams for a number of sports including football, rugby, volleyball and tennis and regularly compete against other colleges and universities in the London area. In addition there are tennis courts and a weight training room. Students are eligible for membership of the University of London Union and Internatioanl Students House. The student centre has a music practice room and lists information on the altest theatre productions, exhibitions, galleries, shows, bars, restaurants and other cultural interests.

Links with Academic Institutions:

At EBS London students study at least one language from French, German, Spanish, Italian, Japanese, Russian or Mandarin Chinese. On completion of Levels 100 and 200 students will spend at least one semester at an institution in a country that has a national language as the language of study. This exchange arrangement allows students to study at co-operating colleges and universities around the world for one or two semesters. Some of the links are with Socrates-Erasmus institutions where the exchanges are assisted with funding from the EU.

Our remarkable graduate employment record is a resounding endorsement of the practical business education and practical business education the EBS London provides.

Links with Industry:

All students at EBS London will complete at least 48 weeks of work experience during their course. This normally takes place in at least 3 countries within large corporations and multinationals. EBS London makes every effort to ensure that students have an individualised Work Experience and Career Objective Programme from Induction day to Graduation Day. This has ensured EBS London's outstanding employment record.

EBS London's host organisations for Work Experience include companies such as Anderson Consulting, Saatchi & Saatchi, Mercedes-Benz, Sotheby's IBM, Sony, Coopers & Lybrand and Reuters. In 1997, 100% of EBS London graduates looking for a position had found one by December of the same year.

Student Testimonials:

"Though I have only been with Procter & Gamble for a short time I believe my education has provided me with proper foundation for a successful career within the company. Though most of my colleagues are older than me and many have a Masters degree, my responsibilities equal theirs and I do not feel less equipped for dealing with the day-to-day work. For example, I was highly complimented on my first presentation. So now I find myself in Stockholm - another day, another country. Again I thank EBS London, for without the experiences gained during four years of studies, I probably would not have found it so easy to accustom myself to the Swedish way of life."
Michael Hollesen, EBS London graduate (1995)

BA (Hons) European Business Administration

A highly respected qualification designed for future executives planning a career in the countries of Europe. In addition to their own language and English, students study two other languages and complete a minimum of 48 weeks work experience in at least two countries

Modular Course?	Yes
Qualifications:	BA Hons; Diploma HE
Application Deadline:	UCAS deadline
Commencement Date:	September and January
Entry Requirement:	Minimum 2 A-levels or equivalent and successful completion of the general entrance test.
Applications to Places:	6:1
Registered:	
Awards:	Exemptions from professional qualifications

	Duration	EC Fees	Non-EC Fees
Full time	4 years	£8340 pa	
Part time			
Sandwich	4 years	£8340 pa	

BA (Hons) International Business Studies (2 languages)

A degree which provides the student with the advantages of EBS London's academic resources with a focus on the globalized business world of today, so that students develop an understanding of modern business practice in diverse international contexts. A strong international focus, enhanced by the combination of a European language with Japanese or Mandarin Chinese and minimum of 48 weeks work experience.

Modular Course?	Yes
Qualifications:	BA Hons; Diploma HE
Application Deadline:	UCAS deadline
Commencement Date:	September and January
Entry Requirement:	Minimum 2 A-levels or equivalent and successful completion
Applications to Places:	6:1
Registered:	200
Awards:	Exemptions from professional qualifications

	Duration	EC Fees	Non-EC Fees
Full time	4 years	£8340 pa	
Part time			
Sandwich	4 years	£8340 pa	

BA (Hons) International Business and Management Studies

This degree shows the importance of the international dimension in the study of business and also gives an emphasis to languages ana management studies. The practical part of these studies is a semester in the USA where the important building of a general knowledge of US business practice takes place. One international business language will be studied and all students will complete at least 48 weeks of work experience.

Modular Course?	Yes
Qualifications:	BA Hons; Diploma HE
Application Deadline:	UCAS deadline
Commencement Date:	September and January
Entry Requirement:	Minimum 2 A-levels or equivalent and successful completion of the General entrance test
Applications to Places:	6:1
Registered:	150
Awards:	Exemption from professional qualifications

	Duration	EC Fees	Non-EC Fees
Full time	4 years	£8340 pa	
Part time			
Sandwich	4 years	£8340 pa	

BA (Hons) International Business Studies (one language)

The language environment for the programme is in either Europe or Asia, which combines well with this degree's broad international perspective on modern business practice. One major international language will be studied. Normally this degree takes three and a half years to complete but optional additional work experience could extend it to four years.

Modular Course?	Yes
Qualifications:	BA Hons; Diploma HE
Application Deadline:	UCAS deadline
Commencement Date:	September and January
Entry Requirement:	Minimum 2 A-levels or equivalent and successful completion of the General entrace test
Applications to Places:	6:1
Registered:	150
Awards:	Exemption from professional qualifications

	Duration	EC Fees	Non-EC Fees
Full time	3.5 years	£8340 pa	
Part time			
Sandwich	4 years	£8340 pa	

BA (Hons) International Management Studies

This degree is only for those who already possess considerable language skills but wish to combine the international focus of an EBS London degree with some valuable experience in the United States. The semester, which may include a specialisation, is a key part of this degree, as is the minimum of 48 weeks work experience.

Modular Course?	Yes
Qualifications:	BA Hons; Diploma HE
Application Deadline:	UCAS deadline
Commencement Date:	September and January
Entry Requirement:	Minimum 2 A-levels or equivalent and successful completion
Applications to Places:	6:1
Registered:	50
Awards:	Exemptions from professional qualifications

	Duration	EC Fees	Non-EC Fees
Full time	4 years	£8340 pa	
Part time			
Sandwich	4 years	£8340 pa	

European School of Management - Oxford

European School of Management

Address:	12 Merton Street
	Oxford
	OX1 4JH
Area:	London and South East England
Phone:	01865 263200
Fax:	01865 251 960

Email: **ctaylor@eap.net**

Website: **http://www.eap.net**

Total Number of Teaching Staff:	27
Research Rating:	n/a
Teaching Rating:	n/a
Additional Rating Information	
Male:Female Student Ratio	
Head of Business School	Professor Chris Halliburton
Admissions Contact	Isabelle Pochic

About the School:

EAP is the European School of Management. Operating in four countries in Europe, it is the region's truly cross-border business school. Unlike most other business schools who add on an international dimension to a national identity, EAP has been international from the start.

Founded in 1973 with a vision to create a pan-European educational facility, EAP has centres in Paris, Oxford, Berlin and Madrid. It has developped strong partnerships in other European countries, North and South America as well as in Asia.

As a European graduate school of management, EAP's mission is to lead the field of cross-border education by providing innovative international management programmes which prepare students for the global business challenges of the 1990s and beyond.

University of Exeter School of Business and Economics

University of Exeter School of Business and Economics

Address:	Streatham Court
	Rennes Drive
	Exeter
	EX4 4PU
Area:	South West England
Phone:	01392 263200
Fax:	01392 263242

Email:

Website: **www.exeter.ac.uk**

Email Application Available?	No
How to apply by email:	
Total Number of Teaching Staff:	50
Staff Teaching Undergraduate Courses	50
Research Rating:	5
Teaching Rating:	Satisfactory
Additional Rating Information	
Male:Female Student Ratio	50:50
Head of Business School	Mr M Timbrell
Head of Undergraduate Studies	Mrs AC Mayes
Admissions Contact	Mrs J Adkins

About the School:
The new purpose-built School of Business and Economics originated with the amalgamation of the Centre for Management Studies and the Department of Economics in August 1997. The new Business School is equipped with all the state-of-the-art facilities you'd expect at one of the UK's most popular universities. We have forged close links with industry and strive to provide the courses needed by both students and employers.

About Undergraduate Studies:
The School of Business and Economics has eight undergraduate degree programmes within the School and a further four in conjunction with other Schools. All our degrees may be taken 'with European Study' – an increasingly popular choice spending the third year abroad, either in academic study or a combination of study and work placement.
Our degrees are otherwise taught over three years and span the wide range of interests within the School –

Accounting, Business Economics, Economics, Statistics and Econometrics, Finance and Management, the latter two being new subject areas which are being built up at the undergraduate level drawing on the considerable expertise already existing at postgraduate level. Exeter graduates remain very sought after by employers.

Facilities:
Our stunning 245 acre campus is renowned throughout the UK and offers an ideal study environment. There is a wide range of sporting facilities, a theatre, concert hall, bars, restaurants, shops, library, accommodation and a bank on campus. Overseas students are guaranteed accommodation with early acceptance of places. The Streatham campus is within the cathredral city boundaries with churches and a mosque near at hand. Exeter is surrrounded by beautiful countryside, with coastline and moors within easy reach. There are excellent rail and road links to London, the rest of the UK and Europe.

Student Testimonials:
'There are various reasons I chose to study at the University of Exeter. Having an interest in business, I tried to compare departments across the country. One way of doing this was to ask professionals which universities they thought highly of – Exeter features high on their lists. When I visited the University, the attractive campus was something which immediately struck me, especially when compared to other concrete city campuses. I found the staff to be extremely helpful, kind and knowledgeable; the other thing I particularly like is the large mixture of students from all around the world. I will be proud of my degree from the University of Exeter.'

General Undergraduate Courses

BA Business and Accounting
Business and Accounting Studies is aimed at students seeking a specialist understanding of accounting as well as a general introduction to a broad range of business subjects. The programme seeks to provide students with a thorough understanding of the subjects covered so that they can cope with the fast changing world of business and accountancy. Accountants and businessmen face an increasingly competitive world due to the globalization of markets and revolutions in information technology. Successful undergraduates for the twenty-first century whether in the field of business or accountancy will require a broad education if they are to seize the most attractive career opportunities. The accounting programmes at Exeter are designed to deliver that education.

Modular Course?	No
Qualifications:	BA; BA Hons

	Duration	EC Fees	Non-EC Fees
Application Deadline:			UCAS deadline
Commencement Date:			October
Entry Requirement:			24 points
Applications to Places:			11:1
Registered:			20
Awards:			n/a

	Duration	EC Fees	Non-EC Fees
Full time	3 years	£1000	£6645
Part time	6 years	pro rata	pro rata
Sandwich			

BA Economic and Statistics/ Management Statistics

These programmes provide a sound base in economics, statistics, accountancy and business computing with practical applications. There are many options to choose from including that of taking a foreign language in the second or third year, and those who are proficient in a language can, of course, study abroad for a year taking some of the management or business-orientated courses offered by several of the foreign universities. For those entering the Accountancy profession the degree offers some exemptions in the Accountancy examinations but the degree is just as suitable for those going into industry, the Civil Service, management consultancy, financial sector or actuarial work.

Modular Course?	No
Qualifications:	BA; BA Hons
Application Deadline:	UCAS deadline
Entry requirements:	20 (22 with General Studies)
Commencement Date:	October
Applications to Places:	8:1
Registered:	28
Awards:	8

	Duration	EC Fees	Non-EC Fees
Full time	3 years	£1000	£6645
Part time	6 years	pro rata	pro rata
Sandwich			

BA Economics and Finance

An increasing number of our graduates in recent years have found employment with financial institutions such as banks, insurance companies, pension funds, investment and unit trusts as well as stockbroking and financial advisory work. This degree programme aims to provide a theoretical background for students who wish to follow a career in the financial area.

Modular Course?	No
Qualifications:	BA; BA Hons
Application Deadline:	UCAS deadline
Commencement Date:	October
Entry Requirement:	22 (24 with General Studies)
Applications to Places:	n/a
Registered:	tbc
Awards:	n/a

	Duration	EC Fees	Non-EC Fees
Full time	3 years	£1000	£6645
Part time	6 years	pro rata	pro rata
Sandwich			

BA Accounting and Financial Studies

Accounting and Financial Studies is designed for students who are interested in following a career in the accounting profession and offers significant exemptions from the examinations of the major professional bodies. The programme seeks to provide students with a thorough understanding of the subjects covered so that they can cope with the fast changing world of business and accountancy. Accountants and businessmen face an increasingly competitive world due to the globalization of markets and revolutions in information technology. Successful undergraduates for the twenty-first century whether in the field of business or accountancy will require a broad education if they are to seize the most attractive career opportunities. The accounting programmes at Exeter are designed to deliver that education.

Modular Course?	No
Qualifications:	BA; BA Hons
Application Deadline:	UCAS deadline
Commencement Date:	October
Entry Requirement:	24 points
Applications to Places:	11:1
Registered:	54
Awards:	52

	Duration	EC Fees	Non-EC Fees
Full time	3 years	£1000	£6645
Part time	6 years	pro rata	pro rata
Sandwich			

BA Business and Management

The SH Business and Management Studies degree is designed to equip graduates for a management career in industry, commerce or the public sector. To this end the programme provides students with a detailed understanding of the functional areas of business and the relationship of management theories and practice to them.

Modular Course?	No
Qualifications:	BA; BA Hons
Application Deadline:	UCAS deadline
Commencement Date:	October
Entry Requirement:	22 (24 with General Studies)
Applications to Places:	33:1
Registered:	35
Awards:	n/a

	Duration	EC Fees	Non-EC Fees
Full time	3 years	£1000	£6645
Part time	6 years	pro rata	pro rata
Sandwich			

BA Business Economics

The objective of this degree programme is to provide graduates with a theoretical and practical understanding of the economic decisions faced by business and its managers and with the ability to analyse the economic and social environment in which these decisions are taken. The programme combines the development of key skills in economic, accounting and social analysis with the application of these skills to the solution of many interacting problems that face business managers. It will appeal particularly to anyone aiming for a career in business.

Modular Course?	No
Qualifications:	BA; BA Hons
Application Deadline:	UCAS deadline
Commencement Date:	October
Entry Requirement:	22 (24 with General Studies)
Registered:	33
Awards:	22

	Duration	EC Fees	Non-EC Fees
Full time	3 years	£1000	£6645
Part time	6 years	pro rata	pro rata
Sandwich			

BA Economics

Modern economics covers a wide range of topics from inflation to the control of monopoly power, from the study of developing countries to the finance of multinational companies. The SH Economics degree programme reflects that breadth of interest in a flexible course designed to cater both for the students who wish to study a broad curriculum and for those who may wish to specialise in a particular area. No previous study of economics is required or assumed. A good pass at GCSE mathematics is essential.

Modular Course?	No
Qualifications:	BA; BA Hons
Application Deadline:	UCAS deadline
Commencement Date:	October
Entry Requirement:	22 (24 with General Studies)
Applications to Places:	8:1
Registered:	54
Awards:	35

	Duration	EC Fees	Non-EC Fees
Full time	3 years	£1000	£6645
Part time	6 years	pro rata	pro rata
Sandwich			

Faculty of Business

Faculty of Business

Address:	Cowcaddens Road
	Glasgow
	G4 0BA
Area:	Scotland
Phone:	0141 331 3000
Fax:	0141 331 3500
Email:	fob@gcal.ac.uk
Website:	www.fob.gcal.ac.uk
Email Application Available?	No
How to apply by email:	
Total Number of Teaching Staff:	212
Staff Teaching Undergraduate Courses	198
Research Rating:	3b
Teaching Rating:	Satisfactory
Additional Rating Information	
Male:Female Student Ratio	50:50
Head of Business School	Professor John Taylor
Head of Undergraduate Studies	
Admissions Contact	

About the School:

The Faculty of Business consists of 10 Departments - Business Administration, Consumer Studies, Economics, Entrepreneurial Studies, Finance and Accounting, Hospitality, Tourism & Leisure Management, Language and Media, Law and Public Administration, Management, Risk & Financial Services. Currently, there are 29 undergraduate programmes and 20 postgraduate and professional programmes. All of the programmes have a strong vocational dimension with many of the full-time programmes including a work placment period. Students have the opportunity to spend one semester at one one of our European partner universities.

The City of Glasgow offers a wide range of social, sporting and cultural facilities, while the surrounding countryside is ideal for outdoor activities such as sailing, walking, climbing, fishing and riding.

About Undergraduate Studies:

Glasgow Caledonian University is a major provider of professional and vocational higher education - serving clients on a national and international basis. The Faculty of Business provides a range of specialist and interdisciplinary programmes, all with a strong vocational emphasis which is reflected in the programme content and teaching and learning strategies used. We are committed to quality in teaching and learning and constantly strive to improve the learning experience for students.

Facilities:

There are loads of sports clubs at Caledonian everything from football to swimming, snow-boarding to Tae Kwon-Do and boxing to badminton. The clubs are suitable for all levels of interest whether you just want to keep yourself in shape or go all the way to national and international championships - students should be able to find something that meets their needs. Sports clubs currently active: Athletics, badminton, basketball (male), basketball (female), boxing, canoeing, climbing, football (male), football (female), go-karting, hillwalking, aerobics, working out in our in-house gym and many more.

Departments/Faculties:

Business Administration
Consumer Studies
Economics
Entrepreneurial Studies
Finance & Accounting
Hospitality, Tourism and Leisure
Language & Media
Law and Public Administration
Management
Risk and Financial Services

Links with Academic Institutions:

The Faculty of Business has links with other academic institutions through the Glasgow Caledonian Affiliate College network and joint programmes offered with other HE institutions. We also have franchise and collaborative links with a number of overseas institutions predominantly in the European Union and USA, but also in Malaysia, Singapore, Kuwait, Uganda, Tanzania, Russia, Oman, China, Poland, Albania and Romania.

Links with Industry:

Departments in the Faculty of Business are encouraged to create mutually beneficial links between themselves and industry, commerce, the public sector and the professions. These include, Stock Exchange, Britannia Life, Scottish Enterprise, Scottish Development Overseas and the LEC Network, ScottishPower, City Building Glasgow, and many more.

Student Testimonials:

"My placement led to a full-time job on graduation" J MacAskill, Graduate, BA (Hons) Business Studies
"I was very impressed by the facilities and the staff" C MacFarlane, Year 4, BA (Hons) Accountancy
"Colleagues now in employment agree they have been able to transfer skills learned in their programme to the workplace" C Broadfoot, Year 2, Diploma in Business Studies

BA/BA (Hons) Business and Languages

Graduates of this programme will develop language, office and information technology skills and expertise - an excellent combination for a career in administration, particularly in the context of the developing European Community. The programme consists of 3 areas - Administration and Information Technology, two European languages and European Legal and Policy Framework. One semester will be spent studying in a European partner institution.

Modular Course?	Yes
Qualifications:	BA; BA Hons
Application Deadline:	UCAS Deadline
Commencement Date:	September
Entry Requirement:	SCE Higher BBB/BBCC; A Level BC
Applications to Places:	4.7:1
Registered:	21
Awards:	0

	Duration	EC Fees	Non-EC Fees
Full time	3-4 years	1000.00	6250.00
Part time			
Sandwich			

BA/BA (HONS) Business Studies

The programme aims to provide a broad education in Business by integrated studies of vocational and academic disciplines. Not only does it aim to develop in students a wide appreciation of relevant Business Disciplines and their importance in solving Business problems, but also allows students to acquire those personal transferable skills necessary for a successful Business career.

Modular Course?	Yes
Qualifications:	BA; BA Hons
Application Deadline:	UCAS deadline
Commencement Date:	September
Entry Requirement:	SCE Higher BBBC; A level BCC
Applications to Places:	13:1
Registered:	70
Awards:	3

	Duration	EC Fees	Non-EC Fees
Full time	3/4 years	1000.00	6250.00
Part time			
Sandwich			

BA/BA (Hons) Consumer and Management Studies

The Consumer and Management Studies (General Route) aims to produce technically proficient, commercially minded graduate managers, who can quickly take up management positions in both domestic and foreign markets, and who can adapt effectively to the challenges of an increasingly 'globalised' business environment.

Modular Course?	Yes
Qualifications:	BA; BA Hons
Application Deadline:	UCAS deadline
Commencement Date:	September
Entry Requirement:	SCE Higher BBC; A Level CD
Applications to Places:	
Registered:	35
Awards:	

	Duration	EC Fees	Non-EC Fees
Full time	3/4 years	1000.00	6250.00
Part time			
Sandwich			

Public Administration and Management

This programme has a number of objectives: knowledge of the system of government, the services it provides and the environment which it operates. The problems and issues faced by policy makers and public sector managers. The programme contains a comprehensive range of academic modules and builds special skills in the areas of : computing, research techniques and presentation. As well as equipping students with the knowledge required to enter the public sector, the skills and techniques gained on this degree provides the foundation for employment in the private sector.

Modular Course?	Yes
Qualifications:	BA; BA Hons; Joint Honours
Application Deadline:	UCAS deadline
Commencement Date:	September
Entry Requirement:	SCE Higher BBBC; A Level BC
Applications to Places:	
Registered:	120
Awards:	

	Duration	EC Fees	Non-EC Fees
Full time	3/4 years	1000.00	6250.00
Part time			
Sandwich			

Business

The programme structure takes full advantage of GCU's modular system to maximise student choice while at the same time ensuring a coherent programme of study leading to a general degree in Business. Subject to having the appropriate knowledge pre-requisites students are able to study any module from over 140 offered by the Faculty of Business. Graduates will have the necessary vocational skills to follow a wide variety of careers in the world of business.

Modular Course?	Yes
Qualifications:	BA; BA Hons
Application Deadline:	UCAS
Commencement Date:	September
Entry Requirement:	SCE Higher BBBC/ A Level BC
Applications to Places:	
Registered:	18
Awards:	

	Duration	EC Fees	Non-EC Fees
Full time	3/4 yrs	1000.00	6250.00
Part time			
Sandwich			

Specialist Undergraduate Course

BA/BA (Hons) Accountancy

Modular Course?	Yes
Qualifications:	BA; BA Hons
Categories:	Finance

BA/BA (Hons) Retail Management

Modular Course?	Yes
Qualifications:	BA; BA Hons
Categories:	Marketing; Small Business; Retailing

Business School

Business School

Address:	Woolwich Campus, Wellington Street
	London
	SE18 6PF
Area:	London and South East England
Phone:	0181 331 9770
Fax:	0181 331 9616
Email:	**l.vellam@gre.ac.uk**
Website:	
Email Application Available?	No
How to apply by email:	
Total Number of Teaching Staff:	75
Staff Teaching Undergraduate Courses	75
Research Rating:	2
Teaching Rating:	Satisfactory
Additional Rating Information	
Male:Female Student Ratio	51:49
Head of Business School	Sue Millar
Head of Undergraduate Studies	Iwona Vellum
Admissions Contact	John Gould

About the School:

Founded in 1890 as the Woolwich Polytechnic, the University of Greenwich has a long history of providing quality courses in Kent and south London. Both part-time day courses and sandwich courses were pioneered at Greenwich. Today, Greenwich is one of the larger new Universities in south-east England with around 1800 full-time and 600 part-time students in the Business School. A range of undergraduate courses are provided on a full and part-time basis.

The Business School is located on two campuses, each with a range of facilities suited to local needs: a city centre location at Woolwich and a professional development centre on a major business park near Maidstone, Kent. The School is continuously updating its course offer, adding career-oriented degrees such as Heritage and Arts Management, and Financial Services to the unique International Business Central Eastern European degree.

About Undergraduate Studies:

The Business School has a portfolio of undergraduate pathways which enable students to study for three years full-time or for four years including a one-year traineeship. Students can incorporate language study and take up work or study placement abroad. Subjects studied in the first year are common to several degrees and it is possible to transfer between named degrees at the end of year one.

Business Studies can be studied as a four-year sandwich degree or as a three-year full-time degree, called Business Administration. Both options enable students to specialise in one of five major areas - Accounting and Finance, Business Economics, Marketing, Operations Management, or Personnel Management, with languages also included.

The Business School offers a number of other pathways which have been developed to enable students to specialise to an even greater degree in the chosen area. The Accounting and Finance pathway provides an opportunity to develop a professional accounting qualification. The newly-developed Economics degrees in Financial Services and Accounting and Information Systems recognise the changing nature of the financial services business, as well as the new career opportunities that are opening up. The newly-developed Heritage Management, Arts Management, Tourism Management exploit the new developments in the service sector.

In the marketing sector, there is a wide choice of courses. As well as the main Marketing degree, there are specialist courses in International Marketing and Marketing Communications. The International Business pathways reflect the increasing internationalism of business with courses such as European Business and European Business (Central/Eastern Europe) providing students with greater awareness of different cultural and business practices, as well as improving language skills. Personnel Management and Operations pathways also reflect the changing nature of business operations. A range of HND and HNC pathways are also offered at the University and Associate Colleges.

Facilities:

The campuses are within easy reach of central London, the political, financial and cultural capital of the UK. London has the largest network of Students' Unions in the country, offering a wide range of subsidised social and cultural activities. Greenwich students have access to these as well as the facilities provided by the University. At Woolwich, a refurbished Union building offers a full range of facilities, while at Avery Hill the new student village provides an attractive residential ambience for student life.

Links with Academic Institutions:

The Business School has links with universities in France, Slovenia, China, Hong Kong and Argentina providing opportunities for student exchanges during the period of study.

Links with Industry:

The Business School has a number of industry links providing consultancy and problem-solving experience during the period of study.

School of Management

School of Management

Address:	Heriot-Watt University
	Riccarton
	Edinburgh
	EH14 4AT
Area:	Scotland
Phone:	0131 451 3557
Fax:	0131 451 3296
Email:	**l.m.mcgill@hw.ac.uk**
Website:	**www.hw.ac.uk/somwww/somweb/**
Email Application Available?	No
How to apply by email:	
Total Number of Teaching Staff:	56
Staff Teaching Undergraduate Courses	56
Research Rating:	3a
Teaching Rating:	Satisfactory
Additional Rating Information	
Male:Female Student Ratio	n/a
Head of School of Management	Professor PG Hare
Head of Undergraduate Studies	
Admissions Contact	Ms S McIntyre

About the School:

The School of Management was created from the Departments of Accountancy and Finance, Business Organisation and Economics to resource a range of undergraduate and postgraduate degrees. The School of Management has a full-time academic staff of over 50 and there are currently 750 undergraduate and 50 postgraduate students. The School awards a range of MA (Hons) degrees after four years, and a range of BA (Ordinary) degrees after three years of study. The postgraduate degrees are the MSc International Banking and Financial Studies, the MSc International Accounting and Financial Studies, MSc Logistics and the MSc Occupational Psychology. All three departments offer opportunities to study for a PhD. In the Department of Economics, this is achieved through the Scottish Doctoral Programme in Economics, provided by a consortium of eight older Scottish universities.

Facilities:

The School is located on the University's Riccarton Campus, a beautiful 380 acre mature woodland site just seven miles from the centre of Edinburgh. There are 1400 beds in the halls of residence on the campus, and the University can normally guarantee a place in hall to all first year students. There is a wide range of facilities on campus including restaurants, shops, banks, Students' Union, and extensive sports facilities. All the cultural, educational, social and sporting amenities of Edinburgh, Britain's most highly-rated city, are easily accessible.

Links with Academic Institutions:

The School has a strong international orientation and has exchange agreements with a number of European universities. A particular feature of the School is its close link with the School of Languages, resulting in the development of a number of joint degrees with a foreign language which require a year of study overseas. The School is the only Scottish member of the European consortium offering the European Master of Business Science programme which aims to develop multi-lingual European business managers. The School also has strong links with universities in Central and Eastern Europe, particularly the Technical University of Budapest, and the College of Finance and Accounting, also in Budapest. The Centre for Economic Reconstruction and Transformation in the Department of Economic is one of the two leading UK centres for the study of transitional problems in Central and Eastern European economies.

Links with Industry:

The School of Management has close links with industry and commerce and its teaching staff are involved in a range of research and consultancy work.

General Undergraduate Courses

MA (Hons) & BA Programme

The School of Management offers degrees in the following subjects: Accountancy and Finance; Management; Economics. Joint degrees are also available in: Accountancy with a European Language; Business and Finance; International Business and Finance; International Business and Languages; Business and Economics; Economics and Languages; Economics and Finance; Accountancy and Information Management; Economics and Accountancy.

All of the above courses are available as MA (Hons) after four years or BA (Ordinary) after three years. They are taught on a modular basis which provides a high degree of flexibility. Students can usually transfer between the various degrees provided they have passed the necessary pre-requisite classes.

The main subjects, together with the range of electives, enable students to select the programme of study most suited to their abilities and the needs of their future careers. The courses have been designed with the requirements of various professional institutions in mind and graduates aiming to take further professional qualifications can often obtain examination exemptions. For example, the degree of MA Accountancy and Finance and MA Accountancy and Information Management are fully accredited by the Institute of Chartered Accountants of Scotland and the Institute of Chartered Accountants in England and Wales, while the degree in Business Organisation provides significant exemptions from the Diploma of the Chartered Institute of Marketing.

Modular Course?	Yes
Qualifications:	BA; MA (Hons)
Application Deadline:	15 December
Commencement Date:	
Entry Requirement:	Accountancy and Finance - SCE Highers ABBB, GCE A-level BCC. Management - SCE Highers ABBB, GCE A-level BCC. Economics - SCE Highers BBBC, GCE A-level CCD
Applications to Places:	
Registered:	
Awards:	

	Duration	EC Fees	Non-EC Fees
Full time	3-4 years	On request	On request
Part time			
Sandwich			

Business School

University of Hertfordshire Business School

Address:	Hertford Campus
	Mangrove Rd
	Hertford
	SG13 8QF
Area:	London and South East England
Phone:	01707 285400
Fax:	01707 285504

Website: http://www.herts.ac.uk/

Email Application Available?	No
How to apply by email:	
Total Number of Teaching Staff:	100
Staff Teaching Undergraduate Courses	90
Research Rating:	3b
Teaching Rating:	Satisfactory
Additional Rating Information	
Male:Female Student Ratio	50:50
Head of Business School	Professor Ben Fletcher
Head of Undergraduate Studies	Mike Rosier
Admissions Contact	Tracey Waters

About the School:

The Business School has its origins in the 1950s and now has some 2000 students and 50 schemes of study. While the School is represented at two campuses and the Business School Development Unit is housed in the Hertfordshire Business Link building in St Albans, its primary base is at Hertford.

The Hertford Campus is set in 100 acres of attractive parkland, only 30 minutes by train from central London. Modern teaching and residential accommodation sits side by side with a magnificent Jacobean mansion house dating from 1630. An excellent on-site Learning Resources Centre combines library and computing facilities. The full range of student services is offered from the campus.

About Undergraduate Studies:

The Business School has an Undergraduate Modular Programme which incorporates a large number of pathways leading to a wide range of awards. These range from Business degrees such as; Business Studies, Accounting, Marketing, Human Resources, Decision Science or Tourism Management, through Economics to Social Science degrees including European Studies, Sociology and Politics.

Facilities:

The Hertford campus is close to the county town of Hertford which offers good shopping and recreation facilities. The majority of full-time Business School students will be based at this campus which has its own sporting facilities including a well-equiped gym, swimming pool and a range of sports pitches. A student bar and late opening coffee shop complement the main cafeteria. The location of the school ensures good car parking facilities. The main University campus at Hatfield, some fifteen minutes drive away, offers further opportunities for student sporting and leisure activity. The University also runs an excellent commercial bus service which links up its campuses across the county.

Departments/Faculties:

The School has four Departments:
Department of Business and Finance
Department of Economics, Statistics and Decision Sciences
Department of Management and Business Information Systems
Department of Social Sciences
Staff are also members of a range of informal academic groups which help co-ordinate research and course development. Nine Centres/Units carry out specialist functions within the School.

Links with Academic Institutions:

Links with other academic institutions range from local 'Associate Colleges' which offer, for example, the University's Diploma in Management Studies, to a range of overseas partners offering both undergraduate and postgraduate programmes. Over 1500 students are on programmes leading to University awards in Hungary, Greece, Germany, Spain, Italy, the Netherlands, Malaysia and China.

Links with Industry:

The commercial work of the School is co-ordinated by the Business School Development Unit. Recent consultancy and training have been provided for such diverse organisations as the Hertfordshire Constabulary, National Westminster Bank, Tesco, ABB and Hertfordshire Business Link. The School has growing success in gaining Teaching Company Schemes.

General Undergraduate Courses

BA (Hons) Business Studies

This programme integrates academic study, skills development and practical training and aims to equip graduates with the knowledge and skills needed by business. Students can select from a wide range of modules including languages. The first two years provide a firm foundation in business education, with the third year spent on industrial placement. . In the final year, students can specialise in Accounting, Management Science, Marketing or Human Resource Management, or follow a general business programme.

Modular Course?	Yes	
Qualifications:	BA Hons	
Application Deadline:	UCAS deadline	
Commencement Date:		
Entry Requirement:	18 points at A-level, including a foreign language, GSCE Maths and English Language, Advanced Level GNVQ with Distinction, with Business as a specified subject, BTEC National Diploma or Certificate with Merits and Distinctions, including Distinction in a foreign language.	
Applications to Places:	6:1	
Registered:	90	
Awards:		

	Duration	EC Fees	Non-EC Fees
Sandwich	4 years	£1000	£6450
Part time	5 years		

BA/BSc Joint Honours

This programme is designed for students who wish to study a set of subjects not available through the single honours programme. Students build a study programme of their own from the wide range available within the Business School, studying two subjects.

Modular Course?	Yes	
Qualifications:	BA; BSc	
Application Deadline:	UCAS deadline	
Commencement Date:		
Entry Requirement:	18 points at A-level, GSCE Maths and English Language, Advanced Level GNVQ with Distinction, BTEC National Diploma or Certificate with Merits and Distinctions.	
Applications to Places:	6:1	
Registered:	100	
Awards:		

	Duration	EC Fees	Non-EC Fees
Full time	3 years	£1000	£6450
Part time			
Sandwich	4 years	£1000	£6450

BA (Hons) International Business Studies

With increasing globalisation, managers need to have an understanding of international business and command of foreign languages. This programme will provide students with a good grounding in business, while developing a range of practical skills and building an understanding of different business cultures. As well as developing competence in two languages other than English, the programme also offers the opportunity to study and work abroad in the third year.

Modular Course?	Yes	
Qualifications:		
Application Deadline:	UCAS deadline	
Commencement Date:		
Entry Requirement:	18 points at A-level, including a foreign language, GSCE Maths and English Language, Advanced Level GNVQ with Distinction, with Business as a specified subject, BTEC National Diploma or Certificate with Merits and Distinctions, including Distinction in a foreign language.	
Applications to Places:	6:1	
Registered:	40	
Awards:		

	Duration	EC Fees	Non-EC Fees
Sandwich	4 years	£1000	£6450

BA (Hons) Accounting; BA (Hons) Accounting and Management Information Systems

These two programmes are designed for students who wish to pursue careers in accounting. The Accounting programme offers a solid foundation in accountancy, together with options which reflect specialisations within the profession. Accounting Management Information Systems is designed to meet the needs of accountants or managers responsible for financial control of an organisation and provides a background in modern accounting practice, management information systems and company law.

Modular Course?	Yes	
Qualifications:	BA Hons	
Application Deadline:	UCAS deadline	
Commencement Date:		
Entry Requirement:	18 points at A-level (16 points for AMIS), GSCE Maths and English Language, Advanced Level GNVQ with Distinction, BTEC National Diploma or Certificate with	
Applications to Places:	6:1	
Registered:	70	
Awards:		

	Duration	EC Fees	Non-EC Fees
Full time	3 years	£1000	£6450
Part time			
Sandwich	4 years		

BA (Hons) Economics; BA (Hons) Business Economics; BA (Hons) International Economics

These three programmes provide an opportunity for students to study Economics within the business environment, showing how it contributes to policy and decision making in both public and private sectors.

Modular Course?	Yes
Qualifications:	BA Hons
Application Deadline:	UCAS deadline
Commencement Date:	
Entry Requirement:	12 points at A-level, GSCE Maths and English Language, Advanced Level GNVQ/BTEC National Diploma or Certificate acceptable.
Applications to Places:	6:1
Registered:	50
Awards:	

	Duration	EC Fees	Non-EC Fees
Full time	3 years	£1000	£6450
Part time			
Sandwich	4 years		

Specialist Undergraduate Course

BSc (Hons) Business Information Systems

Modular Course?	Yes
Qualifications:	BSc/BSc Hons
Categories:	Management; IT Systems

BA/BA (Hons) Tourism Management

Modular Course?	Yes
Qualifications:	BA; BA Hons
Categories:	Leisure

Management Sciences

Modular Course?	Yes
Qualifications:	BSc/BSc Hons
Categories:	Management

HND Business Decision Analysis

Modular Course?	No
Qualifications:	HND
Categories:	Management

BA/BA (Hons) Marketing

Modular Course?	Yes
Qualifications:	BA; BA Hons
Categories:	Marketing

BA/BA (Hons) Human Resources

Modular Course?	Yes
Qualifications:	BA; BA Hons
Categories:	Human Resources

BA/BA (Hons) Asia Pacific Business

Modular Course?	Yes
Qualifications:	BA; BA Hons
Categories:	International Business

Huddersfield University Business School (HUBS)

Huddersfield University Business School

Address:	University Of Huddersfield
	Queensgate
	Huddersfield
	HD1 3DH
Area:	North East England
Phone:	01484 - 422288
Fax:	01484 - 472753
Email:	**hubs@hud.ac.uk**

Website:

http://www.hud.ac.uk/schools/hubs/bushome.htm

Email Application Available?	Yes
How to apply by email:	hubs@hud.ac.uk
Total Number of Teaching Staff:	98
Staff Teaching Undergraduate Courses	98
Research Rating:	2
Teaching Rating:	Satisfactory
Additional Rating Information	
Male:Female Student Ratio	50:50
Head of Business School	David Smith
Head of Undergraduate Studies	Relevant Department
Admissions Contact	Relevant Department

About the School:

HUBS aims to be a collaborative learning community with a clear vocational emphasis and high standards, in which students and staff can satisfy their intellectual and scholarly needs, and develop their potential to progress in the business and professional world of work. Reflecting its strengths, and the main disciplines studied, HUBS is organised into five departments: Accountancy; Economics & Business Studies; Law; Management; and Marketing. All teaching facilities are located on the University's main campus close to the centre of Huddersfield

About Undergraduate Studies:

Undergraduate courses in business have been offered by the University for over twenty five years and there are now some 2,000 students studying on degree and diploma courses in HUBS. Many of the courses are organised on a sandwich basis which involves students spending one year in paid employment. Professional bodies such as the Institute of Marketing, the Institute of Personnel and Development and ACCA grant exemptions to graduates from appropriate courses in HUBS. The University's record of graduates entering employment directly after graduation is extremely good.

Facilities:

The University has recently opened a newly built student village catering for over 1,400 students in high quality residences. Open-air sports facilities are available in the vicinity of this student village and there is a sports hall on the main campus, which is also close to the Huddersfield sports centre.

The Students Union has moved into new premises which offer a good range of social facilities. In the immediate vicinity of the University there are facilities such as a theatre, multi-screen cinema and many clubs. The area also offers opportunities for many outdoor pursuits

Departments/Faculties:

Department of Accountancy (Head: W.W. Teviotdale)
Department of Economics and Business Studies (Head: Dr J R Anchor)
Department of Law (Head: Professor G J Pitt)
Department of Management (Head: Dr M E Waddington)
Department of Marketing (Head: Dr N E Marr)

Links with Academic Institutions:

HUBS has links with academic institutions in many European countries and each year students are offered opportunities to spend part of their period of study, usually one semester, in a university in one of these countries. Students who wish to develop their language skills are able to enrol on the recently validated BA (Hons) International Business which has particularly strong links with overseas academic institutions. There is a substantial body of students from other countries enrolled on courses in HUBS each year.

Links with Industry:

The Business Placement Unit in HUBS has links with over one hundred companies and acts as a co-ordinator to help students find sandwich placements. Many postgraduate students have opportunities to carry out project work for local and national companies as part of their programmes of study. Staff research interests often involve them in working with companies and industries in the UK and overseas

Student Testimonials:

Details are provided in the University's Undergraduate Prospectus which is available from the Registrar's office

BA (Hons) Business Studies

A four year sandwich course offereing opportunities to specialise in the final year

Modular Course?	Yes
Qualifications:	BA
Application Deadline:	normal UCAS
Commencement Date:	September
Entry Requirement:	18 points or equivalent
Applications to Places:	10:1
Registered:	140
Awards:	120

	Duration	EC Fees	Non-EC Fees
Full time			
Part time			
Sandwich	4 years		

BA (Hons) Business and Administration

A three year full-time course involving the study of management issues and problems with particular emphasis on those affecting small and nonprofit organisations as well as more traditional businesses

Modular Course?	Yes
Qualifications:	BA
Application Deadline:	Usual UCAS
Commencement Date:	September
Entry Requirement:	12 points or appropriate GNVQ
Applications to Places:	5:1
Registered:	40
Awards:	New Course
Full time	Three years
Part time	
Sandwich	

HND Business and Management

A two year diploma course which offers the opportunity to progress to a degree course or to seek employment with a nationally recognised qualification

Modular Course?	Yes
Qualifications:	HND
Application Deadline:	Usual UCAS
Commencement Date:	September
Entry Requirement:	6 points; GNVQ or equivalent
Applications to Places:	2:1
Registered:	100
Awards:	100

	Duration	EC Fees	Non-EC Fees
Full time	Two years		
Part time			
Sandwich			

LLB Law

Modular Course?	Yes
Qualifications:	BA
Categories:	Business Law

BA (Hons) Marketing

Modular Course?	Yes
Qualifications:	BA
Categories:	Marketing

BA (Hons) Accountancy and Finance

Modular Course?	Yes
Qualifications:	BA
Categories:	Finance

BA (Hons) Marketing, Retailing and Distribution

Modular Course?	No
Qualifications:	BA
Categories:	Marketing

BA (Hons) Management and Accountancy

Modular Course?	No
Qualifications:	BA
Categories:	Finance; Joint honours

BA (Hons) International Business

Modular Course?	No
Qualifications:	BA
Categories:	International Business

School of Management and School of Accounting Business and Finance

School of Management and School of Accounting Business and Finance

Address:	University of Hull
	Cottingham Road
	Hull
	HU6 7RX
Area:	North East England
Phone:	01482 466 330 (Management)
	or 466 300 (Accounting)
Fax:	01482 466 236 (Management)
	or 466 377 (Accounting)

Email:

Website: www.hull.ac.uk

Email Application Available?	No
How to apply by email:	
Total Number of Teaching Staff:	60
Staff Teaching Undergraduate Courses	60
Research Rating:	3b
Teaching Rating:	Satisfactory
Additional Rating Information	
Male:Female Student Ratio	75:25
Head of Business School	Head of Management: Dr Paul Keys
	Head of Accounting, Business and Finance - Mr Brahim Saadouri
Head of Undergraduate Studies	Dr M Roberts and Mr S Braund
Admissions Contact	Dr M Roberts and Mr S Braund

About the School:

The School of Management and School of Accounting Business and Finance staff possess both high academic credentials and diverse international management and consulting experience. The School has an impressive research programme which has developed over the last few years, and provides and active source of reference and innovation for the taught courses. All courses are taught in a modular format with a strong emphasis on tutor-to-student contact.

Facilities:

The University of Hull occupies a large, green-field campus allowing for expansion without overcrowding. Hull's accommodation is cheaper and more plentiful than in most British University cities, with more than 60% of the full-time students living in university-owned or managed accommodation. Food, recreation and local travel are equally cheap. The University has a strong reputation for the quality of its teaching and research, with Library and Computer and Language Centres which are well-equipped, accessible and spacious.

Hull is close to the countryside and the sea, and has sports and fitness centres and playing fields on the campus. The city provides all the amenities expected from the country's twelfth largest city. On the campus, societies organised by students offer an amazing range of opportunitiesto develop any find of interest.

General Undergraduate Courses

BA Business Studies

This course is designed to provide students with an appreciation of the way a business organisation achieves its objectives. It helps students develop skills that enable them to critically evaluate business situations, understand the different functional areas of business, and understand the nature of business change.

Modular Course?	No
Qualifications:	BA
Application Deadline:	15 December
Commencement Date:	
Entry Requirement:	3 A-levels 24 points, plus O-level Maths or equivalent
Applications to Places:	10:1
Registered:	45
Awards:	

	Duration	EC Fees	Non-EC Fees
Full time	3 years	£1000	£6,200
Part time			
Sandwich			

BA Business Studies and Modern Languages

This course is designed to provide students with a broadly-based foundation in disciplines relevant to the business environment, management, marketing and operational activities within organisations. The first, second and fourth years are spent at Hull with a third year spent working or studying abroad. The language components include courses in the literature, culture and history of the country.

		Modular Course?	No
		Qualifications:	BA
		Application Deadline:	15 December
		Commencement Date:	
		Entry Requirement:	3 A-levels BBB/BBC/BCC depending on the course, plus O-level Maths or equivalent
		Applications to Places:	10:1
		Registered:	27
		Awards:	

	Duration	EC Fees	Non-EC Fees
Full time			
Part time			
Sandwich	4 years	£1000	£6,200

BA Management/BA International Management

This course will develop graduates with the skills and knowledge to understand the role of management in contemporary society, critically assess theories of management and organisation, be aware of the impact of organisations on society, and conceptualise and analyse by use of a systems framework. Students will develop transferable skills appropriate to a wide range of employment situations. In the International programme, the third year is spent studying at a University in the USA or Finland.

Modular Course?		No
Qualifications:		BA
Application Deadline:		15 December
Commencement Date:		
Entry Requirement:		3 A-levels BBB/BBC/BCC depending on the course, plus O-level Maths or equivalent
Applications to Places:		10:1
Registered:		33
Awards:		

	Duration	EC Fees	Non-EC Fees
Full time	3 years	£1000	£6,200
Part time			
Sandwich	4 years	£1000	£6,200

BSc Information Management/ Management Sciences/ Management Sciences International/Computer and Management Sciences

These courses help students understand the scope and limitations of the use of information and decision support systems in management. Students will develop skills in information systems analysis and design, information capture, storage and analysis, the development of decision support systems, and the use

of relevant computer software and application packages.

Modular Course?		No
Qualifications:		BSc
Application Deadline:		15 December
Commencement Date:		
Entry Requirement:		3 A-levels BBB/BBC/BCC depending on the course, plus O-level Maths or equivalent
Applications to Places:		10:1
Registered:		19
Awards:		

	Duration	EC Fees	Non-EC Fees
Full time	3 years	£1000	£6,200
Part time			
Sandwich	4 years	£1000	£6,200

BSc Economics and Management Sciences/ Mathematics and Management Sciences

The Economics degree provides students with a broad-based knowledge of politics, industry and commerce, as well as a working knowledge of the decision-making techniques used by government, business and consumers. The Mathematics degree combines the concepts and rigour of pure mathematics with the application of mathematical techniques in management science.

Modular Course?		No
Qualifications:		BSc
Application Deadline:		15 December
Commencement Date:		
Entry Requirement:		3 A-levels BBB/BBC/BCC depending on the course, plus O-level Maths or equivalent
Applications to Places:		10:1
Registered:		10
Awards:		

	Duration	EC Fees	Non-EC Fees
Part time			
Sandwich	4 years	£1000	£6,200

BSc Accounting/Accounting International

This course is suitable for students who wish to pursue a career in accountancy or related areas. As well as providing an introduction to Accounting, Business and Economics, the course equips students with computing and mathematical tools. A wide range of options allow students to specialise in areas of career interest. For Accounting International the third year is spent studying abroad.

Modular Course?	No

Qualifications:		BSc	
Application Deadline:		15 December	
Commencement Date:			
Entry Requirement:		3 A-levels 20 points, plus	
		O-level Maths or equivalent	
Applications to Places:		10:1	
Registered:		60	
Awards:			

	Duration	EC Fees	Non-EC Fees
Full time	3 years	£1000	£6,200
Part time			
Sandwich	4 years	£1000	£6,200

Kingston Business School

Kingston Business School

Address:	Kingston University
	Kingston Hill
	Kingston Upon Thames
	KT2 7LB
Area:	London and South East England
Phone:	0181 547 2000
Fax:	0181 547 7026
Email:	**business@kingston.ac.uk**
Website:	**http:\\www.king.ac.uk**
Email Application Available?	No
How to apply by email:	
Total Number of Teaching Staff:	110
Staff Teaching Undergraduate Courses	
Research Rating:	3b
Teaching Rating:	Excellent
Additional Rating Information	
Male:Female Student Ratio	50:50
Head of Business School	**Professor David Miles**
Head of Undergraduate Studies	**Professor David Miles**
Admissions Contact	**Undergraduate Admissions Office**

About the School:

Kingston Business School (KBS) comprises over 90 academic staff organised into departments which focus on the principal business functions, each with robust subject authority founded upon strong research and practitioner experience.

Almost 2400 students are currently enrolled on qualification courses, including 1000 mid-career managers attending postgraduate courses, mostly on a part-time basis. Strong relationships are maintained with the professions and industry. The School's educational philosophy is to develop a foundation of sound analytical and critical approaches to problem solving, and to equip students with professional competencies immediately applicable to their employment.

The Business School is located at the University's Kingston Hill campus, a pleasant wooded site within half-an-hour's travel from Central London, adjacent to Richmond Park and the amenities of rural Surrey. The School has convenient access to the motorway network and to Heathrow and Gatwick airports. The Kingston Hill Campus has student residential and social facilities.

About Undergraduate Studies:

The School has a range of quality courses. Particular emphasis is given to the use of information technology; students have open access to local and international academic networks via some 200 prsonal computer workstations. The business curriculum is taught in an international context; an extensive set of opportunities to study and work overseas is on offer for full-time students. A common elective programme ensures a wide range of final year options for all courses, including the BABA (one-year top up after HND). The Business Information Technology and Accounting and Law degrees offer creative mixtures of disciplines within single integrated courses. All first year undergraduates have the opportunity to live in a student hostel if required.

Although the School is large, students have a sense of identity and of belonging to individual courses. Each course has a core team of tutors and administrators responsible for the success of the programme and welfare of their students. There is a wide selection of courses to choose from.

There is ample provision of elective subjects within the courses particularly in the final stages. The courses are both intellectually taxing and designed to help students develop a wide range of personal business skills. Kingston business students are in demand from employers: for industrial placement periods, permanent employment and professional traineeships. Our partnerships with other Universities and Colleges, particularly in the United States and the European Union, offer opportunities for student exchanges and research, supported by a thriving language scheme open to all undergraduate students.

Links with Academic Institutions:

There are franchise links with:
ANE (Academy for National Economy), Moscow
Haarlem Business School in Holland
ICBS Thessaloniki, a private Greek college
There are staff/student exchange links in the US with:
University of North Carolina Charlotte (UNCC) and Grand Valley State University, Michigan
In Europe there are a wide range links under the Socrates Programme.

General Undergraduate Courses

BA Business Studies

Modular Course?	No
Qualifications:	BA
Application Deadline:	UCAS deadlines
Commencement Date:	
Entry Requirement:	CDD to BCC at A-level
Applications to Places:	17:1
Registered:	242
Awards:	

	Duration	EC Fees	Non-EC Fees
Full time	4 years	£1000	£5750
Part time			
Sandwich			

BA Business Studies (European Programme)

Modular Course?	No
Qualifications:	BA
Application Deadline:	UCAS deadlines
Commencement Date:	
Entry Requirement:	CDD to BCC at A-level
Applications to Places:	17:1
Registered:	45
Awards:	

	Duration	EC Fees	Non-EC Fees
Full time	4 years	£1000	£5750
Part time			
Sandwich			

Business Studies (four years with two placement periods); Accounting and Finance (three years full-time); Accounting and Law (three years full-time); Business Information Technology (four years with one year placement); Business Administration (one year extension to Higher Diploma); BTEC Higher Diploma in Business and Finance (two years full-time or three to four years part-time); HD Business and Finance

Modular Course?	No
Qualifications:	HD
Application Deadline:	UCAS deadlines
Commencement Date:	
Entry Requirement:	CDD to BCC at A-level
Applications to Places:	17:1
Registered:	271
Awards:	

	Duration	EC Fees	Non-EC Fees
Full time	2 years	£1000	£5750
Part time			
Sandwich			

BA Business Administration

Follows HD course

Modular Course?	No
Qualifications:	BA
Application Deadline:	UCAS deadlines
Commencement Date:	
Entry Requirement:	CDD to BCC at A-level
Applications to Places:	17:1
Registered:	59
Awards:	

	Duration	EC Fees	Non-EC Fees
Full time	1 year	£1000	£5750
Part time			
Sandwich			

BSc Business Information Technology

Modular Course?	No
Qualifications:	BSc
Application Deadline:	UCAS deadlines
Commencement Date:	
Entry Requirement:	CDD to BCC at A-level
Applications to Places:	17:1
Registered:	220
Awards:	

	Duration	EC Fees	Non-EC Fees
Full time	4 years	£1000	£5750
Part time			
Sandwich			

BA Accounting and Finance

Modular Course?	No
Qualifications:	BA
Application Deadline:	UCAS deadlines
Commencement Date:	
Entry Requirement:	CDD to BCC at A-level
Applications to Places:	17:1
Registered:	299
Awards:	

	Duration	EC Fees	Non-EC Fees
Full time	3 years	£1000	£5750
Part time			
Sandwich			

A recent University decision to modularise means that the structure of the some of these programmes will change from September 1999 but the overall flavour of the courses is likely to remain similar to that described above.

BA Accounting and Law

Modular Course?	No
Qualifications:	BA

Application Deadline:		UCAS deadlines	
Commencement Date:			
Entry Requirement:		CDD to BCC at A-level	
Applications to Places:		17:1	
Registered:		160	
Awards:			

	Duration	EC Fees	Non-EC Fees
Full time	3 years	£1000	£5750
Part time			
Sandwich			

Lancashire Business School

Lancashire Business School

Address:	Preston
	PR1 2HE
Area:	North West England
Phone:	01772 894 606
Fax:	01772 892 904
Email:	**j.boon@uclan.ac.uk**

Website:

Email Application Available?	No
How to apply by email:	
Total Number of Teaching Staff:	125
Staff Teaching Undergraduate Courses	125
Research Rating:	3a
Teaching Rating:	Highly Satisfactory
Additional Rating Information	
Male:Female Student Ratio	50:50
Head of Business School	Alan France
Head of Undergraduate Studies	Phil Hewitt
Admissions Contact	Christine Aveyard

About the School:

Lancashire Business School is one of the largest faculties of the University of Central Lancashire, with almost 200 staff and 4000 students involved in more than 50 different academic programmes. The range includes undergraduate, postgraduate, professional and post-experience courses. The programmes are delivered through the seven academic departments and the Business Development Unit that constitute Lancashire Business School. The academic departments include: Accounting and Financial Services; Management Development; Business Information Management; Organisation Studies; International Business; Journalism; Hospitality and Tourism.

About Undergraduate Studies:

You will find a warm welcome in Lancashire Business School (LBS) and a stimulating set of courses. LBS is one of the main national providers of business and management education, acting as the international gateway to the region.

Facilities:

Lancashire Business School is conveniently located in Preston, the administrative and commercial centre of Lancashire. Preston is situated close to the M6 motorway and on the main London Glasgow railway

line. London is just two and a half hours away and Manchester less than one hour. Areas of outstanding natural beauty such as the Lake District and the Yorkshire Dales are within easy reach and Blackpool, the UK's top leisure attraction is just twenty miles away.

Departments/Faculties:

Accounting and Financial Services
Management Development
Business Information Management
Organisation Studies
International Business
Journalism
Hospitality and Tourism
Business Development Unit
Career Development Unit

Links with Academic Institutions:

The School offers one of the largest programmes of student and staff exchange in the UK providing two-way exchanges with institutions in Europe, China, the USA, South Africa and Australia. In the UK there are strong links, including accreditation, with most of the major professional bodies.

Links with Industry:

The Business School has developed a strong and mutually beneficial relationship with the business and industrial community. In addition to work placements, the School offers one of the largest programmes of student and staff exchange in the UK, providing two-way exchanges with institutions in Europe, China and USA. As well as providing a range of part-time professional and management courses, the School designs and delivers tailor-made training and development programmes for organisations, often working in collaboration with company-based human resource specialists.

General Undergraduate Courses

BA (Hons) Business Studies

This course will develop your intellectual and personal skills in the framework of a rigorous business education. Students spend the third year on placement in industry or commerce. The programme is broadly based and covers the full range of business topics through compulsory modules and options which allow students to develop their own specialisms. There are also opportunities for study or work placement abroad and the study of foreign languages.

Modular Course?	No
Qualifications:	BA Hons
Application Deadline:	UCAS deadline
Commencement Date:	September
Entry Requirement:	A-level 14-18 points depending on course, GCSE Maths

and English Language, Advanced level GNVQ, BTEC HND with Distinctions in appropriate subjects. Candidates without qualifications but with relevant work experience or qualifications are also considered.

Applications to Places:	
Registered:	257
Awards:	

	Duration	EC Fees	Non-EC Fees
Full time	4 years	£1000	£6200
Part time			
Sandwich			

BA (Hons) Marketing

This course is designed to prepare students for a career in any aspect of marketing including marketing research, advertising, public relations or sales management. The programme takes into account industry expectations and links into the professional institutes. It leads to professional exemptions from examinations of bodies such as the Chartered Institute of Marketing and the Market Research Society. There is a strong emphasis on both European and global marketing and students have opportunities for study or work placement abroad and the study of foreign languages.

Modular Course?	No
Qualifications:	BA Hons
Application Deadline:	UCAS deadline
Commencement Date:	September
Entry Requirement:	A-level 14-18 points depending on course, GCSE Maths and English Language, Advanced level GNVQ, BTEC HND with Distinctions in appropriate subjects. Candidates without qualifications but with relevant work experience or qualifications are also considered.

Applications to Places:	
Registered:	136
Awards:	

	Duration	EC Fees	Non-EC Fees
Full time	3 years	£1000	£6200
Part time			
Sandwich			

BA (Hons) Management

This course will provide an exciting and stimulating experience, and a distinctive approach to the study of management which develops communication, interpersonal, groupworking and learning skills, while drawing on both the theory and practice of management. The programme helps students manage their own development and build a commitment to competence.

Modular Course?	No
Qualifications:	BA Hons
Application Deadline:	UCAS deadline
Commencement Date:	September
Entry Requirement:	A-level 14-18 points depending on course, GCSE Maths and English Language, Advanced level GNVQ, BTEC HND with Distinctions in appropriate subjects. Candidates without qualifications but with relevant work experience or qualifications are also considered.

Applications to Places:	
Registered:	143
Awards:	

	Duration	EC Fees	Non-EC Fees
Full time	3 years	£1000	£6200
Part time			
Sandwich			

BA International Business

This challenging programme gives students the opportunity to explore all aspects of the international business environment, and examines the role and operation of international organisations. The programme is multi-disciplinary and covers the core skills needed by international managers, as well as a wide range of specialisms. The programme helps students manage their own development and make informed decisions about their studies and choice of career.

Modular Course?	No
Qualifications:	BA
Application Deadline:	UCAS deadline
Commencement Date:	September
Entry Requirement:	A-level 14-18 points depending on course, GCSE Maths and English Language, Advanced level GNVQ, BTEC HND with Distinctions in appropriate subjects. Candidates without qualifications but with relevant work experience or qualifications are also considered.

Applications to Places:	
Registered:	118
Awards:	

	Duration	EC Fees	Non-EC Fees
Full time	3 years	£1000	£6200
Part time			
Sandwich			

Specialist Undergraduate Course

BA (Hons) Journalism

Modular Course?	No
Qualifications:	BA Hons
Categories:	Journalism

BA (Hons) Public Relations

Modular Course?	No
Qualifications:	BA Hons
Categories:	Marketing

BA (Hons) Hospitality Management/International

Modular Course?	No
Qualifications:	BA Hons
Categories:	Hospitality

BA (Hons) International Tourism

Modular Course?	No
Qualifications:	BA Hons
Categories:	Leisure

BA (Hons) Hospitality Studies

Modular Course?	No
Qualifications:	BA
Categories:	Hospitality

BA (Hons) Accounting

Modular Course?	No
Qualifications:	BA Hons
Categories:	Finance

BA (Hons) International Accounting

Modular Course?	No
Qualifications:	BA Hons
Categories:	Finance

BA (Hons) Financial Services

Modular Course?	No
Qualifications:	BA Hons
Categories:	Finance

BSc (Hons) Business Information Technology

Modular Course?	No
Qualifications:	BSc Hons
Categories:	IT Systems

BA (Hons) Organisation Studies

Modular Course?	No
Qualifications:	BA Hons
Categories:	Management

BA (Hons) Business Enterprise

Modular Course?	No
Qualifications:	BA
Categories:	Small Business

BA (Hons) Human Resource Management

Modular Course?	No
Qualifications:	BA Hons
Categories:	Human Resources

BA (Hons) Accounting and Financial Studies

Modular Course?	No
Qualifications:	BA (Hons)
Categories:	Accounting

Diploma in Personnel Management

Modular Course?	No
Qualifications:	Diploma HE
Categories:	Human Resources

University Diploma in Newspaper Journalism

Modular Course?	No
Qualifications:	
Categories:	Journalism

The Management School

Lancaster University Management School

Address:	Lancaster University
	Lancaster
	LA1 4YX
Area:	North West England
Phone:	+44 1524 594285
Fax:	+44 1524 381454
Email:	A.Bolton@lancaster.ac.uk
Website:	http://www.lancs.ac.uk/users/ manschool/
Email Application Available?	No
How to apply by email:	
Total Number of Teaching Staff:	86
Staff Teaching Undergraduate Courses	65
Research Rating:	5*
Teaching Rating:	Excellent
Additional Rating Information	
Male:Female Student Ratio	53:47
Head of Business School	Professor Stephen Watson (Dean)
Head of Undergraduate Studies	George Long
Admissions Contact	Anne Welsby

About the School:

The Management School is an integral part of Lancaster University, founded in 1964. It is a full-range business school which forms a faculty in its own right. Lancaster is one of three universities to hold the highest possible ratings in Business and Management from the Higher Education Funding Council, for excellence in teaching and 5* in research. The School manages the nearby purpose-designed Lancaster House Training Centre which adjoins a four-star hotel.

About Undergraduate Studies:

Lancaster's undergraduate provision is known for its flexibility. Courses in business, management and economics can be taken for generalist degrees such as the BBA in Management and BSc in Business Studies or for specialist degrees. Variants which include an integral year of work experience or of study at a partner institution in North America, continental Europe or South East Asia, are increasingly popular.
Undergraduate full-time student numbers: 1020.

Facilities:

The parkland campus, three miles south of Lancaster city centre, incorporates a full range of college, cultural, chaplaincy, library, computing, sports and shopping facilities. It provides a safe environment, readily accessible from the M6 and by rail (one hour from Manchester, three hours from London, Edinburgh and Glasgow). Campus accommodation is guaranteed for first-year students, and rents and insurance are below average cost. No other university is so well situated for the outdoor attractions of the Lake District and Yorkshire Dales.

Departments/Faculties:

The Management School comprises Accounting and Finance, Behaviour in Organisations, Economics, Management Learning, Management Science, Marketing, and Management Development Division. The School forms a faculty of the university in its own right.

Links with Academic Institutions:

There are extensive opportunities for study abroad at both undergraduate and postgraduate levels, incorporating reciprocal credit transfer. Lancaster pioneered such arrangements in Europe and has partner institutions in western Europe, North America and in SE Asia. Members of faculty have developed collaborative research with a wide range of business schools.

Links with Industry:

Lancaster has close relationships with British Airways, British Aerospace, Royal and SunAlliance and Bass,and with SMEs. Increasingly such relationships are international and implemented through post-experience Masters programmes. Most Masters programmes incorporate a three-month attachment to a company and several undergraduate programmes include a year's work experience.

Student Testimonials:

"I feel lucky to have been on a course where the relationships between staff and students ensure that you feel more than just another UCAS number." (Sue-Anne Jennings)
"The work has been varied, challenging, interesting and enjoyable. My work experience helped me to get an excellent degree and, what's more, an excellent career." (Collette Curran)
"I was choosy about which university I wanted to go to; Lancaster was my choice because of the reputation of the Marketing Department which is highly regarded in industry. One of the companies which offered me a position targets Lancaster's Marketing students." (Deborah Wiggins)

BBA Management

The BBA is a demanding but stimulating four-year programme which offers an integrated study of management and includes a placement in the third year.

Modular Course?	No
Qualifications:	BBA (Hons)
Application Deadline:	15 December
Commencement Date:	1 October
Entry Requirement:	ABB at A level or equivalent
Applications to Places:	11:1
Registered:	55
Awards:	34

	Duration	EC Fees	Non-EC Fees
Full time	4 years	1000	6550
Part time			
Sandwich			

BBA European Management

The European degree with French, German or Spanish features work experience placements and two years in a leading business schools in Europe.

Modular Course?	No
Qualifications:	BBA (Hons)
Application Deadline:	15 December
Commencement Date:	1 October
Entry Requirement:	ABB at A level or equivalent
Applications to Places:	8:1
Registered:	18
Awards:	9

	Duration	EC Fees	Non-EC Fees
Full time	4 years	£1000	£6550
Part time			
Sandwich			

BSc Business Studies

The BSc in Business Studies is a three-year degree which offers a path similar to the BBA with extensive study opportunities throughout the School.

Modular Course?	No
Qualifications:	BSc Hons
Application Deadline:	15 December
Commencement Date:	1 October
Entry Requirement:	BBB at A level or equivalent
Applications to Places:	14:1
Registered:	New course
Awards:	New course

Full time	3 years	£1000	£6550
Part time			
Sandwich			

BA Accounting and Finance
BSc Finance

Modular Course?	No
Qualifications:	BA Hons; BSc Hons; Joint Honours
Categories:	Finance

BA Economics
BSc International Business (Economics)

Modular Course?	No
Qualifications:	BA Hons; BSc Hons; Joint Honours
Categories:	Finance; International Business; Economics

BSc Management Science
BSc Operations Management

Modular Course?	No
Qualifications:	BSc Hons; Joint Honours
Categories:	Public Sector; IT Systems; Production; Transport

BA Marketing
BA Marketing and Advertising

Modular Course?	No
Qualifications:	BA Hons; Joint Honours
Categories:	Marketing; Small Business

BA Organisation Studies/ Human Resource Management

Modular Course?	No
Qualifications:	BA Hons; Joint Honours
Categories:	Human Resources; Public Sector

University of Leeds

Leeds University

University of Leeds

Address:	Leeds LS2 9JT
Area:	North West England
Phone:	013 233 4469
Fax:	0113 233 4465

Email:

Website: http://www.leeds.ac.uk/bes

Email Application Available?	No
How to apply by email:	
Total Number of Teaching Staff:	95
Staff Teaching Undergraduate Courses	95
Research Rating:	4
Teaching Rating:	Satisfactory
Additional Rating Information	
Male:Female Student Ratio	65:35
Head of Business School	Mr Ken Woolmer
Head of Undergraduate Studies	AJ Jones
Admissions Contact	S North

About the School:

The University of Leeds is one of the largest in the UK, with an international reputation for teaching and research. The Business School covers the full range of disciplines at both undergraduate and postgraduate level, with a staff presently consisting of eighteen professors and more than seventy other staff. More than 2500 are currently studying for the School's specialist first degrees, full-time and part-time.

About Undergraduate Studies:

All programmes are modular, combining core compulsory subjects, options from within the subject area and electives, taken from most fields of study in the University. This flexibility and the extensive range of joint and combined honours schemes gives considerable opportunity to transfer between courses at the end of the first year. The structure also allows increasing specialisation, especially in the third year when students are able to choose from a very wide range of optional subjects.

Facilities:

The School provides a lively and hospitable environment for study with common room facilities, extremely active societies in which many staff actively participate, and good links to the teaching staff of the School through the formal Staff-Student Committee. The University is located close to the City centre, and this has helped to make it the most popular choice for UK students over the last three years.

BA Accounting and Finance

This degree provides a critical understanding of the role of accounting and finance in industry, commerce, and the wider community. It enables graduates to obtain the maximum exemptions from professional accounting examinations (ICAEW). The degree provides training in the acquisition of both computer and numeracy skills as well as those of written and oral presentation.

Modular Course?	Yes
Qualifications:	BA
Application Deadline:	UCAS deadline
Commencement Date:	
Entry Requirement:	Generally, 3 A-levels BBB-BCC, GCSE Maths Grade B, Advanced Level GNVQ plus an additional A-level, BTEC with Distinctions. Mature students with other qualifications and experience considered.
Applications to Places:	18:1
Registered:	146
Awards:	

	Duration	EC Fees	Non-EC Fees
Full time	3 years	On request	On request
Part time			
Sandwich			

BA Management Studies

The degree develops an understanding of complex modern business organisations and provides the skills needed to manage them. Levels 1 and 2 deal with the basics of sound management training, while a very wide range of specialist options in fields such as Personnel or Marketing are available in Level 3. Linked modules in strategic management form the core of the final year of study. Graduate membership of the Institute of Personnel and Development is available to students who graduate on the IPD pathway.

Modular Course?	Yes
Qualifications:	BA
Application Deadline:	UCAS deadline
Commencement Date:	
Entry Requirement:	Generally, 3 A-levels BBB-BCC, GCSE Maths Grade B, Advanced Level GNVQ plus an additional A-level, BTEC with Distinctions. Mature students with other qualifications and experience considered.
Applications to Places:	18:1
Registered:	137
Awards:	

	Duration	EC Fees	Non-EC Fees
Full time	3 years	On request	On request
Part time			
Sandwich			

BA Joint Honours Management and Arabic/Chinese/French/German/Italian/Japanese/Portuguese/Russian/Spanish

The School is actively involved in SOCRATES exchange schemes with leading business schools in France, Germany and Spain so that students on joint honours programmes with French, German and Spanish may spend their year abroad, either following a course of study at one of these Schools or on business placements.

Modular Course?	Yes
Qualifications:	BA Hons; Joint Honours
Application Deadline:	UCAS deadline
Commencement Date:	
Entry Requirement:	Generally, 3 A-levels ABB-BCC, GCSE Maths Grade B, Advanced Level GNVQ plus an additional A-level, BTEC with Distinctions. Mature students with other qualifications and experience considered.
Applications to Places:	18:1
Registered:	142
Awards:	

	Duration	EC Fees	Non-EC Fees
Full time			
Part time			
Sandwich	4 years	On request	On request

BSc Joint Honours Accounting and Computer Studies/Information Systems

These programme provide a critical understanding of the role of accounting and finance in industry, commerce, and the wider community. They also give students a broad appreciation of commercially-orientated computing and the problems of implementing information systems within organisations.

Modular Course?	Yes
Qualifications:	BA Hons; Joint Honours
Application Deadline:	UCAS deadline
Commencement Date:	
Entry Requirement:	Generally, 3 A-levels ABB-BCC, GCSE Maths Grade B, Advanced Level GNVQ plus an additional A-level, BTEC with Distinctions. Mature students with other qualifications and experience considered.
Applications to Places:	18:1
Registered:	29
Awards:	

	Duration	EC Fees	Non-EC Fees
Full time	3 years	On request	On request
Part time			
Sandwich			

BEng/MEng Mechanical and Manufacturing Engineering with Management

This is a joint degree, linking strong engineering training with Management Studies to create a three or four year programme specifically designed to suit future managers in the engineering industry. It unites the complementary strengths of the Schools of Business and Economic Studies and Mechanical Engineering. Selected students with high level results in the second year may be offered a year of study abroad, in France, Germany, Canada or the USA.

Modular Course?	Yes
Qualifications:	BEng/Meng
Application Deadline:	UCAS deadline
Commencement Date:	
Entry Requirement:	Generally, 3 A-levels ABB-BCC, GCSE Maths Grade B, Advanced Level GNVQ plus an additional A-level, BTEC with Distinctions. Mature students with other qualifications and experience considered.
Applications to Places:	18:1
Registered:	34
Awards:	

	Duration	EC Fees	Non-EC Fees
Full time	3-4 years	On request	On request
Part time			
Sandwich			

BA Combined Business Studies (part-time)

This is based closely upon the full-time single honours Management Studies degree, and has been carefully adapted to the needs of those in work. Considerable emphasis is placed on project work designed to apply the academic skills and disciplines to work and business.

Modular Course?	Yes
Qualifications:	BA; Joint Honours
Application Deadline:	UCAS deadline
Commencement Date:	

Entry Requirement:			Generally, 3 A-levels ABB-BCC,
			GCSE Maths Grade B,
			Advanced Level GNVQ plus an
			additional A-level, BTEC
			with Distinctions. Mature students
			with other
			qualifications and experience
			considered.
Applications to Places:			18:1
Registered:			39
Awards:			

	Duration	EC Fees	Non-EC Fees
Full time			
Part time	5-6 years	On request	On request
Sandwich			

BA Accounting and Management Studies

This course offers the benefit of obtaining a joint honours degree in the subject areas of Accounting and Management Studies, with the option for students to choose to specialise in either of these subject areas in their second and third years.

Modular Course?	Yes
Qualifications:	BA
Application Deadline:	UCAS deadline
Entry Requirement:	Generally, 3 A-levels BBB GCSE Maths Grade B, Advanced Level GNVQ plus an additional A-level, BTEC.

Leeds Business School

Leeds Business School

Address:	Beckett Park Campus
	Headingley
	Leeds
	LS6 3QS
Area:	North East England
Phone:	0113 283 2600
Fax:	0113 283 7508
Email:	**Business@lmu.ac.uk**
Website:	**www.lmu.ac.uk/lbs**
Email Application Available?	No
How to apply by email:	
Total Number of Teaching Staff:	287
Staff Teaching Undergraduate Courses	
Research Rating:	n/a
Teaching Rating:	Satisfactory
Additional Rating Information	Business and Management
	(Unit 43) Grade 2
	Politics and International Studies
	(Unit 39) Grade 3b
Male:Female Student Ratio	50:50
Head of Business School	David Green
Head of Undergraduate Studies	
Admissions Contact	The Marketing Unit
	0113 283 7350

About the School:

Leeds Business School has a solid record of achievement in delivering business and management programmes to undergraduates and professionals both in the region and across the UK.

The School provides training and development, on a part-time and credit-rated basis for directors with the Institute of Directors' Diploma and the Masters in Company Direction and for senior managers and professionals in both the public and private sectors. Provision includes tailored in-house programmes, taught part-time and full-time courses and short courses in key areas.

Leeds Metropolitan University has the same mission today as it had at its establishment 23 years ago, to meet the needs of the region's industries and the aspirations of its students for education and training. The broad range of its courses answers these needs, whilst the city of Leeds itself provides arts and leisure pursuits based around a rich cultural heritage. Leeds is home to Opera North, the West Yorkshire Playhouse, the Leeds International Piano Competition and a short drive beyond the centre, the Henry Moore Institute.

About Undergraduate Studies:

Entry requirements, course fees and application forms available on request.
Current courses offered are:
BA (Hons) Accounting & Finance
BSc (Hons) Accounting & Information Systems
BA (Hons) Business Management
BA (Hons) Business Studies
BA (Hons) Public Relations
BA (Hons) Economics & Public Policy
LLB (Hons) Law
BA (Hons) Law with Information Technology
All courses encourage links with employers and some have a sandwich element, allowing students to spend time gaining relevant work experience, at home or abroad.

Facilities:

Leeds Metropolitan University possesses one of the finest sports complexes in British higher education, catering for an extensive programme of recreation activities, classes and sports clubs. The University has recently acquired a £1 million grant from the National Lottery Sports Fund to improve facilities and bring the athletics centre to national competitive standards. The Students Union is established as one of Leeds major venues, playing host to some of the country's best known bands including Kula Shaker, Reef and even Oasis. Organised activities range from Dance nights and hypnotists to Alternative nights and comedians.

Departments/Faculties:

Five Schools:-
- Accountancy and Finance
- Business Strategy
- Economics, Policy and Information Analysis
- Human Resource Management
- Law
Centres and Units:-
- Centre for Director Education
- Policy Research Institute
- European Regional Business and Economic Development Unit
- Centre for Strategic Management
- Human Resource Development Unit
- Thematic Research Centre
- Marketing and Systems Unit

Links with Academic Institutions:

As well as developing partnerships with higher and further educational establishments in the United Kingdom, the School has forged important links with Business Schools and institutions abroad, as far afield as Poland, Spain, Italy, Japan, China, Malaysia, USA, Australia and New Zealand.

Links with Industry:

Leeds Business School has developed strong links with the local business community. The continuing development of partnerships with employers, in the region and beyond, benefits students through work placements and enables companies to take advantage of the School's training, research and consultancy opportunities.

General Undergraduate Courses

BA (Hons) Business Studies

Part of the Business Undergraduate Modular Programme (BUMP), the Business Studies Degree aims to develop knowledge, skills and qualities that will enable graduates to work in a variety of occupations and industrial sectors.

Modular Course?	Yes
Qualifications:	BA Hons
Application Deadline:	August 1998
Commencement Date:	September 1998
Entry Requirement:	Maths and English GCSE - 'B' or above
Applications to Places:	
Registered:	
Awards:	

	Duration	EC Fees	Non-EC Fees
Full time	3 years	£750	£750
Part time			
Sandwich	4 years	£750	£750

BTEC Higher National Diploma in Business

This course is aimed at those students who have not yet made a specific career choice but who wish to pursue a course of general business and management study. The course will be appropriate for those students who wish to take up a career in industry, commerce, the public sector, or the voluntary sector.

Modular Course?	Yes
Qualifications:	HND
Application Deadline:	August 1998
Commencement Date:	September 1998
Entry Requirement:	Maths and English GCSE or equivalent, preferably at Grade C
Applications to Places:	10 : 1
Registered:	
Awards:	

	Duration	EC Fees	Non-EC Fees
Full time	2 years	£750	£750
Part time			
Sandwich			

Specialist Undergraduate Course

BA (Hons) Accounting and Finance

Modular Course?	Yes
Qualifications:	BA Hons
Categories:	Finance

LLB (Hons) Law Programme

Modular Course?	Yes
Qualifications:	LLB (Hons)
Categories:	Business Law; Law

BA (Hons) Economics and Public Policy

Modular Course?	Yes
Qualifications:	BA Hons
Categories:	Human Resources; Finance; Marketing

BA (Hons) Public Relations

Modular Course?	Yes
Qualifications:	BA Hons
Categories:	Marketing

LL.B. (Hons) Law

BA (Hons) Law with Information Technology

Liverpool Business School

Liverpool Business School

Address:	John Foster Building
	98 Mount Pleasant
	Liverpool
	L3 5UZ
Area:	North West England
Phone:	0151 231 3815
Fax:	0151 707 0423

Email: **d.lister@livjm.ac.uk**

Website: **www.livjm.ac.uk/bus/**

Email Application Available?	No
How to apply by email:	
Total Number of Teaching Staff:	130
Staff Teaching Undergraduate Courses	130
Research Rating:	2
Teaching Rating:	Satisfactory
Additional Rating Information	
Male:Female Student Ratio	48:52
Head of Business School	Professor Frank Sanderson
Head of Undergraduate Studies	Dr Keith Lindsay
Admissions Contact	Mr David A Liston

About the School:
Liverpool Business School is situated on the Mount Pleasant campus of John Moores University between the city's two cathedrals. It has 130 staff organised into six subject groups: Business Policy; Marketing; Accountancy and Financial Management; Economic, International Finance and Quantative Methods; and Human Resource Management. It offers a full range of undergraduate, postgraduate and professional programmes as well as conducting extensive consultancy work and research.

About Undergraduate Studies:
The School has developed market-leading expertise in the design, delivery and assessment of business and management programmes which enable participants to apply their learning in the workplace. The School is rapidly expanding its research and consultancy portfolio, focusing on its key strengths in: International Economics and Finance; Human Resource Development; Information Management; Public Service Management. The University offers an Integrated Credit Scheme based on modular programmes delivered within a two semester per year structure. All programmes offer a mix of core and elective modules which can be taken from a wide choice including Marketing, Personnel, Purchasing, Financial Services, Project Management and Multinationals. Entry requirements, deadlines and fee details are available on request.

Facilities:
Liverpool is an attractive city for students with theatres, art galleries, two top football clubs, Aintree and a wide range of other amenities in the city and within the Students' Union.

Specialist Undergraduate Course

BA (Hons) Business Studies

Modular Course?	Yes
Qualifications:	BA
Categories:	Human Resources; Finance; Management

BSc (Hons) Business Information Systems

Modular Course?	Yes
Qualifications:	BSc Hons
Categories:	Finance; Marketing; Management, IT

BA (Hons) International Business Studies

Modular Course?	Yes
Qualifications:	BA Hons
Categories:	International Business, Language

BA (Hons) Public Service Management

Modular Course?	Yes
Qualifications:	BA Hons
Categories:	Public Sector, Local Government

BA (Hons) Accounting and Finance

Modular Course?	Yes
Qualifications:	BA Hons
Categories:	Finance

BA (Hons) Business Administration

Modular Course?	Yes
Qualifications:	BA Hons
Categories:	Human Resources; Finance; Management, HRM

BSc/BA (Hons) Information and Library Management

Modular Course?	Yes
Qualifications:	BA Hons; BSc; Information Management
Categories:	Management, Data Handling, Information Technology

BA (Hons) Joint Programmes (Business, Marketing with other subjects)

Modular Course?	Yes
Qualifications:	BA Hons
Categories:	Marketing; Management, Business

BTEC HND Business

Modular Course?	Yes
Qualifications:	HND
Categories:	Finance; Personnel

BA (Hons) Business Studies (Part-time)

Modular Course?	Yes
Qualifications:	BA Hons
Categories:	Human Resources; Finance; Management, Marketing, HRM, Purchasing

BTEC HNC Business

Modular Course?	No
Qualifications:	HNC
Categories:	Finance; Personnel

London Guildhall University Business School

London Guildhall University Business School

Address:	84 Moorgate
	London
	EC2M 6SQ
Area:	London and South East England
Phone:	0171 320 1616
Fax:	0171 320 1163
Email:	**enqs@lgu.ac.uk**
Website:	**http://www.lgu.ac.uk**
Email Application Available?	No
How to apply by email:	
Total Number of Teaching Staff:	180
Staff Teaching Undergraduate Courses	130
Research Rating:	2
Teaching Rating:	Satisfactory
Additional Rating Information	Research:
	Economics = 3b
	Law = 2
	Business & Management = 1
	Computing Information Systems
	= 1
	Mathematics = 2
Male:Female Student Ratio	50:50
Head of Business School	Susan Proudfoot
Head of Undergraduate Programmes	Eric Collier
Admissions Contact	Centre for Undergraduate
	Programmes

About the School:

London Guildhall University boasts one of the largest business schools in Europe. It has six departments: Accounting and Financial Services; Business Studies; Computing; Information Systems and Mathematics; Economics; Law; and Management and Professional Development, that allows the School to draw on an unrivalled breadth of experience across all courses. The content and range of the portfolio of courses reflects our close links with the City and professional associations, and our unique location in the heart of the City. The programmes maintain a balance between academic, professional and vocational programmes, all of which are designed to equip students for a successful career in business and the professions. The Business School has excellent library facilities in newly-refurbished premises

and specialist subject librarians are on hand to give information and advice. We make extensive use of IT in teaching and the School is well-equipped with mainframe as well as networked mini-computers and micro-computers.

About Undergraduate Studies:

The School offers specialist degree programmes in the following areas: ; BA (Hons) Accounting and Finance; BA (Hons) Business Administration; BA (Hons) Business Studies; BA (Hons) European Business Studies; BA (Hons) Financial Services; BA (Hons) Insurance Studies; LLB (Hons) Business Law; BA (Hons) Economics; BA (Hons) Economic Studies; BA (Hons) Business Economics; BA (Hons) Financial Economics; BA (Hons) Global Economics; BA (Hons) Politics, Philosophy & Economics; BA (Hons) Legal and Economic Studies; BSc (Hons) Business and Information Technology; BTEC HND in Business; BTEC HND in Business and Finance; BTEC HND in Business and Marketing; BTEC HND in Business and Personnel; BTEC HND in European Business; BSc (Hons) Computing and Information Systems; BTEC HND in Computing; BA (Hons) Insurance Studies; LLB (Hons); BA (Hons) Legal Studies; BSc (Hons) Mathematics with Business Applications; BSc (Hons) Multimedia Systems.

Facilities:

The School is located in the heart of London with its attractive combination of ancient landmarks such as St Paul's Cathedral and the Tower of London, and modern icons such as Lloyds Building and the Barbican. With all the theatrical, musical and other amenities it provides a unique environment for study.

Departments:

Accounting and Financial Services
Business Studies
Economics
Management and Professional Development
Law
Computing, Information Systems and Mathematics

Links with Industry:

All departments in the Business School have close links with industry, Livery Companies and the professions.

Student Testimonials:

The University offers one of the most flexible modular programmes in the UK which allows students to study a range of subjects before taking a decision on the specialist subjects they wish to take in the second and third years. Students can study more than one subject throughout a degree by opting for a Joint Honours or Combined Studies degree, such as: Business with Computing; Law with Accounting; Economics with Marketing; Language Studies or Accountancy; Marketing is also available as a specialism. An evening degree programme is now available in: Law; Financial Services; Insurance Studies.

Loughborough University Business School

Loughborough University Business School

Address:	Ashby Road
	Loughborough
	LE11 3TU
Area:	Midlands
Phone:	01509 263171
Fax:	01509 223 960

Email:

Website: www.lboro.ac.uk/departments/bs

Email Application Available?	No
How to apply by email:	
Total Number of Teaching Staff:	57
Staff Teaching Undergraduate Courses	57
Research Rating:	3a
Teaching Rating:	Excellent
Additional Rating Information	
Male:Female Student Ratio	0.74:1
Head of Business School	Professor Sue Cox
Head of Undergraduate Studies	Professor Malcolm King
Admissions Contact	Carol Collier

About the School:

The Business School has grown from being one of the founders of university business education to become one of Europe's premier business schools. Our growth and success come from keeping close to our customers: industry, commerce and the people on our programmes. This has led to many of our programmes being funded by business, particularly in financial services, retailing, automotive industry and engineering. Recent successes include sharing a Queen's anniversary prize for our work in partnership with Rolls Royce and British Aerospace, and one of our MBA students became a regional and national winner of the National Training Award.

We are one of Europe's leading business schools. Our undergraduate degrees, postgraduate programmes, company training courses and research activities all have an international reputation. The quality of our treaching has been rated excellent by the HEFCE. Our undergraduate programmes are practical and commercially orientated, and reflect our extensive links with industry. Our programmes enjoy an excellent reputation with employers, and the career and salary

prospects for our graduates are exceptionally high.

Facilities:

We can offer students one of Britain's greenest and most spacious campuses, with extensive hall and self-catering student accommodation. All enjoy access to the University's internationally renowned sports facilities and the comprehensive amenities of the Students' Union.

General Undergraduate Courses

BSc (Hons) Accounting and Financial Management

This 4-year degree equips students for careers in accounting or industry and commerce. It covers the core accounting subjects required for substantial exemptions from professional examinations and also incorporates the study of other management subjects together with a range of options including languages. The third year is spent in placement in a firm of chartered accountants, or in industry.

Modular Course?	No
Qualifications:	BSc Hons
Application Deadline:	UCAS deadline
Commencement Date:	
Entry Requirement:	Minimum grade C GCSE Maths or
	equivalent. A-levels
	BBC or ACC (excluding General
	Studies). BEC/GNVQ
	applicants considered
	individually.
Applications to Places:	6.7:1
Registered:	234
Awards:	

	Duration	EC Fees	Non-EC Fees
Full time	4 years	£750	£5740
Part time			
Sandwich			

BSc (Hons) Banking and Finance

This 4-year degree, the first of its kind in the country, was developed in partnership with a leading clearing bank. Combining Management, Economics, Banking and Finance, plus a range of options including languages, the degree prepares students for careers in banking, financial services and industry. Students enjoy support from a number of leading financial institutions and the degree provides exemptions from several professional examinations. The third year includes a professional placement.

Modular Course?	No
Qualifications:	BSc Hons

Application Deadline: UCAS deadline
Commencement Date:
Entry Requirement: Minimum grade C GCSE Maths or equivalent. A-levels BBC or ACC (excluding General Studies). BEC/GNVQ applicants considered individually.
Applications to Places: 6.7:1
Registered: 132
Awards:

	Duration	EC Fees	Non-EC Fees
Full time	4 years	£750	£5740
Part time			
Sandwich			

BSc (Hons) Retail Management

This 4-year degree, introduced in 1991 with major financial backing from Sainsbury and C&A, equips students for a career in store management or in specialist retail functions such as buying, merchandising, marketing or logistics. The programme also includes general management subjects plus a range of options including languages. The third year includes a placement in retailing or a related sector.

Modular Course? No
Qualifications: BSc Hons
Application Deadline: UCAS deadline
Commencement Date:
Entry Requirement: Minimum grade C GCSE Maths or equivalent. A-levels BBC or ACC (excluding General Studies). BEC/GNVQ applicants considered individually.
Applications to Places: 6.7:1
Registered: 146
Awards:

	Duration	EC Fees	Non-EC Fees
Full time	4 years	£750	£5740
Part time			
Sandwich			

BSc (Hons) Management Sciences

This 4-year degree provides a broad-based course to equip students for a wide range of careers in management. It focuses on numeracy, information management and information technology and includes the study of other management subjects such as Marketing, Personnel and Finance plus a range of options including languages. The third year includes a placement in industry.

Modular Course? No
Qualifications: BSc Hons
Application Deadline: UCAS deadline
Commencement Date:
Entry Requirement: Minimum grade C GCSE Maths or equivalent. A-levels BBC or ACC (excluding General Studies). BEC/GNVQ applicants considered individually.
Applications to Places: 6.7:1
Registered: 329
Awards:

	Duration	EC Fees	Non-EC Fees
Full time	4 years	£750	£5740
Part time			
Sandwich			

BSc (Hons) Retail Management (Automotive)

This 4-year degree was introduced in 1998 with financial backing from key companies and the two main trade associations. It equips students for a career in automotive distribution management or related sectors. The programme is structured similarly to the Retail Management degree but also includes specialist modules on the automotive industry environment, management of vehicle and fleet sales, and after-sales management. The third year includes a placement in the motor industry.

Modular Course? No
Qualifications: BSc Hons
Application Deadline: UCAS deadline
Commencement Date:
Entry Requirement: Minimum grade C GCSE Maths or equivalent. A-levels BBC or ACC (excluding General Studies). BEC/GNVQ applicants considered individually.
Applications to Places: 6.7:1
Registered: 20
Awards:

	Duration	EC Fees	Non-EC Fees
Full time	4 years	£750	£5740
Part time			
Sandwich			

BA (Hons) International Business

This 4-year degree equips students for careers in management, administration or international business. The programme enables students to study international aspects of management while developing fluency in

French, German or Spanish. In the third year, students have a choice of studying or working abroad, or taking an industrial placement in the UK.

Modular Course?	**No**
Qualifications:	**BA Hons**
Application Deadline:	**UCAS deadline**
Commencement Date:	
Entry Requirement:	**Minimum grade C GCSE Maths or equivalent. A-levels BBC or ACC (excluding General Studies). BEC/GNVQ applicants considered individually.**
Applications to Places:	**6.7:1**
Registered:	**130**
Awards:	

	Duration	EC Fees	Non-EC Fees
Full time	4 years	£750	£5740
Part time			
Sandwich			

Luton Business School

Luton Business School

Address:	Park Square
	Luton
	LU1 3JU
Area:	London and South East England
Phone:	01582 743 121
Fax:	01582 743 143
Email:	**faculty-of-business@luton.ac.uk**
Website:	**http://www.luton.ac.uk/Business**
Email Application Available?	No
How to apply by email:	
Total Number of Teaching Staff:	100
Staff Teaching Undergraduate Courses	100
Research Rating:	2
Teaching Rating:	Satisfactory
Additional Rating Information	
Male:Female Student Ratio	50:50
Head of Business School	Dr Stephen Pettitt
Head of Undergraduate Studies	Russell Kinman
Admissions Contact	

About the School:

Luton Business School is the university's largest faculty with in excess of 100 academic and professorial staff and some 4000 part-time and full-time students studying courses ranging from undergraduate and postgraduate in business and management to those on PhD programmes. The most popular discipline areas include Marketing, Strategic Management, Finance and Accountancy, Human Resource Management, Tourism and International Business. All our programmes incorporate extensive consultation with employers at each stage of design to ensure they relate closely to the requirements of employment in today's global economy. This consultation allows us to develop our programmes to help create career opportunities for our students in new growth sectors.

About Undergraduate Studies:

The majority of our programmes are part of the university Modular Degree Scheme. This enables students to create programmes of study which draw upon their strengths and to meet their personal and career development needs. With a strong vocational and international focus it provides high quality education oriented to the needs of commerce and industry as well as those of the public sector.

Modular Degree Scheme

BA (Hons) Accounting; BA (Hons) Business Administration; BA (Hons) Business Studies; HND Business Studies; BSc (Hons) Business Decision Management; HND Business Decision Management; BSc (Hons) Management Science; BA (Hons) Leisure Management; HND Leisure Management; BA (Hons) Sport and Fitness Management; HND Sport and Fitness Management; BSc (Hons) Sport and Fitness Studies; BA (Hons) Sports Tourism; BA (Hons) Advertising & Marketing Communications; BSc Design Marketing; BA (Hons) International Marketing; BA (Hons) Marketing; BSc Human Resource Management; BA (Hons) Retail Management; BA (Hons) Travel and Tourism; HND Travel and Tourism; BSc (Hons) Hospitality Management

Modular Course?	Yes
Qualifications:	BA; BA Hons; BSc; BSc Hons; HND
Application Deadline:	On request
Commencement Date:	On request
Entry Requirement:	Two passes at A level, and at least four grade C or better GCSEs, including maths and English. A range of alternative qualifications is acceptable, including the various equivalents to A level, an Access pass, or a good (distinctions and merits) pass in BTEC National. Students with a BTEC Higher National Diploma in a suitable area may be able to enrol directly onto Level 2 of the programme. A merit or distinction profile may enable you to enrol on a three-semester programme, completing an honours degree in less than 18 months. The university particularly welcomes applications from older people with work experience, who may not have met the other entry requirements.
Applications to Places:	
Registered:	
Awards:	

	Duration	EC Fees	Non-EC Fees
Full time	2-3 years	On request	On request
Part time	at least four years		
Sandwich	4 years		

Faculty of Management and Business

Faculty of Management and Business

Address:	Aytoun Street
	Manchester
	M1 3GH
Area:	North West England
Phone:	0161 247 3710/3711
Fax:	0161 236 5319
Email:	**m.b.faculty@mmu.ac.uk**
Website:	**http://www.man-bus.mmu.ac.uk**
Email Application Available?	Yes
How to apply by email:	m.b.faculty@mmu.ac.uk
Total Number of Teaching Staff:	150
Staff Teaching Undergraduate Courses	150
Research Rating:	3b
Teaching Rating:	Satisfactory
Additional Rating Information	
Male:Female Student Ratio	45:55
Head of Business School	Professor Andrew Lock
Head of Undergraduate Studies	Relevant Department
Admissions Contact	Relevant Department

About the School:

The Faculty, based in the heart of Manchester, is one of the largest business schools in the country and has been a major provider of business-related education for over 100 years. Some 5000 students, including 1000 postgraduates, study a comprehensive range of full-time, part-time, block release and distance qualification courses from HNC through degree to postgraduate diploma, Masters and PhD levels. The Faculty has strong links with public bodies and professional associations. It is recognised as a Centre of Excellence by the IPD and accredited from AMBA for its MBA course. It is also the North West Centre for the Chartered Institute of Bankers. It has excellent links with international business schools, providing work placement and study abroad, international exchanges and dual qualification courses.

About Undergraduate Studies:

The Faculty has excellent IT and library facilities, and has strong links with public bodies and professional associations. It has been recognised as a Centre of

Excellence by the IPD and is accredited by the AMBA for the MBA course. It is also the North West Centre for the Chartered Institute of Bankers. It also has excellent links with international business schools, providing work placement and study abroad, international exchanges and dual qualification courses. The Faculty is able to provide tailored in-company training and development programmes, customised vocational courses and a range of applied research and consultancy services.

Facilities:

The University's high quality sports and recreation facilities, on four sites in Manchester, are available to all students. Classes are available at all of the sports Centres to suit a range of abilities. There are over 70 different clubs and societies, administered through the Students' Union and its Sports Council. Manchester itself is a thriving city of drama, music, culture and sport. Entertainment venues include the Nynex Arena, Palace Theatre, City Art Gallery, the Museum of Science and Technology and the prestigious Bridgewater Hall, home of the Halle Orchestra. Manchester is also an important financial and commercial centre well served by rail, motorway links and an international airport.

Departments/Faculties:

Accounting and Finance
Business Information Technology
Business Studies
Management
Retailing and Marketing
International Business Unit
Graduate Business School

Links with Academic Institutions:

The Faculty has extensive staff/student exchange links with business schools abroad. It is also involved in a wide variety of funded research projects and collaborative ventures overseas and offers a number of its courses jointly with approved educational establishments abroad.

Links with Industry:

The Faculty provides training and education courses of differing lengths and levels for a range of companies. For example, an open learning degree is provided for management trainees at J Sainsbury and qualification programmes in management development are run in conjunction with a number of blue chip companies. Companies are involved in a number of ways in the undergraduate and postgraduate provisions of the Faculty; for example through student projects, placements, advisory groups and curriculum development.

BA/BSc (Hons) Business & BA/BSc (Hons) Business with Language

This course develops academic and vocational skills and knowledge and provides an industrial placement and a period of study abroad. The course combines core subjects and electives, together with a commissioned group consultancy project. Studies include Marketing, Operations, Business Environment, Business Law, Information Technology, and Business Analysis and Strategy.

Modular Course?	No
Qualifications:	BA Hons; BSc Hons
Application Deadline:	UCAS deadline
Commencement Date:	September
Entry Requirement:	Variable
Applications to Places:	
Registered:	390
Awards:	

	Duration	EC Fees	Non-EC Fees
Full time			
Part time			
Sandwich	4 years	£1000	£6180

BA/BA (Hons) Business Administration

This course develops the academic and vocational skills and knowledge needed for success. It includes the study of the key functions of the business enterprise and combines core subjects with a wide choice of electives to allow students to develop specialisms.

Modular Course?	No
Qualifications:	BA; BA Hons
Application Deadline:	UCAS deadline
Commencement Date:	September
Entry Requirement:	Variable
Applications to Places:	
Registered:	70
Awards:	

	Duration	EC Fees	Non-EC Fees
Full time	I year (post HND)£1000	£6180	
Part time	I year for Hons. £1000	£6180	
Sandwich			

BA (Hons) International Business

This programme, which is a joint venture with institutes in Denmark, Netherlands and North America, concentrates on the development of the international business environment and its impact on company strategies and operations. The programme involves the study of a major European language or Japanese, and gives students the opportunity to spend a year studying abroad.

Modular Course?	No
Qualifications:	BA Hons
Application Deadline:	UCAS deadline
Commencement Date:	September
Entry Requirement:	Variable
Applications to Places:	
Registered:	New course
Awards:	

	Duration	EC Fees	Non-EC Fees
Full time	4 years	£1000	£6180
Part time			
Sandwich			

BA (Hons) Business Studies

The course aims to equip students with HNC or equivalent for management in a wide range of careers. The course is modular and develops skills through project work based on live business situations.

Modular Course?	No
Qualifications:	BA Hons
Application Deadline:	UCAS deadline
Commencement Date:	September
Entry Requirement:	Variable
Applications to Places:	
Registered:	340
Awards:	

	Duration	EC Fees	Non-EC Fees
Full time			
Part time	3 years	£1800	n/a
Sandwich			

BA (Hons) Business in Europe

This degree is a joint venture with institutions of higher education in France, Germany, Italy and Spain, providing students with a joint award. The course covers the determinants of the international business environment and includes study of a language.

Modular Course?	No
Qualifications:	BA Hons
Application Deadline:	UCAS deadline
Commencement Date:	September
Entry Requirement:	Variable
Applications to Places:	
Registered:	217
Awards:	

	Duration	EC Fees	Non-EC Fees
Full time	4 years	£1000	£6180
Part time			
Sandwich			

BSc (Hons) Business Information Technology

This innovative course is designed to prepare graduates for demanding roles in the Information systems field. Modules include Business, Information Technology, Languages, International Studies and there is an industrial placement year.

Modular Course?	No
Qualifications:	BSc; BSc Hons
Application Deadline:	UCAS deadline
Commencement Date:	September
Entry Requirement:	Variable
Applications to Places:	
Registered:	273
Awards:	

	Duration	EC Fees	Non-EC Fees
Full time			
Part time			
Sandwich	4 years	£1000	£6180

BSc/BSc (Hons) Business Information Technology Management

The BSc Business Information Technology Management course provides holders of HND Business Information Technology with a route to graduate status.

Modular Course?	No
Qualifications:	BSc
Application Deadline:	UCAS deadline
Commencement Date:	September
Entry Requirement:	Variable
Applications to Places:	
Registered:	
Awards:	

	Duration	EC Fees	Non-EC Fees
Full time	1 year (post HND)	£1000	£6180
Part time			
Sandwich			

BA (Hons) Accounting and Finance & BA (Hons) Accounting and Finance in Europe

These courses provide a study of the role and techniques of accounting and finance in the UK and Europe. In the European programme, one year is spent studying at a European institution.

Modular Course?	No
Qualifications:	BA Hons
Application Deadline:	UCAS deadline
Commencement Date:	September
Entry Requirement:	Variable

Applications to Places:	
Registered:	341
Awards:	

	Duration	EC Fees	Non-EC Fees
Full time	3-4 years	£1000	£6180
Part time			
Sandwich			

BA (Hons) Financial Services

This course provides a critical awareness of the role, activities, products and performance of the financial services sector. Options include Corporate Strategy, Law and Practice of Banking, Insurance and other relevant disciplines which provide a broadly-based introduction to the financial services sector.

Modular Course?	No
Qualifications:	BA Hons
Application Deadline:	UCAS deadline
Commencement Date:	September
Entry Requirement:	Variable
Applications to Places:	
Registered:	106
Awards:	

	Duration	EC Fees	Non-EC Fees
Full time	3 years	£1000	£6180
Part time			
Sandwich			

BA (Hons) Retail Marketing

This course provides a practical and theoretical introduction to retailing. It provides a foundation in business and retailing and offers a range of electives, including languages.

Modular Course?	No
Qualifications:	BA Hons
Application Deadline:	UCAS deadline
Commencement Date:	September
Entry Requirement:	Variable
Applications to Places:	
Registered:	333
Awards:	

	Duration	EC Fees	Non-EC Fees
Full time			
Part time			
Sandwich	4 years	£1000	£6180

Department of Business and Management, Crewe + Alsager Faculty

Department of Business & Management Studies, Crewe + Alsager Faculty

Address:	Crewe Green Road
	Crewe, Cheshire
	CW1 1DU
Area:	North West England
Phone:	0161 247 5256
Fax:	0161 247 6378
Email:	**S.J.Houghton@MMU.ac.uk**
Website:	**http:\\www.mmu.ac.uk**

Email Application Available?	Yes
How to apply by email:	S.J.Houghton@MMU.ac.uk
Total Number of Teaching Staff:	43
Staff Teaching Undergraduate Courses	35
Research Rating:	3b
Teaching Rating:	Satisfactory
Additional Rating Information	
Male:Female Student Ratio	40:60
Head of Business School	Dr.R.L.Ritchie
Head of Undergraduate Studies	Ms.C.S.Brindley
Admissions Contact	Mr.J.Williams

About the School:

The Department offers a broad portfolio of Business and Management courses, including awards at HND, BA (Hons), post-experience and postgraduate levels. All of the courses have a high degree of vocational orientation through which students develop skills, knowledge and understanding relevant to their chosen careers. The Department has approximately 900 full-time and 450 part-time students and there is a strong emphasis on student-centred and innovative teaching and learning methods.

About Undergraduate Studies:

The Department's recent review of all its undergraduate awards has produced an integrated and comprehensive programme of full and part-time awards. This new programme offers opportunities for each student to achieve their full potential including those with differing entry profiles (e.g. 2 A levels, 1 A level, GNVQ), mature students and overseas students. The opportunity is also available to switch mode from full to part-time or vice-versa without loss of credit or time.

All of the courses have a high degree of vocational orientation through which students develop skills, knowledge and understanding relevant to their chosen careers.

Facilities:

The Crewe + Alsager Faculty is set in a rural campus some thirty miles south of the main University campus in Manchester. The location and size of the Department generates a strong sense of community spirit. The courses and academic staff have a reputation for providing a friendly and supportive environment. The quality of the facilities and the professional expertise of the staff ensure a high quality learning experience for all students. The Department attracts students from a wide international spectrum and provides support for international students in terms of social events, learning support and language tuition. The campus has its own refectory, laundry, shops, banks and other facilities. A full social and cultural programme is offered to students each term led by the Alsager Arts Center. The Faculty also has first-class sports facilities including gymnasium, squash courts, weight-training rooms and thirty-two acres of playing fields.

Departments/Faculties:

The Faculty, with some 5,500 full and part-time students comprises six Departments:-
Business and Management Studies
Humanities and Applied Social Studies
Art, Design and Performance
Environmental and Leisure Studies
Exercise and Sports Science
A number of the undergraduate and postgraduate awards facilitate the study of units from different Departments [e.g. B.Sc.(Hons) Sport and Business]

Links with Academic Institutions:

The Department maintains teaching, research and other collaborative links with several UK and international institutions. Joint research projects with departments at the Aytoun campus of MMU and institutions in France, Israel, Cyprus and Eastern Europe are in progress. Student exchanges with these institutions are a regular feature of most programmes.

Links with Industry:

The Department attracts students from organisations in manufacturing and services as well as the public and health service sectors. Maintaining close links with these organisations, understanding and satisfying their needs is a key feature of the Department's philosophy. This has resulted in Specialist expertise in supporting the needs of the SME sector particularly.

Student Testimonials:
Lucy Watson from Stafford has just completed her first year of the HND in Business Management, with particularly good results in Information Technology and Quantitative Methods. She is now looking forward to her second year of study at the Crewe Campus of the Manchester Metropolitan University. She knows that on successful completion of the HND next academic year, she will have the opportunity of continuing for a further year and gaining a degree in Business Management. "I am impressed with the course", she said. "I was also pleased to find that I could continue to learn a foreign language at the level appropriate to me."

As a student at the Faculty, she settled in quickly and now has a wide circle of friends from many parts of the UK - Manchester, Yorkshire, Wales and Northern Ireland. "I enjoy student life and find the staff friendly too", she says. Lucy is a good ambassador for the local Faculty and enjoys talking to prospective students and showing them around the campus (which she does as a volunteer).

She feels that her course has been useful in preparing her for her vacation work with a large financial organisation in Birmingham. "I was already familiar with computing, and the People and Organisation course was a good preparation for working in a team."

Spencer Davies (BA (Hons) Business Management) was a local student who came to the Crewe Campus having obtained one A Level in History. After he successfully completed the two year HND programme at the local Faculty, he progressed onto the extension degree course. "I have enjoyed my studies at the University and have made many good friends along the way."

General Undergraduate Courses

BA (Hons) Business Management

The Business Management degree is for people who are seeking careers in general business management, but who would like to develop a particular specialism such as information systems, finance and modern languages. There is also the opportunity to follow option routes in Human Resource Management; International Business or Marketing which lead to a named award, ?eg BA (Hons) Business Management (Human Resource Management)?. The advantage of this degree is that it equips graduates with both key functional management and generic skills and management knowledge that can be used in the short term, as well as providing a foundation for lifelong learning.

Modular Course?	No
Qualifications:	BA; BA Hons
Application Deadline:	UCAS deadline
Commencement Date:	October
Entry Requirement:	2 A-levels, typically 12 points, English Language and Maths at GCSE, BTEC National, GNVQ Advanced or equivalent.
Applications to Places:	8:1
Registered:	115
Awards:	26

	Duration	EC Fees	Non-EC Fees
Full time	3 years	£1000	n/a
Part time			
Sandwich			

Higher National Diploma in Business Management

As a nationally recognised higher level qualification it is intended to train people to enter careers which can progress to management positions in industry, commerce and the public sector. It is a practical and intensive programme which links academic study to business and personal skills. The student may through appropriate choice of units achieve one of these named awards:-

HND Business Management
HND Business Management with Sports Studies
HND Business Management with Leisure Studies

One of the key benefits of this programme is that students will normally be able to extend their studies to obtain an honours degree in 12 months (minimum) to 18 months (maximum) depending on the HND profile achieved. Successful HND students who wish to study for a degree whilst working may study part-time for normally two years.

Modular Course?	No
Qualifications:	HND; Leading to Bachelor degree
Application Deadline:	UCAS deadline
Commencement Date:	October
Entry Requirement:	One A level; pass at BTEC National Level; Advanced level GNVQ; or equivalent academic qualification
Applications to Places:	5:1
Registered:	355
Awards:	158

	Duration	EC Fees	Non-EC Fees
Full time	2 years	£1000	On request
Part time			
Sandwich			

BA (Hons) Business Studies

This part-time business studies degree is intended for people with business or management experience who wish to develop their career potential. It is a course of high academic integrity which is specially designed to take account of the needs of the working student. The modular course has been designed to equip students with the necessary knowledge, understanding, decision-making skills and managerial capabilities to handle present and future problems at the national and international level. The total experience gained provides the platform for a successful career in Business Management and may allow progression to the MSc Business Management or other specialist routes.

Modular Course?	No
Qualifications:	BA; BA Hons; Diploma HE
Application Deadline:	October
Commencement Date:	October
Entry Requirement:	Higher National Certificate/
	Diploma in Business
	Studies or Business Management
	or
	Equivalent subject e.g. Retail
	Distribution or equivalent
	Candidates who successfully show,
	through the APL
	(accreditation of prior learning)
	process, that they have
	achieved an equivalent level of
	knowledge and
	understanding or
	Distinction level profile in
	Higher National Diploma in
Applications to Places:	n/a
Registered:	130
Awards:	40

	Duration	EC Fees	Non-EC Fees
Full time			
Part time	2 years	£600 pa	n/a
Sandwich			

HNC in Business Studies

This is a vocational qualification intended for people with and without business experience. The HNC is especially suitable for people who are:
- At the beginning of their career and need to broaden their knowledge of business and how it functions
- Looking to resume a structured career after a break
- Trying to improve their qualifications and career prospects
- Changing the direction of their career and are needing a relevant qualification to help them pursue their ambitions.
- Wishing to progress to a degree level qualification
The course provides a good grounding in Business Studies. Successful HNC students who achieve at least a pass profile have the right to proceed to the BA (Hons) Business Studies degree programme automatically to further their studies. The HNC can also lead to further study for professional qualifications.

Modular Course?	No
Qualifications:	HNC
Application Deadline:	October
Commencement Date:	October
Entry Requirement:	BTEC National award or an ONC/
	D in Business Studies
	or GNVQ Advanced equivalent, or
	3 GCSE passes at
	grade C or above and I A Level
	pass, or qualifications
	which are deemed equivalent to
	the above.
Applications to Places:	2:1
Registered:	50
Awards:	50

	Duration	EC Fees	Non-EC Fees
Full time			
Part time	2 years	£420	n/a
Sandwich			

BA (Hons) Business Management Extension Degrees

The BA/BA (Hons) Business Management extension degrees are a set of inter-linked courses designed as a continuation of the HND Business Management, HND Business Management with Sports Studies and HND Business Management with Leisure Studies. These are: BA/BA (Hons) Business Management; BA/BA (Hons) Business Management with Sports Studies; BA/BA (Hons) Business Management with Leisure Studies. The first year syllabus of the degree programme is studied full-time, and could lead to the award of the degree of BA.

A dissertation, undertaken successfully full-time (one term) part-time (two terms) in the second year of the degree programme allows the award of an honours degree.

The dissertation would be based on the student's workplace, or it could be more theoretical depending on individual interests and circumstances.

Modular Course?	No
Qualifications:	BA; BA Hons
Application Deadline:	UCAS deadline
Commencement Date:	October
Entry Requirement:	HND in Business Management or
	Business Management
	with Sports Studies or Business
	Management with
	Leisure Studies or equivalent.
Applications to Places:	3:1

	Duration	EC Fees	Non-EC Fees
Full time	1.5 years	£1000	n/a
Part time	2 years	£1000	n/a
Sandwich			

Registered: 139
Awards: 87

Specialist Undergraduate Course

BA (Hons) Business Management (Marketing)

Modular Course?	No
Qualifications:	BA; BA Hons; HND; Diploma HE
Categories:	Marketing; Management; Corporate Strategy

BA (Hons) Business Management (Human Resource Management)

Modular Course?	No
Qualifications:	BA; BA Hons; HND; Diploma HE
Categories:	Human Resources; Management; Corporate Strategy

BA (Hons) Business Management (International)

Modular Course?	No
Qualifications:	BA; BA Hons; HND; Diploma HE
Categories:	Management; Corporate Strategy; International Business

BSc & Joint Honours Sport and Business

Modular Course?	No
Qualifications:	BSc; BSc Hons; Joint Honours; HND; Diploma HE
Categories:	Management; Corporate Strategy; Sport

BA Joint Honours Business and Leisure Studies

Modular Course?	No
Qualifications:	BA; BA Hons; Joint Honours; HND; Diploma HE
Categories:	Marketing; Management; Leisure

Manchester School of Management

Undergraduate Office, Manchester School of Management

Address:	PO Box 88
	Manchester
	M60 1QD
Area:	North West England
Phone:	0161 200 3504
Fax:	0161 200 3505
Email:	**msmpg-enq@umist.ac.uk**
Website:	**http://www.umist.ac.uk**
Email Application Available?	No
How to apply by email:	
Total Number of Teaching Staff:	69
Staff Teaching Undergraduate Courses	65
Research Rating:	5*
Teaching Rating:	Excellent
Additional Rating Information	
Male:Female Student Ratio	50:50
Head of Business School	Professor D.A. Littler
Head of Undergraduate Studies	Mrs J Earnshaw
Admissions Contact	Mrs A Beaumont, Undergraduate Office

About the School:

The Manchester School of Management at UMIST is one of the oldest business schools, dating back to 1918. It was one of the earliest UK pioneers of post-experience and postgraduate management education and was among the first UK universities to establish an undergraduate degree in Management in the 1960s. Today it has over 600 undergraduates, 200 postgraduates, 40 research staff and almost 70 academic staff. The School is a member of the Manchester Federal School of Business and Management.

About Undergraduate Studies:

The School, which in The Times Good University Guide is ranked at the top for undergraduate education, has developed an extensive set of undergraduate programmes. These include BSc programmes in Management; International Management with French, German or American Business Studies; Mathematics and Management; Management and Information Technology. By making appropriate selections of options, it is possible to specialise in certain aspects of Management, with the specialisation reflected in the degree title eg BSc in Management (Marketing).

Facilities:

Facilities are available for participation in some forty sports, ranging from Aikido to Windsurfing, via Badminton and Sub-aqua. UMIST has its own five acre sports ground, which caters for soccer and cricket. There is a brand new sports hall comprising an eight-badminton-court-size main hall, dance/areobics studio, martial arts room, squash courts, outdoor basketball/five-a-side pitch, netball.tennis courts and a purpose built fitness suite. The Students Union includes a live music venue, cafe, travel shop and bar. Manchester is an exciting centre for entertainment, sport and culture. The Lake District and Peak District are close at hand.

Departments/Faculties:

The Manchester School of Management is a multi-disciplinary organisation. For administrative and teaching (but not research) purposes, academic staff are grouped into six broad discipline subject groups:
Accounting and Finance
Marketing
Economics
Operations Management/Technology Management
Organisation and Employment Studies
Occupational and Organisational Psychology

Links with Academic Institutions:

The School is a member of the Manchester Federal School of Business and Management, which includes Manchester Business School, Manchester School of Accounting and Finance, and PREST (Programme for Research in Science, Engineering and Technology). The School has postgraduate and undergraduate exchange agreements with several top schools worldwide.

Links with Industry:

The School has extensive research, consultancy and training links with industry through the activities of its Research Centres. The School is also involved in several Teaching Company Schemes whereby MSM acts in partnership with a company to train young graduates working on applied projects in industry.

General Undergraduate Courses

BSc Management

This programme is long-established but continually evolving. The first year provides a foundation of core management disciplines and all courses are compulsory, while the second and third years offer a wide range of options covering many areas of management. These include Accounting, Marketing, Psychology, Law, Industrial relations, Economics, Operations and Production. This allows students to specialise, or not as they wish, and build a degree programme tailored to their own needs. Students who specialise in certain areas during their second and third years are able to have that specialisation reflected in their degree title. These include: BSc in Management (Accounting and Finance); BSc in Management (Decision Science); BSc in Management (Employment and Organisation); BSc in Management (Human Resources); BSc in Management (International Business Economics); BSc in Management (International Studies); BSc in Management (Marketing); BSc in Management (Operations and Technology).

Modular Course?	Yes
Qualifications:	BSc Hons
Application Deadline:	UCAS deadline
Commencement Date:	Late September
Entry Requirement:	3 A-levels at Grade A B B
Applications to Places:	
Registered:	
Awards:	

	Duration	EC Fees	Non-EC Fees
Full time	3 years	£750 (under review)	£6800
Part time			
Sandwich			

BSc in International Management with French

This four-year programme is designed to educate and develop students who will have both management knowledge and skills and a high level of business capability in the French language as well as a real understanding of the business culture of French-speaking countries. The degree is taught jointly by Manchester School of Management and the Department of Language Engineering. The third year is spent in a carefully chosen French-language Business School/ University.

Modular Course?	Yes
Qualifications:	BSc Hons
Application Deadline:	UCAS deadline
Commencement Date:	Late September
Entry Requirement:	ABB at A-level, including B in French
Applications to Places:	
Registered:	
Awards:	

	Duration	EC Fees	Non-EC Fees
Full time	4 years	£750 (under review)	£6800
Part time			
Sandwich			

BSc in International Management with German

This four year degree programme is designed to educate students with a high-level of management-orientated capability in the German language and insight into the business culture of German-speaking countries. The programme is taught jointly by the Manchester School of Management and the Department of Language Engineering. The third year is spent in a carefully selected German or Austrian Business School/ University with strengths in management studies.

Modular Course?	Yes
Qualifications:	BSc Hons
Application Deadline:	UCAS deadline
Commencement Date:	Late September
Entry Requirement:	BBB at A-level, including B in German
Applications to Places:	
Registered:	
Awards:	

	Duration	EC Fees	Non-EC Fees
Full time	4 years	£750 (under review)	£6800
Part time			
Sandwich			

BSc in Internatonal Management with American Business Studies

In addition to studying the fundamental disciplines of management and the major functional areas, students follow courses based on American Society, Politics, Economics and Business. Their third year is spent (as part of an exchange programme) in Business/ Management Schools in Leading USA/Canadian universities. They live and study with American students, and prepare for an International Management project completed in the fourth year of study in Manchester.

Modular Course?	Yes
Qualifications:	BSc Hons
Application Deadline:	UCAS deadline
Commencement Date:	Late September
Entry Requirement:	ABB at A-level
Registered:	
Awards:	

	Duration	EC Fees	Non-EC Fees
Full time	4 years	£750 (under review)	£6800
Part time			
Sandwich			

BSc in Management and Information Technology

This programme is concerned with the study of the use of information technology in a management context. It aims to produce graduates who are creative and innovative thinkers, and who have good communication skills as well as a good technical grounding in IT systems. Therefore applications are encouraged from candidates with both arts and/or science backgrounds. The programme does not have any prerequisites in terms of qualifications in mathematics.

Modular Course?	Yes
Qualifications:	BSc Hons
Application Deadline:	UCAS deadline
Commencement Date:	Late September
Entry Requirement:	BBB at A-level
Applications to Places:	
Registered:	
Awards:	

	Duration	EC Fees	Non-EC Fees
Full time	3 years	£750 (under review)	£6800
Part time			
Sandwich			

Middlesex University Business School

Middlesex University Business School

Address:	Middlesex University Business School
	The Burroughs
	London
	NW4 4BT
Area:	London and South East England
Phone:	0181-362-5000
Fax:	0181-202-1539
Email:	**ADMISSIONS@MDX.AC.UK.**
Website:	**http://www.mdx.ac.uk**

Email Application Available?	No
How to apply by email:	
Total Number of Teaching Staff:	210
Staff Teaching Undergraduate Courses	140
Research Rating:	3b
Teaching Rating:	Highly Satisfactory
Additional Rating Information	
Male:Female Student Ratio	50:50
Head of Business School	Professor David Kirby
Head of Undergraduate Studies	Ms Mary Simpson
Admissions Contact	Sheila Sharp

About the School:

Middlesex University Business School (MUBS) delivers high quality undergraduate, postgraduate, and professional courses and is one of the largest Business Schools in the UK. MUBS attracts students from Europe, North and South America and the Far East and established links to educational institutions around the world. Based at the Hendon campus it is within easy commuting distance of cental London giving students easy access to the capital's rich store of academic, cultural, artistic and social facilities.

About Undergraduate Studies:

Middlesex University is an innovative university with a record of achievement established in a little over two decades. It has a modular academic structure which offers unrivalled freedom for undergraduate students to combine a diverse range of subjects and follow programmes of study tailored to their particular needs and interests.

Facilities:

Middlesex University has extensive sports and leisure facilities at each of its campuses. At the Hendon campus, home of the Business School, is the recently built Burroughs Sports Club. Facilities include a fully furnished gymnasium, sauna and steam rooms and a sports hall which caters for badminton, basketball, volleyball, table tennis and other team and individual sports. There is an astroturf and planning has been received to develop a number of facilities for racket sports including Squash, Lawn tennis and Real tennis.

Departments/Faculties:

The Business School consists of the following Academic Groups: Accountancy & Finance, Economics, Entrepreneurship & Economic Development, Human Resource Management, Law, Mangement Strategy, Marketing and Mathematics & Statistics.

Links with Academic Institutions:

Middlesex Univesity's links with higher education institutions in Europe and further afield are a particular strength. Middlesex was a pioneer in developing opportunities for students to spend time studying or working in another country and consistently comes top of the UK league table for the number of European exchanges it organises.

Links with Industry:

MUBS has extensive placement and sponsorship links with private and public service industries/organisations including many nationally and internationally known. MUB enjoys external accreditation from organisations including the Assocation of MBAs, Institute of Personnel and Development (as a Centre of Excellence), Chartered Institute of Marketing, Law Society, Accounting and many more.

Student Testimonials:

"Firms who survive are those that keep up with the pacemaker. The Middlesex course gave me a broad vision in all aspects of managing my on business. I thoroughly recommend the university to anyone who wishes to establish a sound academic foundation for the future."

Kihor Patel, BA Accounting & Finance, Independent Retailer Excellence Award 1995

General Undergraduate Courses

BA (Hons) Business Administration

Designed to equip students with knowledge, skills and capability for today's business environment.

Modular Course?	No
Qualifications:	BA
Application Deadline:	15 Dec
Commencement Date:	21 Sept
Entry Requirement:	16 Points at A Level Merit at A
	GNVQ Maths/Eng -

		GCSE 'C'
Applications to Places:		6 : 1
Registered:		96
Awards:		211

	Duration	EC Fees	Non-EC Fees
Full time	Three Years	£1,000	£6,400
Part time			
Sandwich			

BA (Hons) Business Studies

Designed to equip students with knowledge, skills and capability for today's business environment.

Modular Course?	No
Qualifications:	BA
Application Deadline:	15 Dec
Commencement Date:	21 Sept
Entry Requirement:	16 Points at A Level Merit at A GVNQ Maths/Eng - GCSE 'C'
Applications to Places:	6 : 1
Registered:	162
Awards:	102

	Duration	EC Fees	Non-EC Fees
Full time			
Part time			
Sandwich	Four years	£1,000	£6,400

BA (Hons) Business Economics

To acquire a good knowledge of Economic principles and an in-depth knowledge of most areas relevant to business.

Modular Course?	No
Qualifications:	BA
Application Deadline:	15 Dec
Commencement Date:	21 Sept
Entry Requirement:	16 Points at A Level Merit at A GNVQ Maths/Eng - GCSE 'C'
Applications to Places:	5 : 1
Registered:	33
Awards:	11

	Duration	EC Fees	Non-EC Fees
Full time	Three years	£1,000	£6,400
Part time			
Sandwich	Four years	£1,000	£6,400

BA (Hons) International Management

To prepare students for a challenging career in international business

Modular Course?	No
Qualifications:	BA

Application Deadline:	15 Dec
Commencement Date:	21 Sept
Entry Requirement:	16 Points at A Level Maths/Eng - GCSE 'C'
Applications to Places:	4 : 1
Registered:	36
Awards:	New Prog from Sept '96

	Duration	EC Fees	Non-EC Fees
Full time			
Part time			
Sandwich	Thin - Four years	£1,000	£6,400

BSc Mathematics for Business

Offers a firm grounding in mathematics, an understanding of, and skills in, operational research and statistics.

Modular Course?	No
Qualifications:	BSc
Application Deadline:	15 Dec '96
Commencement Date:	21 Sept '97
Entry Requirement:	8 Points at A Level including GCSE 'C' in Maths
Applications to Places:	
Registered:	
Awards:	10

	Duration	EC Fees	Non-EC Fees
Full time			
Part time			
Sandwich	Four years	£1,000	£6,400

Specialist Undergraduate Course

LLB Law

Modular Course?	No
Qualifications:	BA Hons
Categories:	Business Law

BA (Hons) Marketing

Modular Course?	No
Qualifications:	BA Hons
Categories:	Marketing

BA (Hons) Human Resource Management

Modular Course?	No
Qualifications:	BA Hons
Categories:	Human Resources

BA (Hons) Hospitality Management

Modular Course?	No

BA (Hons) Accounting and Finance

Napier University Business School

Napier University Business School

Address:	9 Sighthill Court
	Edinburgh
	EH12 4BN
Area:	Scotland
Phone:	0131 455 3460
Fax:	0131 455 3593
Email:	k.mackay@napier.ac.uk
Website:	http:/www.napier.ac.uk
Email Application Available?	Yes
How to apply by email:	
Total Number of Teaching Staff:	120
Staff Teaching Undergraduate Courses	90
Research Rating:	n/a
Teaching Rating:	Satisfactory
Additional Rating Information	
Male:Female Student Ratio	40:60
Dean of Business School	Mr Jack Worden
Head of Undergraduate Studies	Mr Ross Hamilton
Information office:	0131 455 3369

About the School:

The Business School is the largest faculty of Napier University and covers the disciplines of Human Resource Management, Strategic Management, Business Operations Management, Hospitality and Tourism Management, Languages, Information Management, Marketing and Accounting & Finance. The School offers Masters degrees, postgraduate diplomas, undergraduate programmes and courses leading to professional qualifications. The Business School reputation for academic excellence is enhanced and supported by complimentary research and consultancy.

About Undergraduate Studies:

Napier Business School offers a wide range of degree, honours degree and joint honours degree courses as well as certificate and diploma courses. Our modular programme allows students flexibility in course choice and deciding their ultimate degree programme. Each level is equivalent to one year full time study. An honours/joint honours degree consists of four levels of study, with an ordinary degree consisting of three levels of study .

Facilities:

The Sighthill campus has a Sports Centre with facilities for football, squash, volleyball, badminton, hockey, judo, fencing and table tennis and there is a climbing wall and multi-gym. The Craiglockhart campus has a swimming pool (with disabled access) and classes are run in swimming and aqua-aerobics. For the non-sporty there are many other clubs and societies including a Chinese/Asian Society which among other events hold a Chinese New Year celebration.

Departments/Faculties:

Napier University Business School is organised as a matrix structure which consists of eight cognate groups as follows:
Human Resource Management, Marketing, Languages, Accounting & Finance, Business Operations Management, Information Management, Hospitality & Tourism Management and Strategic Management.

Links with Academic Institutions:

The Business School has links with Kingston University in England and Haarlem in Holland through a consortium MBA programme. The distance learning MBA programme is currently delivered in Mauritius and South Africa. The BA (Hons) Accounting is delivered in Hong Kong through its City University.Napier University is part of the beautiful city of Edinburgh and host to ten international festivals a year. It is a lively city and ideal for student life.

Links with Industry:

The Business School has extensive links with many large organisations through consultancy and training programmes including private and local government sector employers.

General Undergraduate Courses

BA (Hons) Business Studies

This course is the traditional "sandwich" form of business undergraduate degree programme, incorporating a one year paid work based learning in level 3.

Modular Course?	Yes
Qualifications:	BA; BA Hons; Joint Honours
Application Deadline:	end Aug
Commencement Date:	late Sept
Entry Requirement:	SCE H Grade BBCC or GCE A Level CDD
Applications to Places:	
Registered:	90
Awards:	

	Duration	EC Fees	Non-EC Fees
Full time	4 years	£1000 pa	£6,100
Part time	5 years	£650 pa	
Sandwich	4 years	£500 per year	

BA (Hons) Accounting

Modular Course? | Yes
Qualifications: | BA; BA Hons
Categories: | Finance

BA (Hons) Marketing Management

Modular Course? | Yes
Qualifications: | BA; BA Hons
Categories: | Marketing; Small Business

BA (Hons) Languages and Export Management

Modular Course? | Yes
Qualifications: | BA; BA Hons
Categories: | Export; International Business

BA (Hons) Business Information Management

Modular Course? | Yes
Qualifications: | BA; BA Hons
Categories: | Corporate Strategy; IT Systems

BA (Hons) Hospitality (Hotel and Catering Management)

Modular Course? | Yes
Qualifications: | BA Hons
Categories: | Human Resources; Hospitality; International Business

BA (Hons) Hospitality (Tourism Management)

Modular Course? | No
Qualifications: | BA Hons
Categories: | Human Resources; Hospitality; Leisure

BA Hotel Services Management

Modular Course? | Yes
Qualifications: | BA
Categories: | Hospitality; International Business

Joint Honours

A wide variety of Joint Honours programmes is also available. These include certain combinations of the single Honours Degrees shown above and other major/minor combinations, e.g. Accounting with Entrepreneurship, Business Studies and Human Resource Management, Hospitality with Human Resource Management etc.

Please contact the Business School Information Office for full details of these programmes.

Faculty of Management and Business

Faculty of Management and Business

Address:	Park Campus
	Boughton Green Road
	Northampton
	NN2 7AL
Area:	Midlands
Phone:	01604 735500
Fax:	01604 721214

Email:

Website: http://www.nene.ac.uk

Email Application Available?	No
How to apply by email:	
Total Number of Teaching Staff:	105
Staff Teaching Undergraduate Courses	40
Research Rating:	1
Teaching Rating:	Satisfactory
Additional Rating Information	
Male:Female Student Ratio	45:55
Head of Business School	Mrs Diane Hayes
Head of Undergraduate Studies	Mr Malcom Lacey
Admissions Contact	Mrs Judy Jordan

About the School:

Nene-University College Northampton has approximately 10,000 students following undergraduate and post-graduate courses across most disciplines. The Faculty of Management and Business has developed significantly over the last fifteen years and covers the disciplines of: Information Systems; Accounting and Finance; Economics; Law; Business and Management. It provides a broad range of courses from Certificate to Masters level, as well as Professional qualifications for around 2,300 full-time and 1,300 part-time students. The Faculty is housed in purpose built accommodation on a 70 acre parkland campus on the edge of Northampton.

This includes the residential Sunley Management Centre which is used for corporate training and consultancy work. The international policy ensures that there are active links with universities throughout Europe, and that many European students visit Nene on exchange each year. There has been significant investment in both library and IT resources for students.

Facilities:

Northampton is centrally located with easy access to London and other parts of the country. Recreational, sporting and cultural activities flourish in the town and on campus. Sporting facilities include football, basketball, hockey and cricket and there are also clubs for mountaineering, skiing, flying and parachuting. Drama and music are also popular with brass band, choir, symphony and chamber orchestras. There are residential facilities for 1400 students on campus, with many en-suite facilities.

Departments/Faculties:

School of Law and Accountancy
School of Business and Management
School of Information Systems

Links with Academic Institutions:

The Faculty has links with partner institutions in France, at Groupe ESC, Poitiers and in The Netherlands at Hogeschool Drenthe, Emmen. The Faculty's international policy ensures that there are active links with universities throughout Europe, and many European students visit Nene on exchange each year.

Links with Industry:

Nene - University College Northampton has strong training links with many major companies in the East Midlands and nationally via Sunley Management Centre. Current corporate clients include Scania GB, NFC, Rank Organisation, Whitbread, H.M. Treasury and Northamptonshire County Council.

General Undergraduate Courses

BA Business Studies

This course balances the intellectual elements associated with undergraduate study and the vocational needs of employment. This balance is achieved through a core business programme, a varied approach to business options, the development of transferable skills and the choice of a placement year in industry or a combined work and study year in Europe. Options, including foreign languages, provide an opportunity to specialise in areas such as Finance, Accounting, Marketing, Human Resource Management, Operations Management and Entrepreneurship.

Modular Course?	No
Qualifications:	BA
Application Deadline:	UCAS deadlines
Commencement Date:	
Entry Requirement:	12 points at A-level, GCSE Maths grade C minimum
Applications to Places:	4:1
Registered:	342
Awards:	

	Duration	EC Fees	Non-EC Fees
Full time			
Part time			
Sandwich	4 years	£1000	£6495

BA European Business

A sandwich course with a third year spend either studying at a partner University or on a work placement in France, Germany, Italy, Spain, Switzerland, Belgium or Austria. In the first year language development is integrated into a broad business education which develops competence and awareness within a European perspective. The final year develops the strategic dimensions of business and allows further specialisation through option paths while continuing language development.

Modular Course?	No
Qualifications:	BA
Application Deadline:	UCAS deadlines
Commencement Date:	
Entry Requirement:	8 points at A-level, GCSE Maths grade C minimum
Applications to Places:	4:1
Registered:	105
Awards:	

	Duration	EC Fees	Non-EC Fees
Full time			
Part time			
Sandwich	4 years	£1000	£6495

BA Business Administration and Management

This course is designed for students with a high level of attainment in HND Business and Finance. The core includes Strategic Management, Information Management and Financial Management, with options in European Business Law, Strategic Marketing, Managing Organisations and People and Entrepreneurship and New Ventures.

Modular Course?	No
Qualifications:	BA
Application Deadline:	UCAS deadlines
Commencement Date:	
Entry Requirement:	HND Business with Merit profile in year 2
Applications to Places:	4:1
Registered:	98
Awards:	

	Duration	EC Fees	Non-EC Fees
Full time	1 year	£1000	£6495
Part time			
Sandwich			

BA Business Enterprise

The programme aims to provide an intellectually demanding and satisfying course of study in business, focusing on issues and skills important to small and medium sized enterprises (SMEs). The programme is designed to increase the employability of graduates within business, through the development of appropriate transferrable skills, business knowledge and understanding, and a well motivated attitude to enterprise and entrepreneurship. In addition to enhancing employment prospects in the small and medium size business, the programme will also produce graduates who are able to start up, and maintain, their own business.

Modular Course?	No
Qualifications:	BA
Application Deadline:	UCAS deadlines
Commencement Date:	
Entry Requirement:	12 points at A-level
Applications to Places:	4:1
Registered:	20
Awards:	

	Duration	EC Fees	Non-EC Fees
Full time	3 years	£1000	£6495
Part time			
Sandwich			

Combined Honours Programme: BA Business Administration with Law or Economics or Information Systems or Management Science

Offers the opportunity to study on a combined programme taking a major, minor and elective combination. Many other options available combining business studies with social science, the humanties, arts or science.

Modular Course?	No
Qualifications:	BA
Application Deadline:	UCAS deadlines
Commencement Date:	
Entry Requirement:	8 points at A-level
Applications to Places:	4:1
Registered:	n/a
Awards:	

	Duration	EC Fees	Non-EC Fees
Full time	3 years	£1000	£6495
Part time			
Sandwich			

BA Accounting and Finance

Modular Course?	No
Qualifications:	BA
Categories:	Finance

BA Business Information Systems

Modular Course?	No
Qualifications:	BA
Categories:	Management

BSc Computing

Modular Course?	No
Qualifications:	BSc
Categories:	IT Systems

LLB

Modular Course?	No
Qualifications:	LLB
Categories:	Business Law

School of Management

Department of Management Studies

Address:	Armstrong Building
	University of Newcastle upon Tyne
	Newcastle upon Tyne
	NE1 7RU
Area:	North East England
Phone:	0191 222 5353
Fax:	0191 222 5857
Email:	School.of.Management@ncl.ac.uk
Website:	http:\\www.ncl.ac.uk

Email Application Available?	No
How to apply by email:	
Total Number of Teaching Staff:	40
Staff Teaching Undergraduate Courses	30
Research Rating:	2
Teaching Rating:	Satisfactory
Additional Rating Information	
Male:Female Student Ratio	65:35
Head of Business School	Dr Roger Vaughan
Head of Undergraduate Studies	T Boland
Admissions Contact	Dr Mike Cox & Dr Norman Jackson

About the School:

Management has been taught and researched at the University of Newcastle for fifty years. Newcastle School of Management's philosophy of business education is founded on three strengths. Firstly, we are business-oriented having strong links with leading UK and international companies. Secondly, our University provides a wide range of elective subjects. Finally, Newcastle's research excellence is reflected in its innovative Management School programmes. We educate managers for the realities of tomorrow's global business environment.

About Undergraduate Studies:

The School's undergraduate courses have a modular structure. In addition to single honours programmes, there are a wide variety of joint honours degrees spanning faculties and subjects. New entrants will join approximately 300 undergraduates and a further 150 postgraduates on specialist and MBA programmes. Strong links with business schools in Europe are enabling us to develop opportunities to study abroad as part of our programmes. The School's graduates can be found in senior positions from the North East of England to the Pacific Rim.

Facilities:

In a dramatic setting on the River Tyne, Newcastle upon Tyne combines a compact, historic city centre with excellent arts, sports and leisure facilities and, just a few miles away, the beautiful countryside and coastline of Northumberland. The University's facilities from sports centres to its own theatre are available to all School of Management students. Not surprisingly, Newcastle upon Tyne is one of the most popular university choices in the UK.

Departments/Faculties:

The School of Management is a cross-faculty organisation involving a number of departments and research centres including Management Studies, Accounting and Finance, Agricultural Economics and Food Marketing, Economics, Education, Law, Mechanical Materials and Manufacturing Engineering, the Centre for Urban and Regional Development and the Engineering Design Centre.

Links with Academic Institutions:

We have increasingly close relationships with business schools abroad, especially in Norway, Denmark and France, as well as exchange agreements with Universities in Spain, Germany, Austria, Greece and Turkey. With the development of European Economic and Monetary Union, and the globalisation of business and political activity, managers are increasingly required to operate across national boundaries, and these opportunities play an essential part in preparing our students for the challenges of management.

Links with Industry:

The School of Management has close links with a number of employers, which include them taking MBA graduates, providing consultancy projects for MBA students to take as part of their programme, and providing advice and guidance about the relevance and content of the School's programmes.

General Undergraduate Courses

BA (Hons) Business Management

This vocationally-orientated degree prepares undergraduates for careers in private and public sector management. It is designed to develop the ability to set overall objectives for an organisation, motivate employees, and control and co-ordinate activities in such a way that objectives are attained. The course offers a wide range of options including languages.

Modular Course?	Yes
Qualifications:	BA Hons

Application Deadline:		UCAS deadline	
Commencement Date:			
Entry Requirement:		24 points at A-level or equivalent, GCSE Maths, A-level in Modern Languages for international courses.	

Applications to Places:

Registered:

Awards:

	Duration	EC Fees	Non-EC Fees
Full time	3 years	On request	On request
Part time			
Sandwich			

BA (Hons) European Business Management; BA (Hons) International Business Management

In view of the increasing internationalisation of business within the Single European Market, these 4-year programmes provide a broad educational base for a career in management, as well as developing fluency in another language and improving awareness of cultural differences. The courses offer a wide range of options and the opportunity to spend the third year studying in a European business school.

Modular Course?	Yes
Qualifications:	BA Hons
Application Deadline:	UCAS deadline
Commencement Date:	
Entry Requirement:	24 points at A-level or equivalent, GCSE Maths, A-level in Modern Languages for international courses.

Applications to Places:

Registered:

Awards:

	Duration	EC Fees	Non-EC Fees
Full time	4 years	On request	On request
Part time			
Sandwich			

Specialist Undergraduate Course

BA (Hons) Accounting with Law

Modular Course?	No
Qualifications:	BA Hons
Categories:	Finance

BA (Hons) Accounting with Economics

Modular Course?	No
Qualifications:	BA Hons
Categories:	Finance

BA (Hons) Accounting with Financial Analysis

Modular Course?	No
Qualifications:	BA Hons
Categories:	Finance

BSc (Hons) Rural and Environmental Economics

Modular Course?	No
Qualifications:	BSc Hons
Categories:	Agriculture

BSc (Hons) Rural Environmental Management

Modular Course?	No
Qualifications:	BSc Hons
Categories:	Agriculture

BSc (Hons) Agri-Business Management and Food Marketing

Modular Course?	No
Qualifications:	BSc Hons
Categories:	Agriculture

Business School

University of North London Business School

Address:	University of North London
	Stapleton House
	277-281 Holloway Road
	London
	N7 8HN
Area:	London and South East England
Phone:	0171 753 5052
Fax:	0171 753 5051
Email:	admissions@unl.ac.uk
Website:	www.unl.ac.uk

Email Application Available?	No
How to apply by email:	
Total Number of Teaching Staff:	128
Staff Teaching Undergraduate Courses	128
Research Rating:	2
Teaching Rating:	Satisfactory
Additional Rating Information	
Male:Female Student Ratio	50:50
Head of Business School	Jean Fawcett
Head of Undergraduate Studies	Bob Morgan
Admissions Contact	Karl Lester

About the School:

The Business School offers a wide range of full and part-time undergraduate diplomas and degrees which share a commitment to ensuring that students gain a sound understanding of the essential theoretical disciplines whilst developing an ability to apply knowledge to realistic business situations. Emphasis is also placed on the development of social and personal skills including information technology and effective communication. Undergraduate teaching is informed by the extensive research work focused in the School's four specialist Research Centres.

About Undergraduate Studies:

The Business School encompasses a modular degree scheme which allows students to choose either a Single Honours or a Combined Honours degree from over 20 subjects. All students will gain a sound understanding of business functions and business practice with the option of specialisation in one or two areas. The scheme includes a business skills unit, modern language option plus the opportunity for work placements in the UK or overseas. The School has an excellent record in graduate employment.

Facilities:

The University has over 14000 students with a diversity of background, experience, age and ethnicity. There is a thriving social life which includes a comprehensive range of sporting activities from archery to skiing. The Student Union organises frequent social events and supports over 100 clubs and societies. Owing to its location, the University offers the pleasures of London on its doorstep including theatres and clubs, museums and galleries as well as Camden Lock, Covent Garden, Soho and the West End.

Links with Academic Institutions:

The School maintains excellent links with leading organisations and recent research projects include: Tourism Development for the World Bank; Lottery Fund Disposition for the Millenium Commission; and Transport Planning for the European Union.

General Undergraduate Courses

The Business School Degree Scheme

Students can choose either a Single Honours or a Combined Honours (two subjects) degree. The Scheme ensures that all students, irrespective of subject choice, will gain an understanding of the financial, economic, social, marketing, human resource, quantitative and legal aspects of business and will be able to take advantage of personal development workshops including information technology and interpersonal skills. The programmes are intended to support students career aspirations, giving exemptions to professional bodies such as IPD, ACCA or CIPS where appropriate. They encourage students to develop the intellectual framework and personal skills required for a successful career in a wide range of business environments. Close links are maintained with employers and national professional associations to ensure that programmes are relevant to the needs of both students and business. Many programmes provide opportunities for international placement and exchange and the study of a European language. The Scheme also provides opportunities to participate in EU sponsored ERASMUS exchanges in Europe and in study exchanges with our partner institutions in the USA.

Modular Course?	Yes
Qualifications:	BA Hons
Application Deadline:	15 December
Commencement Date:	
Entry Requirement:	2 A-level passes and 3 other subjects at GCSE or O-level, or 3 A-level passes with passes in 2 other subjects at GCSE or O-level. (An AS-Level is regarded as equivalent

to half an A-level).
BTEC National Diploma or
Certificate at a good standard,
or the agreed equivalent of the
Business Education
Council or Scottish Vocational
Education Council.
GNVQ with an overall merit
grade. A match between
optional units in the GNVQ and
the chosen degree
programme will be expected.
With some degree
programmes there may be a
requirement for candidates to
have completed additional
units.
All undergraduate programmes
will require GCSE grade C
or above, or equivalent, in
English Language and
Mathematics.

Applications to Places:	20:1
Registered:	
Awards:	

	Duration	EC Fees	Non-EC Fees
Full time	3-4 years	£1500 pa	£5990 pa
Part time			
Sandwich			

Single Honours Degree Programme

A Single Honours degree consists of a coherent pathway of modules which focuses on one area whilst still allowing some choice and flexibility. This programme is appropriate for students who have a clear idea of the subjects they are interested in. Subjects on offer include: Accounting and Finance; Business Administration; Economics and Finance; Business Studies; Facilities Management; Hospitality Management/International Hospitality Management; International Business; Leisure and Tourism Management/International Leisure and Tourism Management. Many of the Single Honours degrees are four year programmes and involve a one year work placement.

Modular Course?	Yes
Qualifications:	BA Hons
Application Deadline:	15 December
Commencement Date:	
Entry Requirement:	2 A-level passes and 3 other subjects at GCSE or O-level, or 3 A-level passes with passes in 2 other subjects at GCSE or O-level. (An AS-Level is regarded as equivalent

to half an A-level).
BTEC National Diploma or
Certificate at a good standard,
or the agreed equivalent of the
Business Education
Council or Scottish Vocational
Education Council.
GNVQ with an overall merit
grade. A match between
optional units in the GNVQ and
the chosen degree
programme will be expected.
With some degree
programmes there may be a
requirement for candidates to
have completed additional
units.
All undergraduate programmes
will require GCSE grade C
or above, or equivalent, in
English Language and
Mathematics.

Applications to Places:	20:1
Registered:	
Awards:	

	Duration	EC Fees	Non-EC Fees
Full time	3-4 years	£1500 pa	£5990 pa
Part time			
Sandwich			

Combined Honours Degree Programme

There is a range of Joint and Major/Minor Combined Honours degrees available in the Scheme; the degree title (i.e. whether Joint or Major/Minor) depends on how many modules are taken in each subject area. Students choose two from: Accounting; Arts Management; Business Economics; Business Operations Management; Economics; Events Management; Facilities Management; Human Resource Studies; Hospitality Management; International Business; Business Law; Leisure Studies; Marketing; Retail Management; Sports Management; Tourism Studies.

Modular Course?	Yes
Qualifications:	BA Hons
Application Deadline:	15 December
Commencement Date:	
Entry Requirement:	2 A-level passes and 3 other subjects at GCSE or O-level, or 3 A-level passes with passes in 2 other subjects at GCSE or O-level. (An AS-Level is regarded as equivalent to half an A-level). BTEC National Diploma or Certificate at a good standard, or the agreed equivalent of the

Business Education
Council or Scottish Vocational
Education Council.
GNVQ with an overall merit
grade. A match between
optional units in the GNVQ and
the chosen degree
programme will be expected.
With some degree
programmes there may be a
requirement for candidates to
have completed additional
units.
All undergraduate programmes
will require GCSE grade C
or above, or equivalent, in
English Language and
Mathematics.

Applications to Places:
Registered:
Awards:

	Duration	EC Fees	Non-EC Fees
Full time	3-4 years	£1500 pa	£5990 pa
Part time			
Sandwich			

programme will be expected.
With some degree
programmes there may be a
requirement for candidates to
have completed additional
units.
All undergraduate programmes
will require GCSE grade C
or above, or equivalent, in
English Language and
Mathematics.

Applications to Places: 20:1
Registered:
Awards:

	Duration	EC Fees	Non-EC Fees
Full time	Various	£1500 pa	£5990 pa
Part time	Various	£115 per unit	£115 per unit
Sandwich			

BTEC Diplomas and Certificates

The School offers the following programmes at Certificate or Diploma level: Business Management: HND and HNC, together with specialist awards in Accounting, Marketing, Human Resources, and Operations Management; Hospitality and Business Management: HND; Tourism Management: HND; Sport and Leisure Management: HND; Interfaculty Studies.

Modular Course? No
Qualifications: HNC; HND
Application Deadline: 15 December
Commencement Date:
Entry Requirement: 2 A-level passes and 3 other
subjects at GCSE or O-level,
or 3 A-level passes with passes in
2 other subjects at
GCSE or O-level. (An AS-Level is
regarded as equivalent
to half an A-level).
BTEC National Diploma or
Certificate at a good standard,
or the agreed equivalent of the
Business Education
Council or Scottish Vocational
Education Council.
GNVQ with an overall merit
grade. A match between
optional units in the GNVQ and
the chosen degree

Newcastle Business School

Newcastle Business School

Address:	Ellison Building
	Ellison Place
	Newcastle Upon Tyne
	NE1 8ST
Area:	North East England
Phone:	0191 227 4433
Fax:	0191 227 3893

Email:

Website: http://www.unn.ac.uk/corporate/nbsdepts.htm

Email Application Available?	No
How to apply by email:	
Total Number of Teaching Staff:	219
Staff Teaching Undergraduate Courses:	219
Research Rating:	2
Teaching Rating:	Excellent
Additional Rating Information	
Male:Female Student Ratio	50:50
Head of Business School	Professor DTH Weir
Head of Undergraduate Studies	Mr G Moore
Admissions Contact	Alison Venis

About the School:

Newcastle Business School which operates from three sites in the North East was assessed as excellent in 1994. It is the largest business school in the North East with more than 4000 students and it offers a complete range of courses from Certificate and Diploma to Masters level. The campuses at Carlisle and Longhirst in Northumberland mean that it can now offer business education to students throughout the North at undergraduate and postgraduate levels. The School has developed an extensive and well-respected network of international links, and study opportunities abroad are available to many students.

About Undergraduate Studies:

Newcastle is famous for its night life and student life is rich and varied. The city has seven theatres and a huge choice of cinemas, restaurants, live music venues and clubs. Sports facilities in the city and the University are very good and the whole region offers a wealth of unspoilt beautiful countryside.

BA (Hons) Business Administration

This programme offers a broad business education with opportunities to specialise in Finance, Human Resource Management, and Marketing. There are 3 entry points, with direct entry to year 3 for HND Business graduates.

Modular Course?	Yes
Qualifications:	BA Hons
Commencement Date:	
Entry Requirement:	12 A level points or GCSE Maths and English, BTEC National Diploma with Distinctions, Advanced GNVQ with Distinctions or Merit.
Applications to Places:	5:1
Registered:	245
Awards:	

	Duration	EC Fees	Non-EC Fees
Full time	1-3 years	£1000	£5600
Part time			
Sandwich			

BA (Hons) Business Studies

This course equips graduates with capability to assume responsible roles in business and also to obtain exemptions from professional examinations of bodies such as IPD and CIM. The first two years develop broad skills and knowledge, while the third year provides an opportunity to apply the knowledge through a work placement. The final year offers specialisms such as Finance, Personnel, Marketing and Information Systems.

Modular Course?	Yes
Qualifications:	BA Hons
Application Deadline:	UCAS deadline
Commencement Date:	September
Entry Requirement:	Individual course requirements on request. Generally, three grade C A-levels plus GCSE Maths and English, BTEC National Diploma with Distinctions, Advanced GNVQ with Distinctions.
Applications to Places:	6:1
Registered:	458
Awards:	

	Duration	EC Fees	Non-EC Fees
Part time	4-5 years	£1000	£5600
Sandwich	4 years	£1000	£5600

BA (Hons) International Business Studies

This course gives students the skills, knowledge and capability to contribute effectively to international business. In the first two years, skills in Finance, Marketing and Information Systems are combined with language studies, with a choice of French, German, Spanish or Russian. The third year is spent studying and working abroad. In the final year, students continue studies in Strategic Analysis and Management, choose from a wide range of business options and complete an individual project.

Modular Course?	Yes
Qualifications:	BA (Hons)
Application Deadline:	UCAS deadline
Commencement Date:	September
Entry Requirement:	Three A-levels plus GCSE Maths and English or BTEC National Diploma with Distinctions, Advanced GNVQ with Distinctions and Merits.
Applications to Places:	5:1
Registered:	271
Awards:	

	Duration	EC Fees	Non-EC Fees
Full time	4 years	£1000	£5600
Part time			
Sandwich			

BA (Hons) International Business Administration

The aim of this course is to produce graduates with the competences and linguistic skills to operate as managers in the world of international business. It is specifically designed for overseas or European applicants for whom English is a second language. UK students with considerable experience abroad may also apply.

Modular Course?	Yes
Qualifications:	BA (Hons)
Application Deadline:	UCAS deadline
Commencement Date:	September
Entry Requirement:	Individual course requirements on request. Three grade C A-levels and GCSE Maths and English, or BTEC National Diploma with Distinctions, Advanced GNVQ with Distinctions.
Applications to Places:	5:1
Registered:	34
Awards:	

	Duration	EC Fees	Non-EC Fees
Full time	1 or 3 years	£1000	£5600
Part time			
Sandwich			

BA (Hons) Human Resource Management

This course provides a general grounding in business in the first year, with increasing specialisation in HRM in the second year. The third year is spent in a supervised work placement, while in the final year, students continue studies in Strategic Analysis and Management, and complete an individual project.

Modular Course?	Yes
Qualifications:	BA Hons
Commencement Date:	September
Entry Requirement:	Individual course requirements on request. Three grade C A-levels plus GCSE Maths and English, BTEC National Diploma with Distinctions, Advanced GNVQ with Distinctions.
Applications to Places:	5:1
Registered:	104
Awards:	

	Duration	EC Fees	Non-EC Fees
Full time	4 years	£1000	£5600
Part time			
Sandwich			

BA (Hons) Accountancy; Diploma of Higher Education in Accounting

This group of courses provide a choice of studies and opportunities to obtain qualifications for a career in accountancy or financial services. The degree courses provide opportunities to specialise in areas such as Financial Accounting, Financial Management, or Management Accounting. Professional exemptions from examinations of ACCA, CIMA may be gained on these courses.

Modular Course?	Yes
Qualifications:	BA Hons; Diploma HE with merit
Application Deadline:	UCAS deadline
Commencement Date:	September
Entry Requirement:	Individual course requirements on request. Generally, three A-levels 18 points for BA (Hons) with GCSE Maths and English, BTEC National Diploma with Distinctions, Advanced GNVQ with Distinctions and Merits. Twelve points at A level for DipHE or equivalent.
Applications to Places:	4:1
Registered:	228
Awards:	

	Duration	EC Fees	Non-EC Fees
Full time	2-3 years	£1000	£5600

BA (Hons) Financial Services

The course is aimed at students who have an interest in the areas of business finance and financial services who may be considering a career in these sectors of the economiy. The course shares a common first year with BA (Hons) Accountancy, allowing greater flexibility.

Modular Course?	Yes
Qualifications:	BA Hons
Application deadline:	UCAS
Commencement Date:	September
Entry regs:	14 points at A level or equivalent
Application ration	4:1
Registered:	83

	Duration	EC Fees	Non-EC Fees
Full time	3 years	£1000	£5600

BA (Hons) Accounting and Finance Top Up

This course provides a full time conversion for students who have completed part or all of their professional training in accounting who wish to obtain an honours degree in Accounting and Finance.

Modular Course?	Yes
Qualifications:	BA Hons
Commencement Date:	September
Entry Requirement:	Individual course requirements on request. ACCA papers 1-10
Applications to Places:	3:1
Awards:	

	Duration	EC Fees	Non-EC Fees
Full time	1 year	£1000	£5600
Part time			
Sandwich			

BA (Hons) Marketing

This course provides a general grounding in business in the first year, with increasing specialisation in Marketing in the second year. The third year is spent in a supervised work placement to develop business and marketing experience, while in the final year, students continue studies in Strategic Analysis and Management, with greater specialisation in marketing subjects and complete an individual marketing-based project. The degree has been awarded maximum exemptions from the Chartered Institute of Marketing.

Modular Course?	Yes
Qualifications:	BA Hons
Application Deadline:	UCAS deadline
Commencement Date:	September
Entry Requirement:	Individual course requirements on request. Three grade C A-levels plus GCSE Maths and English, BTEC National Diploma with Distinctions, Advanced

GNVQ with Distinctions and Merits.

Applications to Places:	6:1
Registered:	195
Awards:	

	Duration	EC Fees	Non-EC Fees
Sandwich	4 years	£1000	£5600

BA (Hons) Travel and Tourism Management/BA (Hons) Travel and Tourism (completion)

This course, which was the first of its kind in the UK, aims to develop business graduates who are knowledgeable about the structure, operation and impact of the travel and tourism industry. The degree was developed in association with the ABTA National Training Board and is recognised by leading organisations in the field.

Modular Course?	Yes
Qualifications:	BA Hons
Application Deadline:	UCAS deadline
Commencement Date:	September
Entry Requirement:	Individual course requirements on request. Three grade C A-levels plus GCSE Maths and English, BTEC National Diploma with Distinctions, Advanced GNVQ with Distinctions and Merits.
Applications to Places:	5:1
Registered:	235
Awards:	

	Duration	EC Fees	Non-EC Fees
Full time	1 or 4 years	£1000	£5600
Sandwich	4 years	£1000	£5600

BSc (Hons) Business Information Technology (Completion); BSc (Hons) Business Information Systems; BSc (Hons) Business Systems and Information Technology

This group of courses focus on business and strategic issues in information technology and provide a firm grounding in the way IT can be applied to business problems. Students gain a broad based business education to degree standard in addition to a high level of technical IT skills.

Modular Course?	Yes
Qualifications:	BSc Hons FT/SW

Application Deadline:		UCAS deadline
Commencement Date:		September
Entry Requirement:		Individual course requirements on request. BSc BIT - HND BIT with merits in final year units. BSc BIS - 18 points at A level or equivalent. BSc BSIT - 12 points at A level or equivalent.
Applications to Places:		4:1
Registered:		240
Awards:		

	Duration	EC Fees	Non-EC Fees
Full time	1-3 years	£1000	£5600
Sandwich	4 years	£1000	£5600

BA (Hons) Logistics and Supply Chain Management

A one year top up degree for holder's of related HNDs, this course encourages the development of functional expertise as well as an understanding of the strategic significance of the supply chain philosophy.

Modular Course?	Yes
Qualifications:	BA Hons
Commencement Date:	September
Entry Requirement:	Individual course requirements on request. HND in Business and Finance or equivalent with Merits in final year units.
Applications to Places:	5:1
Registered:	30
Awards:	

	Duration	EC Fees	Non-EC Fees
Full time	1 year	£1000	£5600

University of Nottingham Business School

University of Nottingham Business School

Address:	The University of Nottingham
	University Park
	Nottingham
	NG7 2RD
Area:	Midlands
Phone:	0115 951 5252
Fax:	0115 951 5262
Email:	
Website:	http://www.nottingham.ac.uk/unbs

Email Application Available?	No
Total Number of Teaching Staff:	33
Staff Teaching Undergraduate Courses	33
Research Rating:	4
Teaching Rating:	Excellent
Additional Rating Information	
Male:Female Student Ratiostudents.	57:43
Head of Business School	Professor B Chiplin
Head of Undergraduate Studies	Dr A Bruce
Admissions Contact	Mrs H Whalley (0115 951 5251)

About the school:

The University of Nottingham Business School is a leading centre of management education. The School places strong emphasis on research and includes the internationally-known Centre for Management Buy-Out Research. It received an excellent rating for teaching and has strong liks with many industrial and commercial organisations. From October 1999 the School will occupy state-of-the-art accommodation to meet the needs of the 21st century business, and the building is one of the flagship projects on the University's new campus.

About Undergraduate Studies:

In all of its undergraduate programmes, the School is committed to maintaining the standards which earned its 'excellent' rating in the 1994 HEFCE assessment. Course content, delivery modes and assessment systems are monitored continually and a strong spirit of innovation ensures a stimulating and dynamic learning environment which emphasises the importance of the link between excellent teaching and the research

expertise of lecturing staff.

Facilities:

The University offers first-class sporting and social facilities and there are a large number of active student societies. The main University is located in a beautiful parkland campus, a short distance from the new Business School, and two miles from the centre of Nottingham, the thriving commercial and cultural capital of the East Midlands.

Links with Academic Institutions:

The School has MBA exchange agreements with WHU Koblenz (Germany), ESC Rennes, ESC Pau (France), Dalhousie University (Canada) and has plans to develop further links during 1998.

Links with Industry:

The School has excellent links with industry and has several sponsored Chairs; The Boots Professor of Accounting & Finance, the Norwich Union Professor of Insurance Studies, the Midland Bank Chair in the Management of Financial Studies, the Worshipful Company of Insurers Chair in Insurance Management and the Christel DeHaan Chair in International Tourism and Travel. The Centre for Management Buy-out Research is funded by Touche Ross and Barclay Development Capital Ltd.

Student Testimonials:

"Overall, I felt the standard of teaching was excellent, staff were always accessible for questions, and constructive in their advice. I enjoyed the course thoroughly and would recommend it to anybody."
"I very much enjoyed my time at Nottingham. I believe that the standard of teaching was excellent and the course has given me a good start to my working life. Group work and presentations especially helped, as did computer work."

General Undergraduate Courses

BA Industrial Economics

The principal aim of the course it to offer a programme which provides a strong case of material in theoretical and applied Microeconomics, with a focus on the modern business enterprise and its operating environment. Around this core, students have the opportunity to assemble a programme which reflects their particular enthusiasm and requirements.
This degree is accredited at foundation level by the Institute of Chartered Accountants in England and Wales. Students who take certain Marketing modules gain full exemption from the Institute of Marketing's Certificate examinations.

Modular Course?	Yes
Qualifications:	BA Hons

Application Deadline:	UCAS deadline		
Commencement Date:	October		
Entry Requirement:	ABB at A level and GCSE Maths		
	Grade B		
Applications to Places:	20:1		
Registered:	70		
Awards:			

	Duration	EC Fees	Non-EC Fees
Full time	3 years		
Part time			
Sandwich			

BA Management Studies

This course provides students with a broad, thorough and fully-integrated introduction to the ideas and practices of management. It has as its focus the concept of the organisation and its operating environment and sets out to provide an understanding of the way in which organisations might be made to operate more effectively.

This degree is accredited at foundation level by the Institute of Chartered Accountants in England and Wales. Students who take certain Marketing modules gain full exemption from the Institute of Marketing's Certificate examinations

Modular Course?	Yes
Qualifications:	BA Hons
Application Deadline:	UCAS deadline
Commencement Date:	October
Entry Requirement:	ABB at A level and GCSE Maths
	Grade B
Applications to Places:	20:1
Registered:	40
Awards:	

	Duration	EC Fees	Non-EC Fees
Full time	3 years		
Part time			
Sandwich			

BA Management Studies with French

This course is jointly organised by the Business School and the Department of French. The aim of the course it to respond to a growing demand for graduates who combine expertise in Management Studies, French language and French business practice. The third year of the programme is spent in France or a French-speaking country. During this year students may undertake a supervised placement, a course of study at a recognised institution of higher education or a combination of the two.

Modular Course?	Yes
Qualifications:	BA Hons
Application Deadline:	UCAS deadline
Commencement Date:	October

Entry Requirement:	ABB (including French at A		
	level)		
	Grade B Maths GCSE		
Applications to Places:	20:1		
Registered:	25		
Awards:			

	Duration	EC Fees	Non-EC Fees
Full time	4 years		
Part time			
Sandwich			

BA Management Studies with German

This course is jointly organised by the Business School and the Department of German. The aim of the course it to respond to a growing demand for graduates who combine expertise in Management Studies, German language and German business practice. The third year of the programme is spent in Germany or a German-speaking country. During this year students may undertake a supervised placement, a course of study at a recognised institution of higher education or a combination of the two.

Modular Course?	Yes
Qualifications:	BA Hons
Application Deadline:	UCAS deadline
Commencement Date:	October
Entry Requirement:	ABB (including German at A
	level)
	Grade B Maths GCSE
Applications to Places:	20:1
Registered:	20
Awards:	

	Duration	EC Fees	Non-EC Fees
Full time	4 years		
Part time			
Sandwich			

BA Management Studies with Spanish

This course is jointly organised by the Business School and the Department of Hispanic Studies. It aims to combine an understanding of the modern commercial enterprise with Spanish language ability and a familiarity with the history, culture, economy and social institutions of Spanish speaking countries. The third year of the programme is spent in Spain or a Spanish-speaking country. During this year students may undertake a supervised placement, a course of study at a recognised institution of higher education or a combination of the two.

Modular Course?	Yes
Qualifications:	BA Hons
Application Deadline:	UCAS deadline

Commencement Date:		October	
Entry Requirement:		ABB (including Spanish at A level)	
		Grade B Maths GCSE	
Applications to Places:		20:1	
Registered:		10	
Awards:			

	Duration	EC Fees	Non-EC Fees
Full time	4 years		
Part time			
Sandwich			

Commencement Date:		October	
Entry Requirement:		ABB (including a language at A level)	
		Grade B Maths GCSE	
Applications to Places:		20:1	
Registered:		5	
Awards:			

	Duration	EC Fees	Non-EC Fees
Full time	3 years		
Part time			
Sandwich			

BA Management Studies with Portuguese

This course is jointly organised by the Business School and the Department of Hispanic Studies. It aims to combine an understanding of the modern commercial enterprise with Portuguese language ability and a familiarity with the history, culture, economy and social institutions of Portuguese speaking countries. The third year of the programme is spent in Portugal or a Portuguese speaking country. During this year students may undertake a supervised placement, a course of study at a recognised institution of higher education or a combination of the two.

Modular Course?	Yes
Qualifications:	BA Hons
Application Deadline:	UCAS deadline
Commencement Date:	October
Entry Requirement:	ABB (including a language at A level)
	Grade B Maths GCSE
Registered:	5
Awards:	

	Duration	EC Fees	Non-EC Fees
Full time	4 years		
Part time			
Sandwich			

BA Management Studies with East European Studies

This course aims to combine an expertise in management studies with a high level of proficiency in language and an in-depth knowledge of economics, social and political aspects of transition in post-socialist countries. The course consists of three elements: (1) Management Studies, (2) an East European language, (3) East European area studies. The course provides students with sufficient skills to pursue a career in a wide range of activities involving Eastern Europe and the former Soviet Republics.

Modular Course?	Yes
Qualifications:	BA Hons
Application Deadline:	UCAS deadline

BSc Chemistry and Management Studies

A joint honours degree in Chemistry and Management Studies

Modular Course?	Yes
Qualifications:	BSc Hons
Application Deadline:	UCAS deadline
Commencement Date:	October
Entry Requirement:	24 points and GCSE Maths Grade B. Good pass in Chemistry at A level.
Applications to Places:	20:1
Registered:	n/a
Awards:	

	Duration	EC Fees	Non-EC Fees
Full time	3 years		
Part time			
Sandwich			

BSc Computer Science and Management Studies

A joint honours degree in Computer Science and Management Studies.

Modular Course?	Yes
Qualifications:	BSc Hons
Application Deadline:	UCAS deadline
Commencement Date:	October
Entry Requirement:	24 points and GCSE Maths Grade B
Applications to Places:	20:1
Registered:	n/a
Awards:	

	Duration	EC Fees	Non-EC Fees
Full time	3 years		
Part time			
Sandwich			

Nottingham Business School

Nottingham Business School

Address:	Burton Street
	Nottingham
	NG1 4BU
Area:	Midlands
Phone:	0115 941 8418
Fax:	0115 948 6512
Email:	**Sheilah.Han@ntu.ac.uk**
Website:	**http://www.nbs.ntu.ac.uk**
Email Application Available?	No
How to apply by email:	
Total Number of Teaching Staff:	144
Staff Teaching Undergraduate Courses	
Research Rating:	3a
Teaching Rating:	Excellent
Additional Rating Information	
Male:Female Student Ratio	52:48
Head of Business School	Professor Martin Reynolds
Head of Undergraduate Studies	
Admissions Contact	

About the School:

Nottingham Business School is one of the UK's leading business schools and has earned an international reputation for its teaching, research and consultancy. It is one of the few business schools to have received an Excellent rating from the Higher Education Funding Council, and this reflects the strong partnerships between staff, students and employers which have put the School at the forefront of educational development in business and management studies.

About Undergraduate Studies:

The Business School seeks to produce graduates and diplomats who are self-reliant, confident, and intellectually equipped to meet the demands of a managerial career stretching well into the next century. To meet an ever-changing, increasingly technological and international environment, the Business School's courses are constantly refined in terms of content, assessment and delivery.

Facilities:

The Nottingham Trent University enjoys an excellent location in a compact, vibrant and sophisticated city, set in the heart of England. Famed for its legends and its lace, Nottingham has been dubbed the Queen of the

Midlands with major surveys declaring it the UK's leading city for quality of life. It offers a vibrant environment in which to learn, provides excellent recreational and entertainment facilities, and is easily accessible. The University has invested heavily in the provision of high quality residential accommodation for new students and the Students' Union provides a lively and wide-ranging programme of activities.

General Undergraduate Courses

BA (Hons) Accounting and Finance

This is a vocationally-relevant course for people seeking a career in accountancy, financial management or management accounting functions in industry and commerce. It also provides a valuable grounding in finance for people specialising in other careers such as marketing or personnel management. Students are encouraged to see financial management within the context of business decision making, and are introduced to other topics such as Information Technology, Law and Organisational Behaviour. Students can take options beyond the core subjects such as Marketing, IT, or Languages, or can study accounting topics such as Financial Management, Auditing or Tax in greater depth.

Modular Course?	No
Qualifications:	BA Hons
Application Deadline:	On request
Commencement Date:	
Entry Requirement:	Normally, GCSE passes at Grade C or above in at least three subjects, including English and Maths, 8 points at A-level for Diploma courses, 16 points at A-level for degree courses.
Applications to Places:	15:1
Registered:	300
Awards:	

	Duration	EC Fees	Non-EC Fees
Full time	3-4 years	On request	
Part time			
Sandwich			

BA (Hons) Business Information Services

This programme is firmly business-based and is ideal for students who may have been put off traditional BIS courses by their emphasis on technology. The first stage introduces basic concepts about information technology applications, while at the second stage students look at the implementation of information systems in organisations, considering selection, design, human

ictors and management processes. The third stage
ikes a more strategic look at the impact of IT in
rganisations, showing how they can be used to gain
ompetitive advantage. The course involves no
rogramming but develops skills in using popular
ackages such as databases and spreadsheets.

odular Course?	No
ualifications:	BA Hons
pplication Deadline:	On request
ommencement Date:	
ntry Requirement:	Normally, GCSE passes at Grade C or above in at least three subjects, including English and Maths, 8 points at A-level for Diploma courses, 16 points at A-level for
pplications to Places:	15:1
egistered:	130
wards:	

	Duration	EC Fees	Non-EC Fees
ill time	4 years	On request	
art time			
andwich			

3A (Hons) Business and Quality Management

This course provides a unique opportunity to study
Quality in relation to traditional business functions such
s Marketing, Human Resources, Finance and Strategic
Management. The course takes a practical view of
Quality, providing an introduction to quantitative
methods which underpin quality processes and tools. A
vide range of options, together with a placement year
make this an extremely flexible course.

odular Course?	No
ualifications:	BA Hons
pplication Deadline:	On request
ommencement Date:	
ntry Requirement:	Normally, GCSE passes at Grade C or above in at least three subjects, including English and Maths, 8 points at A-level for Diploma courses, 16 points at A-level for degree courses.
pplications to Places:	15:1
egistered:	140
wards:	

	Duration	EC Fees	Non-EC Fees
ill time	4 years	On request	
art time			
andwich			

BA (Hons) Business Studies

The course aims to provide a forward-looking but
generalist base of knowledge for people who intend to
pursue management careers. The basic business
disciplines of Economics, Law, Accounting and
Quantitative Methods are established in the first year
then applied through the remainder of the course to key
business issues such as the nature of management,
decision making, the business environment and business
policy. A wide range of study options expand the core
material by developing technical skills and more
specialist knowledge to suit individual interests and
objectives. The course also offers the opportunity to
study at leading European institutions in Holland and
Denmark.

Modular Course?	No
Qualifications:	BA Hons
Application Deadline:	On request
Commencement Date:	
Entry Requirement:	Normally, GCSE passes at Grade C or above in at least three subjects, including English and Maths, 8 points at A-level for Diploma courses, 16 points at A-level for degree courses.
Applications to Places:	15:1
Registered:	650
Awards:	

	Duration	EC Fees	Non-EC Fees
Full time	4 years	On request	
Part time			
Sandwich			

BA (Hons) European Business

This course encourages flexibility, empathy and cultural
awareness relevant to business in Europe and beyond
and develops business, language and personal skills.
Languages are studied in the first two years, and the
course offers two placements one in a UK and one in
French, German or Spanish company. Students spend
the whole of the third year abroad.

Modular Course?	No
Qualifications:	BA Hons
Application Deadline:	On request
Commencement Date:	
Entry Requirement:	Normally, GCSE passes at Grade C or above in at least three subjects, including English and Maths, 8 points at A-level for Diploma courses, 16 points at A-level for degree courses.
Applications to Places:	15:1
Registered:	250
Awards:	

	Duration	EC Fees	Non-EC Fees
Full time	4 years	On request	
Part time			
Sandwich			

Applications to Places:	15:1
Registered:	180
Awards:	

BA (Hons) Financial Services

This course concentrates on the key themes of Business Organisations, Financial Services, Business Strategy, Management, and Personal Skills. Students can take a specialist route covering topics such as Lending, Risk, Law and Regulations in more detail, or choose more general options such as Languages, Accounting, Economics, Marketing or Human Resource Management.

Modular Course?	No
Qualifications:	BA Hons
Application Deadline:	On request
Commencement Date:	
Entry Requirement:	Normally, GCSE passes at Grade C or above in at least three subjects, including English and Maths, 8 points at A-level for Diploma courses, 16 points at A-level for degree courses.
Applications to Places:	15:1
Registered:	140
Awards:	

	Duration	EC Fees	Non-EC Fees
Full time	4 years	On request	
Part time			
Sandwich			

BA (Hons) International Hospitality Management; BA (Hons) Hotel and Catering Management

These two courses prepare students for a business-oriented career in the hospitality industry. The course has an international perspective and includes the study of a foreign language. The BA (Hons) Hotel and Catering Management course is a top-up for students who have achieved good results at HND level and want to obtain a degree.

Modular Course?	No
Qualifications:	BA Hons
Application Deadline:	On request
Commencement Date:	
Entry Requirement:	Normally, GCSE passes at Grade C or above in at least three subjects, including English and Maths, 8 points at A-level for Diploma courses, 16 points at A-level for degree courses.

	Duration	EC Fees	Non-EC Fees
Full time	1 or 4 years	On request	
Part time			
Sandwich			

Diploma in Higher Education in Accounting

The course is designed for students who want to pursue a career in accounting and gain professional qualifications.

Modular Course?	No
Qualifications:	Diploma HE
Application Deadline:	On request
Commencement Date:	
Entry Requirement:	Normally, GCSE passes at Grade C or above in at least three subjects, including English and Maths, 8 points at A-level for Diploma courses, 16 points at A-level for degree courses.
Applications to Places:	15:1
Registered:	n/a
Awards:	

	Duration	EC Fees	Non-EC Fees
Full time	2-3 years	On request	
Part time			
Sandwich			

Open University Business School

Open University Business School

Address:	Open University
	Walton Hall
	Milton Keynes
	MK7 6AA
Area:	London and South East England
Phone:	01908 653 449
Fax:	01908 654 320
Email:	crel-gen@open.ac.uk
Website:	http://oubs@open.ac.uk

Email Application Available?	No
How to apply by email:	
Total Number of Teaching Staff:	1000
Staff Teaching Undergraduate Courses	40
Research Rating:	3a
Teaching Rating:	Excellent
Additional Rating Information	
Male:Female Student Ratio	70:30
Head of Business School	Professor David Asch
Head of Undergraduate Studies	Julian Batsleer
Admissions Contact	Course Development and Sales

About the School:

The Open University is Europe's largest and most innovative university with a world-wide reputation for the quality of its courses and teaching methods. The OU Business School was founded in 1983 to offer practicising managers the benefits of distance learning. Already over 190,000 managers have studied with the OUBS in the UK, the Republic of Ireland, Continental Europe and beyond. Management development with the OUBS is relevant, practical, rigorous and sociable - a mix of working to your own schedule in your own time and studying with other managers at tutorials, residential schools and study groups - a mix given the highest possible rating of Excellent by the HEFCE and a mix that has earned us the Queen's Award for Export Achievement.

About Undergraduate Studies:

The Professional Certificate and Diploma in Management provide a firm grounding in key management issues and a range of tools and techniques for all managers. There are no prior qualifications required to enter the Certificate programme and successful completion of the Certificate and Diploma allows direct access to Stage 2 of the OUBS MBA. The

two programmes can be completed in two years.

Links with Academic Institutions:

IPD, CIMA, Paris Chamber of Commerce, LINK (Russia), Singapore Institute of Management, Open Learning Institute Hong Kong, University of Asmara (Eritrea), British Council (USA)

Student Testimonials:

'Having a demanding full-time job, I needed my studies to be flexible. I did not have time to attend classes everyday, so I chose distance learning and the OUBS was the best option.' Tomas Pallas Aparisi, European Commission.

'Throughout the course you learn the theories but also how those ideas can be used to the benefit of the individual and the company.' Caroline Bailey, Business Development Manager, Thresher.

General Undergraduate Courses

The Capable Manager

The Capable Manager will develop your management skills and techniques and challenge the way you currently view your role and function. All four key management roles – people, marketing, information/resources and finance are covered. More than half the course is devoted to managing people, because this is by far the most important managerial role – managers achieve results through people. The rest of the course is equally divided between marketing, information and finance.

Modular Course?	No
Qualifications:	Professional Certificate in Management
Application Deadline:	March or September
Commencement Date:	May or November
Entry Requirement:	None
Applications to Places:	1:1
Registered:	2500
Awards:	2125

	Duration	EC Fees	Non-EC Fees
Full time			
Part time	1 year	£1500	On request
Sandwich			

Managing Development and Change

This course is concerned with the management of people in the context of organisational change. It provides a programme of learning and development for mid-level managers. The course will improve your effectiveness at individual, team and organisational levels. The key theories, skills and competencies are all covered: managing performance and learning; skills in selection, appraisal and personal development;

managing conflict and diversity; building team effectiveness; planning, managing and implementing change and managing people and change in a complex and dynamic environment.

Modular Course?	No
Qualifications:	Professional Diploma in Management
Application Deadline:	March or September
Commencement Date:	May or November
Entry Requirement:	None, but to obtain the Professional Diploma in Management, the Professional Certificate in Management and Managing Resources for the Market must be successfully completed also.
Applications to Places:	1:1
Registered:	1700
Awards:	1450

	Duration	EC Fees	Non-EC Fees
Full time			
Part time	6 months	£950	On request
Sandwich			

Managing Resources for the Market

This course is vital for managers preparing themselves for more senior positions. It will help you to manage your internal resources more effectively and react to volatile external markets more responsively. The course has been designed to foster the skills, confidence and sense of responsibility necessary for successfully managing an organisation's separately accountable functions. It deals with the management of information and resources so that the needs of key customers can be satisfied regularly and consistently.

Modular Course?	No
Qualifications:	Professional Diploma in Management
Application Deadline:	March or September
Commencement Date:	May or November
Entry Requirement:	None, but to obtain the Professional Diploma in Management, the Professional Certificate in Management and Managing Development and Change must be successfully complete also.
Applications to Places:	1:1
Registered:	1550
Awards:	1300

	Duration	EC Fees	Non-EC Fees
Full time			
Part time	6 months	£950	On request
Sandwich			

Said Business School, University of Oxford

aid Business School

---

ddress:	The Radcliffe Infirmary
	Woodstock Road
	Oxford
	OX2 6HE
rea:	London and South East England
hone:	01865 228 470
ax:	01865 228 471
mail:	**enquiries@sbs.ox.ac.uk**
Vebsite:	**www.sbs.ox.ac.uk**

mail Application Available?	No
pply via UCAS	
otal Number of Teaching Staff:	27
aff Teaching Undergraduate Courses	
esearch Rating:	4
eaching Rating:	Satisfactory
dditional Rating Information	
ale:Female Student Ratio	n/a
ead of Business School	Professor J A Kay
ead of Undergraduate Studies	Dr D Faulkner
dmissions Contact	Undergraduate Admissions Office

About the School:

he University of Oxford, the most ancient university in he English-speaking world, was established in 1231. he Faculty of Management, created in 1998, is the oungest faculty within the University, and is already leveloping courses which are setting the agenda for ew management in the new millennium. The Faculty omprises the Said Business School together with empleton College. The raison d'être of the Faculty is to rovide; an international environment for scholarship, tudents and staff; one which is fully integrated into the Jniversity of Oxford, drawing on its diverse resources n all disciplines related to management; one which is ntelligent, bringing the highest calibre students to study ogether; and one which is individual, bringing the Dxford tutorial system into business education. The aculty of management offers management and business eaching in the following undergraduate degrees in ollaboration with the Oxford faculties of Engineering nd Economics.

Economics and Management

Economics & Management is a three year joint degree course which provides an opportunity to combine the traditional areas of economics with a range of management disciplines from Accounting and Finance to Marketing and Operations Management.

Modular Course?	No
Qualifications:	BA
Application Deadline:	15 October 1998
Commencement Date:	11 October 1999
Entry Requirement:	On request
Applications to Places:	n/a
Registered:	160
Awards:	

	Duration	EC Fees	Non-EC Fees
Full time	3 years	On request	On request
Part time			
Sandwich			

School of Business

School of Business

Address:	Wheatley Campus
	Wheatley
	Oxford
	OX33 1HX
Area:	London and South East England
Phone:	01865 485908
Fax:	01865 485830
Email:	business@brookes.ac.uk
Website:	www.brookes.ac.uk/business/

Email Application Available?	Yes
How to apply by email:	business@brookes.ac.uk
Total Number of Teaching Staff:	100
Staff Teaching Undergraduate Courses	100
Research Rating:	1
Teaching Rating:	Satisfactory
Additional Rating Information	Our understanding for 'teaching' is 'approved quality' 1990 for the School. Next review 2000/2001 to be confirmed.
Male:Female Student Ratio	44:56
Head of Business School	Professor Mary Benwell
Head of Undergraduate Studies	Howard Brown (Deputy Head)
Admissions Contact	Mike Haffey (Senior Admissions Tutor)

About the School:

The School of Business is one of the largest Schools in the University and provides practice orientated education, training, development and consultancy. It is very active internationally with links to educational institutions throughout the world. There is a strong emphasis on interactive teaching methods in all programmes. The University was a pioneer of modular programmes in the 1970s and is constantly updating its approach to teaching and course delivery. HEFCE assessors have drawn attention to the School's achievements in cultivating an innovative climate and in the development of competence related approaches.

About Undergraduate Studies:

Courses are within the Modular Programme of the University enabling Joint Honours as well as Single Honours degrees to be offered. The School has built up considerable expertise in offering sandwich courses with a network of supportive employers. This programme has been extended to Europe with partner institutions enabling both academic study and work experinece to be undertaken in France or Germany, for example.

The School seeks to 'add value' by working with professional bodies, where applicable eg in Marketing (CIM) and Accountancy.

Facilities:

The University runs a wide range of public lectures enabling students to listen to and talk with national and international figures. Cultural life on campus is rich and varied. Art, Music and Drama are well represented. The Students' Union is a major resource for our students and operates from the Helena Kennedy Centre, a complex housing student services, shops, travel agency etc and large events arena. Over 60 student run clubs and societies operate. The University boasts a state-of-the-art centre for sport, with a main sports hall accommodating a health suite, squash, badmington courts, heavy weights room, climbing room and tower. Outdoor sport (tennis, rugby, football, crickets rowing etc) is well catered for with floodlit and artificial turf facilities.

Departments/Faculties:

Economics
Accountancy
Management Development and Human Resource Management
Marketing and Services Management
Operations Management and MIS
Business Organisation Skills and Strategy

Links with Academic Institutions:

The School has formal links with colleges, polytechnics and Universities throughout the world, enabling students to either participate in exchange programmes or undertake more extensive programmes of study. There are partners in France, Germany, Hungary and Spain, the USA, Australia and Japan as well as the several countries in South East Asia.

Links with Industry:

The School has strong links with local employers in the public and private sector for designing and operating tailor made courses as well as participation in general programmes, such as the DMS and MBA. The emphasis on practice education has resulted in many links to industry for work placements, sponsorship of projects, and research as well as future employment of our students
More overseas links have recently been developed to support our increasing emphasis on international applications of management.

Student Testimonials:

' I enjoyed your course very much. It was interesting..too bad you were only teaching me one module!' A L, Marketing student
'The service offered by the Placement Office was superb enabling me to choose between placement opportunities. Thank you'. Business sandwich student.

Thanks for all your personal help and my degree has enabled me to obtain an excellent job in the banking industry in Bejiing'. BC Acounting and Marketing student

General Undergraduate Courses

Business and Management

The course provides an understanding of the nature, role, significance and content of managerial activities as undertaken in a range of organisations. It also develops skills necessary to working effectively in those organisations. The course offers up nine specialist pathways as well as an optional work placement year.

Modular Course?	No
Qualifications:	BA Hons
Application Deadline:	UCAS
Commencement Date:	September
Entry Requirement:	GCSE Maths (B preferred), English , 3*A Levels (CCC) or acceptable equivalents
Applications to Places:	20:1
Registered:	120
Awards:	100

	Duration	EC Fees	Non-EC Fees
Full time	3 years	£1000 pa	£6600 pa
Part time	max 8 years	£160 per module	na
Sandwich	4 years	£1000 per year	£6600 per annum

European Business Studies

A 4 year 'sandwich' course studied in Oxford and France or Germany providing opportunities to study business subjects, develop foreign language skills and to study and work abroad.

Modular Course?	Yes
Qualifications:	BA Hons; Diploma HE; German and/or French degree equivalents. Dual qualification award.
Application Deadline:	UCAS
Commencement Date:	September
Entry Requirement:	GCSE Maths (B) and English. A level French or German and 2 other A levels or equivalents
Applications to Places:	4:1
Registered:	50
Awards:	50

	Duration	EC Fees	Non-EC Fees
Full time	4 years	£1000 pa	£6600 pa
Part time	na	na	na
Sandwich	4 years	£6600 per annum	

Joint Honours

The opportunity to combine any two individual subjects offered within the Modular Programme of the University. There are 6 Business Subjects: (Accountancy, Business Administration, Economics, Marketing, Retailing, Tourism) and over 50 other single subject choices available to students.

Modular Course?	No
Qualifications:	BA Hons; BSc Hons; Joint Honours; Diploma HE; Qualification depends on subjects selected and student choice
Application Deadline:	UCAS
Commencement Date:	September
Entry Requirement:	GCSE Maths (B) and English and 3 A Levels or equivalent. Some subjects may require specialist GCSE or A levels.
Applications to Places:	10:1
Registered:	200 +
Awards:	200+

	Duration	EC Fees	Non-EC Fees
Full time	3 years	£1000 pa	£6600 pa
Part time	up to 8 years	£160 per module	na
Sandwich	na		

International Business and Management

A one academic year programme for business students with entry qualifications equivalent to the first 2 years of this international business degree. There is a choice of 7 specialist pathways leading to named awards.

Modular Course?	No
Qualifications:	BA Hons
Application Deadline:	UCAS
Commencement Date:	September
Entry Requirement:	HND or Diploma equivalent to first 2 years of an hons degree
Applications to Places:	3:1
Registered:	30
Awards:	30

	Duration	EC Fees	Non-EC Fees
Full time	Normally 1 year	£4500	£6600
Part time	na		
Sandwich	na		

International Banking and Finance

A one academic year programme for business/banking students with entry qualifications equivalent to the first two years of this international business and banking degree.

Modular Course?	Yes
Qualifications:	BA Hons
Application Deadline:	UCAS
Commencement Date:	September
Entry Requirement:	HND or Diploma equivalent to first 2 years of a hons degree
Applications to Places:	2:1
Registered:	20
Awards:	10

	Duration	EC Fees	Non-EC Fees
Full time	Normally 1 year £4500		£6600
Part time	na		
Sandwich	na		

Specialist Undergraduate Course

Marketing Management

Modular Course?	Yes
Qualifications:	BA Hons; Diploma HE; Exemptions from some CIM examinations
Categories:	Marketing; Small Business; Corporate Strategy

Business Economics

Modular Course?	Yes
Qualifications:	BA Hons; Diploma HE
Categories:	Corporate Strategy; Business combined with economics

Accounting and Finance

Modular Course?	Yes
Qualifications:	BA Hons; Diploma HE; Exemptions from professional bodies eg up to 8 ACCA exemptions
Categories:	Finance

International Business Management, includes 7 options matched to typical HND majors internationally

Modular Course?	Yes
Qualifications:	BA Hons; Diploma HE
Categories:	International Business

International Banking and Finance

Modular Course?	Yes
Qualifications:	BA Hons; Diploma HE
Categories:	Finance; International Business

Department of Management & Marketing

University of Paisley, Department of Management & Marketing

Address:	High Street
	Paisley
	PAI 2BE
Area:	Scotland
Phone:	0141 848 3000
Fax:	0141 848 3395

Email:

Website: www.paisley.ac.uk

Email Application Available?	No
How to apply by email:	
Total Number of Teaching Staff:	37
Staff Teaching Undergraduate Courses	37
Research Rating:	n/a
Teaching Rating:	n/a
Additional Rating Information	
Male:Female Student Ratio	50:50
Head of Business School	
Head of Undergraduate Studies	Professor RGL von Zugbach
Admissions Contact	Dr Alisdair Galloway

General Undergraduate Courses

BA Business and Management

Undergraduate degree focusing on the practice of management and the development of management skills, making significant use of simulation within and outwith the classroom. Between second and third years, many students take advantage of the opportunity to go on a year's placement to gain practical experience.Graduates are entitled to associate membership of the Institute of Management, and full membership on attainment of sufficient practical experience. As well as mainstream management modules, students also select from specialist courses in HRM, or Marketing or Finance.

Modular Course?	Yes
Qualifications:	BA; BA Hons; Diploma HE
Application Deadline:	UCAS deadline
Commencement Date:	Late September
Entry Requirement:	A-level - I @ B and I @ C: or

| | | | |
| I @ C and 2 @ D. |
| Scottish Highers - 3 @ B and I |
| @ |

Applications to Places:	3:I
Registered:	70
Awards:	44

	Duration	EC Fees	Non-EC Fees
Full time	3-4 years	£1000	
Part time			
Sandwich			

Specialist Undergraduate Course

BA Business and Management

Modular Course?	Yes
Qualifications:	BA; BA Hons; Diploma HE
Categories:	Human Resources; Marketing; Management

Plymouth Business School

University of Plymouth Business School

Address:	Drake Circus
	Plymouth
	PL4 8AA
Area:	South West England
Phone:	01752 232 800
Fax:	01752 232 853
Email:	admissions-l@pbs.plym.ac.uk
Website:	http://www.pbs.plym.ac.uk
Email Application Available?	No
How to apply by email:	
Total Number of Teaching Staff:	80
Staff Teaching Undergraduate Courses	
Research Rating:	2
Teaching Rating:	Satisfactory
Additional Rating Information	
Male:Female Student Ratio	50:50
Head of Business School	Professor Peter Jones
Head of Undergraduate Studies	
Admissions Contact	01752 232804/07/63/82

About the School:

The University of Plymouth Business School is the major provider of business and management programmes west of Bristol with over 2000 students and some 80 full-time staff. The School is largely self-contained with subject expertise in: Accounting and Finance; Economics; Law; Business Operations; Marketing; Business Strategy; Human Resource Management; Information Technology. The School is based in its own new well-equipped building with specialist facilities including a management suite dedicated to postgraduate programmes, a language resource centre and laboratories, and a unique aroma room for perfumery business cources.

The School offers a wide range of flexible modular programmes, and teaching is based on small tutorial groups providing personal attention and competency-based learning for students who want to practice management rather than talk about it.

About Undergraduate Studies:

Facilities:

Plymouth Business School is situated in a delightful location in a historic city surrounded by the sea and many areas of outstanding natural beauty, including the

amous Plymouth Hoe with stunning views of Plymouth
Sound, and historic harbour. Plymouth is ideal for sport
with a wide choice of team games, golf or wind-surfing,
sailing and scuba diving. There is a thriving international
culture within the University plus the facilities of a lively
city with cinemas, night spots, music venues, a leisure
complex that stages top music performers and the
acclaimed Theatre Royal.

Portsmouth Business School

University of Portsmouth Business School

Address:	Locksway Road
	Milton
	Portsmouth
	PO4 8JF
Area:	London and South East England
Phone:	01705 844202
Fax:	01705 844059

Email:

Website:

Email Application Available?	Yes
How to apply by email:	Admissions Tutors may be
	contacted via the university
	website - http://www.port.ac.uk
Total Number of Teaching Staff:	120
Staff Teaching Undergraduate Courses	
Research Rating:	3b
Teaching Rating:	Highly Satisfactory
Additional Rating Information	
Male:Female Student Ratio	50:50
Head of Business School	Mr Mike Dunn
Head of Undergraduate Studies	Dr Ray French
Admissions Contact	01705 844068

About the School:

The Business School provides a range of flexible and relevant programmes at both undergraduate and postgraduate level in business, accounting and economics There are 1900 undergraduate students in the School, including international students from all continents. The School has a long-standing commitment to vocational education and has provided postgraduate management training and undergraduate sandwich business courses for forty years. There are extensive overseas links with European countries, and in North America and South East Asia, and wide ranging links with employing organisations. Good computing facilities are offered in the School's twelve computing laboratories.

About Undergraduate Studies:

A high proportion of undergraduates in the School are enrolled on sandwich courses, spending their third year on industrial and commercial training placements. The BA Business Studies course was one of the first of its kind established in the UK and was built upon a successful relationship with, and sponsorship by, major employers.

Facilities:

With over 14,000 students in the University the Students' Union operates over a hundred clubs and societies serving a wide range of sporting, social, musical and cultural interests. The Business School has a branch of the Students' Union with its own catering and bar facilities.

Departments/Faculties:

Department of Business and Management
Department of Accounting and Management Science
Department of Economics
Centre for Quality and Project Management
Portsmouth Management Centre (the short course unit of the School)

Undergraduate Programme Area

All courses in the School belong to this Programme Area and there is scope to transfer between programmes, all of which are organised in units of study and are credit-rated.

Links with Academic Institutions:

Portsmouth Business School is recognised as one of the few Centres of Excellence of the Institute of Personnel Development. The School has numerous international links, including the distinctive BA European Business. Several management programmes are provided in Malaysia, Hong Kong, Greece and Holland.

Links with Industry:

Over six hundred firms participate in the School's undergraduate training placement programme which is managed by a dedicated unit. An Advisory Board of leading industrialists gives guidance on the School's course portfolio.

General Undergraduate Courses

Business Studies

The business pathways are a blend of theory and practice. The programme combines the very best from traditional business education and applies the latest knowledge and techniques to enable students to identify, understand and resolve business issues and problems. A key feature of this programme is the broad range of optional units.

Modular Course?	No
Qualifications:	BA Hons
Application Deadline:	UCAS Deadline
Commencement Date:	September
Entry Requirement:	3 Cs A Level or GNVQ
	(Distinction) + GCSE Grade B
	Maths
Applications to Places:	10:1
Registered:	166
Awards:	202

	Duration	EC Fees	Non-EC Fees
Full time			
Part time			
Sandwich	4 years	£1000 (max)	£5000

BA (Hons) European Business (EBP)

This programme is an international business course which has been developed to meet the requirements of the European Internal Market. The structure and content of the course are designed to overcome the difficulties facing international organisations in finding multilingual and internationally mobile employees.

Modular Course?	No
Qualifications:	BA Hons
Application Deadline:	UCAS Deadline
Commencement Date:	September
Entry Requirement:	20 points A level (to include Grade C in Language)
Applications to Places:	10:1
Registered:	49
Awards:	39

	Duration	EC Fees	Non-EC Fees
Full time	4 years	£1000 (max)	£5000
Part time			
Sandwich			

BA Accounting

This course is designed for students who wish to take up a career as a Chartered, Certified Management or Public Sector accountant or wish to follow a career where accountancy is a major component.

Modular Course?	No
Qualifications:	BA Hons
Application Deadline:	UCAS deadline
Commencement Date:	September
Entry Requirement:	16 points A level
Applications to Places:	10:1
Registered:	
Awards:	

	Duration	EC Fees	Non-EC Fees
Full time	3 years	£1000 (max)	£5000
Part time			
Sandwich	4 years	£1000 (max)	£5000

BA Economics

This single honours course provides an excellent opportunity for those who wish to study the subject in some depth. At the same time as undertaking a rigorous treatment of the subject matter, the student is permitted to select those areas of economics of greatest interest, through a wide choice of options.

Modular Course?	No
Qualifications:	BA Hons

Application Deadline:	UCAS deadline
Commencement Date:	September
Entry Requirement:	18 points A level
Applications to Places:	10:1
Registered:	
Awards:	

	Duration	EC Fees	Non-EC Fees
Full time	3 years	£1000 (max)	£5000
Part time			
Sandwich			

BA Accounting & Business Information Systems

This course is designed both for those wishing to prepare for a career in accounting or finance, and for students wishing to take up employment in more general management positions, particularly in those areas relating to information systems and technology.

Modular Course?	No
Qualifications:	BA Hons; Joint Honours
Application Deadline:	UCAS deadline
Commencement Date:	September
Entry Requirement:	16 points A level
Applications to Places:	10:1
Registered:	
Awards:	

	Duration	EC Fees	Non-EC Fees
Full time	3 years	£1000 (max)	£5000
Part time			
Sandwich	4 years	£1000 (max)	£5000

BA(Hons) Business Administration

This is the three year, full-time version of the Business Studies Degree. Here students proceed from Level 2 to 3 and are not required to complete an industrial placement.

Modular Course?	No
Qualifications:	BA Hons
Application Deadline:	UCAS Deadline
Commencement Date:	September
Entry Requirement:	3 C's A Level or GNVQ (Distinction) + GCSE Grade B Maths
Applications to Places:	10:1
Registered:	
Awards:	

	Duration	EC Fees	Non-EC Fees
Full time	3 years	£1000 (max)	£5000
Part time			
Sandwich			

BA (Hons) International Business Studies

This variant of the BA Business Studies course enables students to spend one semester studying in an English-speaking partner university abroad (North America or Scandinavia) and also to complete a work placement overseas. In the final year students specialise in international business topics.

Modular Course?	No
Qualifications:	BA Hons
Application Deadline:	UCAS deadline
Commencement Date:	September
Entry Requirement:	3 C's A Level or GNVQ (Distinction) + GCSE Grade B Maths
Applications to Places:	10:1
Registered:	
Awards:	

	Duration	EC Fees	Non-EC Fees
Full time			
Part time			
Sandwich	4 years	£1000 (max)	£5000

Specialist Undergraduate Course

BA (Hons) Hospitality Management

Modular Course?	Yes
Qualifications:	BA Hons; with Tourism pathway
Categories:	Hospitality; Leisure

BA (Hons) Business Economics with Business Law

Modular Course?	Yes

BA (Hons) International Finance & Trade

Modular Course?	Yes
Qualifications:	BA Hons
Categories:	Finance

BA (Hons) Business Economics

Modular Course?	Yes
Qualifications:	BA Hons
Categories:	

BA (Hons) Financial Services

Modular Course?	Yes

Qualifications:	BA Hons
Categories:	Finance

BA (Hons) Accounting with Law/Finance

Modular Course?	Yes
Qualifications:	BA Hons
Categories:	Finance; Business Law

Queen's School of Management

Queen's School of Management

Address:	Lanyon Building
	Belfast
	BT7 1NN
Area:	Northern Ireland
Phone:	01232 273 622
Fax:	01232 328 649

Email:

Website: http://www.qub.ac.uk

Email Application Available?	No
How to apply by email:	
Total Number of Teaching Staff:	22
Staff Teaching Undergraduate Courses	22
Research Rating:	n/a
Teaching Rating:	n/a
Additional Rating Information	
Male:Female Student Ratio	50:50
Head of Business School	
Head of Undergraduate Studies	Professor Alan Sangster
Admissions Contact	Dr Peter Dunne (BSc Finance); Dr Dave Newman (BSc Information Management); Mr Mike Pogue (BSc Accounting); Ms Pauline Maclaran (BSc Management)

About the School:

The Queen's University of Belfast was originally established as 'Queen's College, Belfast' by Queen Victoria in 1845 as one of three colleges in Ireland. It was raised to the status of a full university in 1908 with its own Charter and Statutes.

About Undergraduate Studies:

The School offers small scale, high quality undergraduate programmes in four key areas: BSc Management; MSc Accounting; BSc Information Management; BSc Finance. All the School's courses appreciate the relevance of practical experience and the increasing importance of languages in the business and management environment.

Facilities:

Queen's is situated on the popular south side of the city in what 'Country Life' magazine described as 'a perfect Victorian suburb', yet it is only a mile from the centre of the city. This is the area where a large number of the

young people of Belfast live, work and play. Belfast's 'golden mile' stretches from the city's Grand Opera House which has been refurbished in the Victorian tradition of Matchem's 1895 original design. Since it re-opened in 1980, audiences have enjoyed the best of international touring companies.

When Queen's College opened in 1849 there were 20 professors and 90 matriculated students; we have now together around 1,200 full-time academic staff, including 127 professors, and almost 11,500 full-time students who attend courses and undertake research in Agriculture & Food Science, Arts, Economics & Social Sciences, Medicine & Health Sciences, Science, Engineering, Education, Law and Theology. The University is ideally placed in this cultural thoroughfare and beside the main site are numerous theatres, club venues, bookshops, bistros, pizzeria, health food emporia and fashion shops.

Since the original 1845 foundation, Queen's has always adhered to the principle of strictly non-denominational teaching and this is included in its Charter. In two particular respects the 1908 Charter was notably ahead of its time: it made provision for a student on the governing body (the Senate) and made women eligible equally with men to hold any office or enjoy any advantages of the University.

Queen's is unique as a university in having its own international arts festival. In two and a half weeks each November, the Festival offers more than 200 performances in every area of the arts. Alongside major visiting orchestras and top classical musicians are to be found a wide ranging theatre programme, jazz and folk music, and a whole host of lighter events.

Over the years Queen's has become a well established institution with a national and international reputation. At the regional level it plays a significant role in the educational, professional, industrial and cultural life of the Province.

Although Queen's is a comparatively old institution, it has a distinctly modern outlook. An example of this forward-looking policy is our programme of giving every student the opportunity to gain computing experience. In 1996 Queen's recorded its highest ever undergraduate intake. With new additions to its range of courses, it is confident of consolidating its position well into the future as one of the most progressive

General Undergraduate Courses

BSc Accounting

The BSc (Accounting) degree offers a firm base for either further academic study or for taking the professional examinations of the main professional bodies. It is recognised by the accounting profession, industry, commerce and the public sector as a degree which attracts only school leavers of the very highest calibre and, as a result, our graduates are much sought after.

The employment record of graduates in Accounting from Queen's is excellent. The degree in Accounting will give exemption from the whole of Professional I and Professional II examinations of the Institute of Chartered Accountants in Ireland. These are the most generous exemption s offered to any degree. Exemptions are also available from the examination of CIMA, ACCA and CIPFA.

Modular Course?	Yes
Qualifications:	BSc Hons
Application Deadline:	UCAS deadline
Commencement Date:	September
Entry Requirement:	26 A-level points
Applications to Places:	8:1
Registered:	70
Awards:	

	Duration	EC Fees	Non-EC Fees
Full time	3 years	£1000 pa	£5620 pa
Part time			
Sandwich	1 year	£1000 pa	£5620 pa

BSc Management

The BSc Management degree aims to prepare managers for the complexities of the 21st century. The school has excellent teaching facilities including an excellent computer suite enabling students to use a range of software and access external databases and information sources. Research-led teaching is a feature of the curriculum. The academic staff maintain a high level of contact with business and private sector organisations and are actively engaged in research across a broad spectrum of management topics. All students study 18 modules in their degree programme, six in each year of study. The final degree classification for each student is based on the one module studied in the second and third years.

Modular Course?	Yes
Qualifications:	BSc Hons
Application Deadline:	UCAS deadline
Commencement Date:	September
Entry requirement:	26 A-level points
Applications to Places:	20:1
Registered:	50
Awards:	

	Duration	EC Fees	Non-EC Fees
Full time	3 years	£1000 pa	£5620 pa
Part time			
Sandwich	1 year	£1000 pa	£5620 pa (plus language)

BSc Finance

The primary aim of the BSc Finance degree is to turn out students with a rigorous grounding in theory, techniques and tools required for operating in today's financial environments. Given this aim, two aspects of

the programme are of prime importance:
I; The strong emphasis which is placed on the development of qualitative skills, particularly in the general areas of accountancy and statistical analysis.
ii. The placement year. A year of professional experience between the second and final years of the degree.

Staff are aided by the fact that they are active in using state-of-the-art techniques and computer equipment.

Modular Course?	Yes
Qualifications:	BSc Hons;
Application Deadline:	UCAS deadline
Commencement Date:	September
Entry Requirement:	24 A-level points
Applications to Places:	9:1
Registered:	40
Awards:	

	Duration	EC Fees	Non-EC Fees
Full time	4 years	£1000 pa	£5620 pa
Part time			
Sandwich	1 year	£1000 pa	£5620 pa

BSc Information Management

Information Management is the study of management and information systems in organisations. It includes a significant grounding in Information Technology as well as in management. The degree aims to prepare managers for the complexities of the twenty-first century. The School has excellent teaching facilities including an excellent computer suite enabling students to use a range of software and access external databases and information sources. Research-led teaching is a feature of the curriculum. The academic staff maintain a high level of contact with business and private sector organisations and are actively engaged in research across a broad spectrum of management topics. All students study 18 modules in their degree programme, six in each year of study. The final degree classification for each student is based on the 12 modules studied in second and third years.

Modular Course?	Yes
Qualifications:	BSc Hons; BA Hons
Application Deadline:	UCAS deadline
Commencement Date:	September
Entry Requirement:	22 A-level points
Applications to Places:	11:1
Registered:	30
Awards:	

	Duration	EC Fees	Non-EC Fees
Full time	3 years	£1000 pa	£5620 pa
Part time			
Sandwich	1 year	£1000 pa	£5620 pa (plus language)

School of Business

Royal Agricultural College School of Business

Address:

	Cirencester
	GL7 6JS
Area:	South West England
Phone:	01285 652 531
Fax:	01285 641 659
Email:	admissions@royagcol.ac.uk
Website:	http://www.royagcol.ac.uk/extranet/
	schools/sob

Email Application Available?	No
How to apply by email:	
Total Number of Teaching Staff:	55
Staff Teaching Undergraduate Courses	
Research Rating:	n/a
Teaching Rating:	n/a
Additional Rating Information	
Male:Female Student Ratio	50:50
Head of Business School	Jonathan Turner
Head of Undergraduate Studies	
Admissions Contact	Gail Young/Sue Burton

About the School:

The College is the only business school dedicated to the agrifood business sector and specialises in courses related to the food industry and related sectors, rural affairs and farm management. As well as offering a comprehensive range of undergraduate, postgraduate and post-experience courses the College operates the Centre for Agrifood Business Research, which carries out contract research and is very active in management development and consultancy in the UK and overseas.

About Undergraduate Studies:

The School operates a wide range of vocationally-oriented pathways within a moular scheme. Based on a BSc (Hons) Business Management, students can chose Agrifood, Finance, Marketing, Human Resource Management or International Degrees. Other main pathways include: Rural Land Management; Agriculture and Land Management; International Agriculture; Horticultural Management; Mechanisation Management; Equine Management; Crop Technology. All of these courses include significant management elements.

Facilities:

The Students' Union offers a full range of clubs and societies and there are extensive sporting facilities, including a nearby leisure centre.

General Undergraduate Courses

BSc (Hons) Business Management

This course combines business management with economics, policy, and biotechnology relating to the food and agribusiness sector. Compulsory modules include Business Policy, Management Skills, Business Law, Research Methods, Agrifood Issues and Management Decision Making. It also includes a language module and an optional 5 month or one year study placement. In addition to these core subjects students can specialise in: Finance, Marketing, Human Resource Management and International Business.

Modular Course?	No
Qualifications:	BSc Hons
Application Deadline:	On request
Commencement Date:	On request
Entry Requirement:	On request
Applications to Places:	2:1
Registered:	360
Awards:	

	Duration	EC Fees	Non-EC Fees
Full time	2 to 4 years	On request	On request
Part time			
Sandwich			

The Management School

University of Salford Faculty of Business and Management

Address:	Salford
	M5 4WT
Area:	North West England
Phone:	0161 745 5350
Fax:	0161 745 5022
Email:	
Website:	
Email Application Available?	No
How to apply by email:	
Total Number of Teaching Staff:	175
Staff Teaching Undergraduate Courses	175
Research Rating:	1
Teaching Rating:	Satisfactory
Additional Rating Information	
Male:Female Student Ratio	50:50
Head of Business School	Professor Kenneth Gee
Head of Undergraduate Studies	Nigel Hall
Admissions Contact	Mike Crosbie

About the School:

The Faculty was launched in August 1996 as a result of a merger between University College Salford and the University of Salford and now has around 125 full-time staff and 3000 students. All departments are located on the main campus, close to the Library and Computer facilities. The Faculty has its own training restaurant and language laboratories. Salford offers a full range of academic and professional management programmes and enjoys close links with local employers through its part-time courses and short-course provision.

About Undergraduate Studies:

Salford is a linear university, bringing together the best of the old university traditions with the dynamism of the polytechnics' strengths in Business and Management education. The Faculty's strong vocational tradition in all degree and postgraduate programmes ensures an excellent employment record for graduates.

Facilities:

Salford is located just 10 minutes from the centre of Manchester close to the river on a parkland site. The University has Faculties for creative and performing arts providing a rich cultural environment for management students.

Departments/Faculties:

The Faculty consists of five departments: Business Studies; Leisure and Hospitality Studies; Management School; Professional Studies; Quality Management.

General Undergraduate Courses

BSc (Hons) Business Studies

All students enrol initially on the BSc (Hons) Business Studies degree. They can then decide whether to study a broad range of subjects, leading to the award of BSc (Hons) Business Studies, or choose a particular specialism such as: BSc (Hons) Business Studies with Financial Management; BSc (Hons) Business Studies with Human Resource Management; BSc (Hons) Business Studies with International Business; BSc (Hons) Business Studies with Law; BSc (Hons) Business Studies with Marketing Management; BSc (Hons) Business Studies with Quantitative Business Management.

Other undergraduate courses: BA (Hons) Applied Consumer Studies; BA (Hons) Food Industry Management; BA (Hons) Hospitality Management; BA (Hons) Leisure Management; BA (Hons) Quality Management; BSc (Hons) Finance and Accounting; HND/HNC courses; Dip HE in Accounting; Graduate Membership of Institute of Meat.

Modular Course?	No
Qualifications:	BA Hons; BSc Hons; HNC; HND;
	Diploma HE
Application Deadline:	1 September
Commencement Date:	
Entry Requirement:	Normal entry requirements
Applications to Places:	6:1
Registered:	550
Awards:	

	Duration	EC Fees	Non-EC Fees
Full time	3-4 years	£750	£5750
Part time			
Sandwich			

Sandwell College

Sandwell College

Address:	Wednesbury Campus
	Woden Road South
	Wednesbury
	WS10 0PE
Area:	Midlands
Phone:	0121 556 6000
Fax:	0121 556 6080

Email:

Website:

Email Application Available?	No
How to apply by email:	
Total Number of Teaching Staff:	
Staff Teaching Undergraduate Courses	
Research Rating:	n/a
Teaching Rating:	n/a
Additional Rating Information	
Male:Female Student Ratio	50:50
Head of Business School	Keith Hall
Head of Undergraduate Studies	Robert Hunt
Admissions Contact	Keith Hall

About the School:
Sandwell College has offered BTEC Higher programmes for 30 years. The courses are well-recognised and highly rated nationally and internationally. The School has recently moved to purpose-built accommodation at the Wednesbury campus which provides a pleasant learning environment with excellent facilities.

About Undergraduate Studies:
The College has well-qualified experienced staff operating a tutorial system to help students with studies and career advice. There is a choice of college accommodation and modern custom-built facilities.

Facilities:
There is an active Students Union and the College is well-situated to provide easy access to all parts of the West Midlands and the many sporting and social facilities on offer.

BTEC Higher National Diploma
The College offers a choice of HNDs in Marketing, Personnel, Finance, and Business. All students complete a number of mandatory units and choose from a range of options to suit individual requirements. Successful completion enables students to gain access to one-year top-up degree programmes, professional courses and a range of careers in the public and private sectors.

Modular Course?	No
Qualifications:	HND
Application Deadline:	September
Commencement Date:	
Entry Requirement:	
Applications to Places:	3:1
Registered:	120
Awards:	

	Duration	EC Fees	Non-EC Fees
Full time	2 years	On request	On request
Part time			
Sandwich			

Sheffield University Management School

Sheffield University Management School

Address:	9 Mappin Street
	Sheffield
	S1 4DT
Area:	North East England
Phone:	0114 222 3368
Fax:	0114 222 3348
Email:	**SUMS@sheffield.ac.uk**
Website:	**http://www.sums.ac.uk/mba**
Email Application Available?	Yes
How to apply by email:	www.sums.ac.uk/mba/ appform.htm
Total Number of Teaching Staff:	56
Staff Teaching Undergraduate Courses	52
Research Rating:	4
Teaching Rating:	Satisfactory
Additional Rating Information	Neither Accounting nor Leisure Management have yet been reviewed for teaching status.
Male:Female Student Ratio	60:40
Head of Business School	Professor Ian Gow
Head of Undergraduate Studies	Mr David Shearn
Admissions Contact	Ms Samina Ahmed

About the School:

The School is accommodated in a new building within the University's campus and just 5 minutes walk from the city centre. The building meets the full range of student needs, including teaching areas, 5 computer labs (one for dedicated postgraduate use), separate undergraduate and postgraduate reading and common rooms. A specialist library and bookshop is opposite the School.

The University of Sheffield has long been valued for its research and is currently ranked fourth in the latest assessment of UK universities. Currently the School is closely involved with a range of national projects, including the Sheffield-based National Centre for Popular Music and the new National Sports Institute.

About Undergraduate Studies:

Our degree programmes are concerned with the study of businesses and their management. We are as much concerned with the management of schools, hospitals and the police as with profit-making organisations. Accounting is not treated as a narrow professional activity, but as a subject with broad contemporary social and organisational applications.

Busines Studies is multi-disciplinary, drawing upon such subjects as economics, mathematics, information technology and the behavioural sciences; its applications cover finance, marketing, operations, human resources and accounting.

Facilities:

The Sports Council has designated Sheffield as its first National City of Sport. In addition to the University's own extensive sporting facilities, the city boasts an Olympic standard swimming pool, an international athletics stadium, and a 12,000 seat indoor arena. Bursaries are available for outstanding sportsmen and women.

Our Students' Union was described by The Higher as a "shining example of a union which provides excellent commercial services while placing a premium on improving welfare provision". Most students become involved in activities organised by its societies - over 130 groups covering political, academic, national, religious and other recreational interests.

Departments/Faculties:

Division of Accounting
Division of Human Resource Management
Division of Marketing
Division of Management Sciences
Division of International Business Strategy
Division of Leisure Management

Links with Academic Institutions:

There is a study-abroad option through exchange programmes in three other leading European business schools who teach in English - the University of Aalborg, Denmark, Group ESC Rennes and EDHEC, Nice, France.

Our staff also have many research links with other academic institutions throughout the world.

Links with Industry:

Our staff have strong research and business contacts; in particular there are active links with accountancy firms. Students on our Executive - MBA are sponsored by many regional companies. Currently the School is closely involved with a range of national projects including the Sheffield-based National Centre for Popular Music and the new National Sports Institute.

We offer Company-specific courses for Nippon Lever, KOBACO, the Korean Broadcasting Association and many others sponsored by the British Council.

BA in Business Studies

Busines Studies is multi-disciplinary, drawing upon such subjects as economics, mathematics, information technology and the behavioural sciences; its applications cover finance, marketing, operations, human resources and accounting.

Modular Course?	Yes
Qualifications:	BA Hons
Application Deadline:	UCAS-determined
Commencement Date:	September 1998
Entry Requirement:	ABB-BBC
Applications to Places:	22:1
Registered:	150
Awards:	140

	Duration	EC Fees	Non-EC Fees
Full time	3 years	£1,000	£6,800
Part time			
Sandwich			

BA in Business Studies and a European language

The three taught years are as with the single honours Business Studies degree, but half will be spent studying in the language department. An additional year, year three, will be spent abroad. For all other details, see single honours Business Studies.

Modular Course?	Yes
Qualifications:	Joint Honours
Application Deadline:	UCAS-determined
Commencement Date:	Sep 98
Entry Requirement:	BBB
Applications to Places:	22:1
Registered:	40
Awards:	30

	Duration	EC Fees	Non-EC Fees
Full time	4 years		
Part time			
Sandwich			

Accounting & Financial Management

Accounting is not seen as a narrow professional activity but as a subject with broad contemporary social and organisational applications. Dual degrees are available with Economics, Information Management, or Mathematics.

Modular Course?	Yes
Qualifications:	BA Hons; Joint Honours
Application Deadline:	UCAS-determined
Commencement Date:	September 1998
Entry Requirement:	BBB

Applications to Places:	11:1
Registered:	100
Awards:	70

	Duration	EC Fees	Non-EC Fees
Full time	3 years		
Part time			
Sandwich			

BA in Business Studies and Economics or Information Management or Japanese Studies or Chinese Studies or Korean Studies or Mathematics

Teaching is shared evenly between the relevant two departments. Students will have a wide range of choice in the Business Studies of the course, allowing them to specialise in those aspects of the subject which interest them.

Modular Course?	Yes
Qualifications:	Joint Honours
Application Deadline:	UCAS-determined
Commencement Date:	September 1998
Entry Requirement:	ABB-BBC
Applications to Places:	10:1
Registered:	150
Awards:	140

	Duration	EC Fees	Non-EC Fees
Full time	3 years		
Part time			
Sandwich			

167

Department of Management

School of Management

Address:	University of Southampton
	Highfield
	Southampton, Hampshire
	SO17 1BJ
Area:	London and South East England
Phone:	01703 593076
Fax:	01703 593844
Email:	mbamail2@soton.ac.uk
Website:	http://www.soton.ac.uk/~mgtweb
Email Application Available?	No
How to apply by email:	Enquiries:
	mbamail2@soton.ac.uk
Total Number of Teaching Staff:	57
Staff Teaching Undergraduate Courses	57
Research Rating:	5
Teaching Rating:	n/a
Additional Rating Information	
Male:Female Student Ratio	55:45
Head of Business School	Professor George McKenzie
Head of Undergraduate Studies	Professor CB Chapman
Admissions Contact	Mrs Louise Roberts

About the School:

The University of Southampton has delivered accounting and management education for over fifty years for both undergraduate and postgraduate students. The School of Management is located in refurbished accommodation on the main campus with special teaching, study and computer facilities. In the 1996 Research Assessment Exercise the Department of Management achieved the excellent rating of 5, which placed it in the top 10 (out of 100) schools in Business and Management.

About Undergraduate Studies:

We offer a wide range of degrees covering Accounting and Management Sciences, including combinations with Law, Finance, Modern Languages (French, German or Spanish), Economics, Music, Physics, Mathematics. Our programmes are as flexible as possible, particularly in the first year, when transfer between degrees may be possible. You will be taught using a mixture of lectures and classes during which you will not only cover academic material, but also a variety of transferable skills (presentation skills, communication, time management, teamwork), which are invaluable for any future career.

Facilities:

Southampton boasts many historical attractions and the selection of shops and amenities expected of a modern city. There are many pubs, clubs and restaurants to choose from and a number of theatres. There is a wide range of sports facilities including a dry ski slope and the area is ideal for sailing and water sports. Southampton has its own Premier League football club and is home to Hampshire Cricket Club.
Southampton has a superb location on the South Coast, close to the beautiful New Forest. The University has an active Students' Union with a wide range of clubs and societies for all interests.

Departments/Faculties:

The School has four teaching and research interest groups in: Accounting and Finance, Banking, Information Systems, and Management Sciences.

Links with Academic Institutions:

The School participates, at undergraduate level, in the SOCRATES exchange with partner universities in Belgium, Spain, Germany and Italy.

Links with Industry:

Companies sponsoring MBA students include British Gas, British Telecom, Flight Refuelling, GEC, IBM, Vosper Thornycroft, and a number of public sector organisations. Research and consultancy is undertaken for many organisations which strengthens the School's links with industry, commerce and the public sector.

Student Testimonials:

"I decided to apply for an Accounting and Spanish degree in order to be conversant with commerce and be able to run my own business. With Spanish my opportunities at the end of the course should be further enhanced. I am delighted to say that a year down the line all my expectations (about student life) have proved justified. The University itself has a relaxed, friendly environment. Most social events are organised by the Students' Union and you have the opportunity to meet a lot of people with the same interests as yourself. The University of Southampton has something for everyone, both academically and socially."

General Undergraduate Courses

Management Sciences with Physics/Music/Mathematics/ Economics

Management study with one of the above

Modular Course?	No
Qualifications:	BSc Hons
Application Deadline:	UCAS deadline
Commencement Date:	

Entry Requirement:			22/24 points
Applications to Places:			
Registered:			
Awards:			

	Duration	EC Fees	Non-EC Fees
Full time	3 years	£1000	£6700
Part time			
Sandwich			

Finance with Economics/ Mathematics

Finance and one of the above subjects

Modular Course?	No
Qualifications:	BSc Hons
Application Deadline:	UCAS deadline
Commencement Date:	
Entry Requirement:	22/24 points
Applications to Places:	
Registered:	
Awards:	

	Duration	EC Fees	Non-EC Fees
Full time	3 years	tba	£6700
Part time			
Sandwich			

Accounting and Economics

Modular Course?	No
Qualifications:	BSc Hons; Joint Honours
Application Deadline:	UCAS deadline
Commencement Date:	
Entry Requirement:	24 points
Applications to Places:	
Registered:	
Awards:	

	Duration	EC Fees	Non-EC Fees
Full time	3 years	£1000	£6700
Part time			
Sandwich			

Specialist Undergraduate Course

Accounting and Law

Modular Course?	No
Qualifications:	BSc Double Honours
Categories:	Finance; Law

Accounting and Finance

Modular Course?	No
Qualifications:	BSc Hons; Joint Honours
Categories:	Finance

Accounting or Management Sciences and a Modern Language (French, German or Spanish)

Modular Course?	No
Qualifications:	BSc Hons; Joint Honours
Categories:	Finance; International Business; Management Science

Management Sciences and Accounting

Modular Course?	No
Qualifications:	BSc Hons; Joint Honours
Categories:	Finance; Accounting; Management Science

Management Sciences

Modular Course?	No
Qualifications:	BSc Hons
Categories:	Management Science

Southampton Business School

Southampton Business School

Address:	Southampton Institute
	East Park Terrace
	Southampton
	SO14 0YN
Area:	South West England
Phone:	01703 319 000
Fax:	01703 237 529
Email:	SBS@solent.ac.uk
Website:	http://www.solent.ac.uk/sbs/
	index.html

Email Application Available?	No
How to apply by email:	
Total Number of Teaching Staff:	125
Staff Teaching Undergraduate Courses	125
Research Rating:	2
Teaching Rating:	Satisfactory
Additional Rating Information	Accountancy received the 2
	Business and Management 1
Male:Female Student Ratio	50:50
Head of Business School	Professor John Latham
Associate Dean	Professor Gerald Vinten
Head of Undergraduate Studies	Tom Thomas
Admissions Contact	John Flanagan

About the School:

Founded in September 1997 on the merger of the Business Management and Business Finance Faculties, building on the strengths of both. The School is one of the largest in the UK, and so has critical mass across a wider number of specialisms. The acquisition of skills and competencies, which employers increasingly expect, is central to all course provision, as is a strong international dimension. Staff take leading roles in professional bodies, and students consistently obtain prizes in professional examinations. The School constantly refelcts on and improves its learning, teaching and assessment strategies. Teaching and library facilities are excellent. with electronic access.

Facilities:

A sports hall and fitness suite has sauna and solarium. Daily fitness classes include circuit training, step aerobics and aerobics. Coaching is provided in netball, rugby (men and women), soccer, water polo, basketball, fencing and Tae-kwon-Do. There are two playing fields,

and a Waterborne Activities Centre, with dinghy, keelboat and powerboat courses. Leadership, teamwork and qualification schemes also operate. An Olympic style swimming pool is being constructed in the city, with a financial contribution from the Institute, and with student access. Competitive national and international sports are pursued. A Students' Union building hosts a range of other social activities.

Departments/Faculties:

Marketing
Strategy
Accountancy
Economics and Business Modelling
Human Resources Management

Links with Academic Institutions:

An active student exchange programme with many overseas universities such as Maine (USA), Bishops (Canada), Genoa (Italy) and Skovde (Sweden). The Product Centred International Marketing Model (PCIMM) involves 150 students following a global interactive marketing course with Wisconsin Stout University, the University of Maine and Champlain College, Vermont, with plans to expand across the globe.

Links with Industry:

Institute of Internal Auditors (Past President), Royal Society of Health (Current Chairman), Royal Society {for the Encouragement} of Arts {Manufactures and Commerce} (Council member), Institute of Management (Branch Chair), Institute of Personnel and Development, Chartered Institute of Marketing, Chartered Institute of Management Accountants, twinning with top UK advertising agency through the Institute of Practitioners in Advertising.

General Undergraduate Courses

BA (Hons) Business Studies

A vocationally based course with a 48 week industrial placement for full-time students in year 3. Students can, through options, specialise in areas such as Finance, Personnel, Tourism, or Marketing, or develop linguistic skills. At final level, students are required to complete a problem based business project, usually related to their placement experience. A prize, sponsored by Marks and Spencer plc, is awarded to the best placement project.

Modular Course?	No
Qualifications:	BA Hons
Application Deadline:	UCAS deadline
Commencement Date:	
Entry Requirement:	A-level points vary by course.
	GNVQ Merit applications
	welcome. Mature applicants
	considered on the basis of

experience rather than academic qualifications.

	Applications to Places:	9:1
Registered:	550
Awards:	

	Duration	EC Fees	Non-EC Fees
Full time	4 years	£1000	£5200
Part time	variable	£1000	£5200
Sandwich			

BA (Hons) Business Administration

This course aims to produce highly marketable graduates by providing a mixture of academic rigour and vocational skills. It provides a significant measure of flexibility for the students through its inclusion in the common level 1 of the Business School Undergraduate Programme, and its option choices, many of which are of an international dimension, at levels 2 and 3. Successful completion of the course may also provide exemptions to several professional bodies.

Modular Course?	No
Qualifications:	BA Hons
Application Deadline:	UCAS deadline
Commencement Date:	
Entry Requirement:	A-level points vary by course. GNVQ Merit applications welcome. Mature applicants considered on the basis of experience rather than academic qualifications.
Applications to Places:	9:1
Registered:	440
Awards:	

	Duration	EC Fees	Non-EC Fees
Full time	3 years	£1000	£5200
Part time	variable	£1000	£5200
Sandwich			

BA (Hons) International Business

The programme is designed to enable students to develop business skills and then to apply them to the international business environment. In doing so they will appreciate the cultural as well as the national differences when trading with other countries. All students undertake a period of study abroad, in Spain, Germany, France, Italy, Finland, Sweden, USA or Canada.

Modular Course?	No
Qualifications:	BA Hons
Application Deadline:	UCAS deadline
Commencement Date:	
Entry Requirement:	A-level points vary by course. GNVQ Merit applications

welcome. Mature applicants considered on the basis of experience rather than academic qualifications.

	Applications to Places:	9:1
Registered:	100
Awards:	

	Duration	EC Fees	Non-EC Fees
Full time	3 years	£1000	£5200
Part time			
Sandwich			

BA (Hons) Accountancy

This single honours degree programme establishes the accountancy underpinning relevant to CCAB professional qualification. It also provides aspiring businessmen/women with an opportunity to develop a sound financial knowledge base for future career selection.

Modular Course?	No
Qualifications:	BA Hons
Application Deadline:	UCAS deadline
Commencement Date:	
Entry Requirement:	A-level points vary by course. GNVQ Merit applications welcome. Mature applicants considered on the basis of experience rather than academic qualifications.
Applications to Places:	9:1
Registered:	150
Awards:	

	Duration	EC Fees	Non-EC Fees
Full time	3 years	£1000	£5200
Part time			
Sandwich			

Specialist Undergraduate Course

BA (Hons) Marketing

Modular Course?	No
Qualifications:	BA Hons
Categories:	Marketing

BA (Hons) Marketing Design

Modular Course?	No
Qualifications:	BA Hons
Categories:	Marketing

BA (Hons) Human Resource Management

Modular Course?	No
Qualifications:	BA Hons
Categories:	Human Resources

BA (Hons) Accountancy and Law

Modular Course?	No
Qualifications:	BA Hons
Categories:	Finance; Business Law

BA (Hons) Sports Studies with Business

Modular Course?	No
Qualifications:	BA Hons
Categories:	Leisure

BA Financial Services

Modular Course?	No
Qualifications:	BA
Categories:	Finance

HND in Business and Leisure Studies

Modular Course?	No
Qualifications:	HND
Categories:	Leisure

South Bank Business School

South Bank Business School

Address:	103 Borough Road
	London SE1 0AA
Area:	London and South East England
Phone:	0171 815 8281
Fax:	0171 815 8250
Email:	**enrol@sbu.ac.uk**
Website:	**http:www.sbu.ac.uk**
Email Application Available?	Yes
How to apply by email:	enrol@sbu.ac.uk
Total Number of Teaching Staff:	200
Research Rating:	3a
Teaching Rating:	Excellent
Additional Rating Information	3A European Studies
	3B Business & Management
	Languages - Excellent (22),
	Business & Management -
	Satisfactory
Male:Female Student Ratio	46:54
Head of Business School	Professor Nick Rowe
Head of Undergraduate Studies	Mr Nick Richards
Admissions Contact	Paul Prendergast (ft) or Hrilina
	Ghosh (p/t)
Director of Undergraduate Programmes	Mr Roger Smith

About the School:
The South Bank Business School offers a wide range of undergraduate, postgraduate and post-experience courses, both full time and part time, in Business, Marketing, Languages and European Studies, Accountancy, Finance, Law and Management (including Hotel and Tourism Management and Arts Management). The Business School has approximately 5,000 students of whom approximately 3,500 are on undergraduate programmes. The School's academic activities are supported by a modern library, a Learning Resource Centre housing a modern languages centre and up to date computer facilities for open access, CD ROM, satellite communications and conferencing. The South Bank Business School is located on the main University campus in South East London, approximately 10-15 minutes walking distance from Westminster, Waterloo and London Bridge.

About Undergraduate Studies:
The undergraduate programme offers a wide range of full and part-time courses, including: Business Studies; Accounting and Finance Management; Arts

Management; Law; Languages; Human Resource Management; Marketing; Hotel and Tourism; Management Professional Education. Courses available are: BA (Hons) Business studies; BA Business Administration; BA (Hons) Business Studies with a language; HND Business Studies; BA (Hons) Accounting and Finance; Foundation course in Accountancy; ACCA Professional Accountancy Course; LLB Hons (Law); BA(Hons) Modern Languages and International Business; European Business Certificate; BA (Hons) Hotel Management; BA(Hons) Tourism Management; BA Arts Management; BA Hons International Tourism and Hotel Management; Common Foundation Course (For International Students only) Combined Honours; Law Field; Economics Field; Management Field; Human Resource Field, Accounting Field, Marketing Field, Tourism Field and Modern Languages Field.

Facilities:
There is a large indoor sports centre within the Business School building in London Road. This sports provision caters for a large number of indoor and outdoor pursuits, including a wide programme of activities available to students and staff. The School is located on the central campus about one mile from the South Bank Arts complex, the West End and the City so that students have easy access to the wealth of activities which the capital city offers. The students union has excellent facilities with entertainment venues and shops on the main campus together with social clubs and societies.

Departments/Faculties:
The Business School comprises eight academic divisions which contribute to all undergraduate, postgraduate and post-experience courses. The Divisions are: Accounting Strategy and Marketing; Economics Finance; Quantitative and Information Systems; Human Resource Management Modern Languages Leisure and Tourism Industries Law

Links with Academic Institutions:
The Business School has excellent links with a large number of overseas institutions. Over a long period of time the School has developed links with institutions in the Scandinavian countries (Norway, Denmark, Sweden, Finland); with many other EU countries including Germany, France, Spain, Greece and Italy as well as with North America, India, Pakistan, Thailand and other South East Asian countries.

Links with Industry:
There is a strong tradition of co-operation with Business, industries and the professions. The Business School Association comprises over 250 companies and external organisations and works closely with academic staff in the design of courses; skills development; student placements; research; consultancy etc. There are a number of externally sponsored prizes awarded and also regular contributions from guest speakers.

Business School

Staffordshire University Business School

Address:	Brindley Building
	Leek Road
	Stoke
	ST4 2DF
Area:	Midlands
Phone:	01782 294 000
Fax:	01782 747 006

Email:

Website: http://web.staffs.ac.uk/schools/

business/welcome.htm

Email Application Available?	No
How to apply by email:	
Total Number of Teaching Staff:	150
Staff Teaching Undergraduate Courses	150
Research Rating:	2
Teaching Rating:	Satisfactory
Additional Rating Information	
Male:Female Student Ratio	50:50
Head of Business School	Chris Brownless
Admissions Contact:	Fiona Coventry
	01782 294177

About the School:

The Business School has over 180 staff, almost 3000 full-time and 1700 part-time students, and offers major programmes from campuses in Stoke and Stafford. Programmes are offered in all areas of business management, including: Economic Analysis; Forecasting and Environment; Marketing; Accounting and Finance; Management of Operations and Information; Management of Human Resources; Development of Business Strategies; Property and Construction Management; and specialist skills such as Quantity and Valuation Surveying.

About Undergraduate Studies:

We offer a wide range of courses at undergraduate and postgraduate level, all offering flexibility and breadth of choice. Staff have carried out consultancy for many UK and international organisations and this is reflected in a number of centres that combine and focus expertise.

Facilities:

We are located in the heart of the UK with easy access to city and open country, and we can offer accommodation on campus. Stafford and Stoke both offer a good choice of nightlife with live music widely available. Most major stores can be found in the area

and there is an award-winning shopping centre close to Stoke. The Festival Park in Hanley offers a wide choice of recreation including bowling, swimming, snooker and cinemas on a 23 acre site, while there is a wealth of cultural activity close to the campuses including museums, art galleries and libraries. Both campuses have all-weather sports pitches and indoor sports facilities.

General Undergraduate Courses

Degrees in Business

The courses include: BA (Hons) Business Studies; BA (Hons) Marketing; BA (Hons) Business with Operations Management; BA (Hons) Human Resource Management; BA (Hons) International Business Management; BA (Hons) International Finance and Business; BA (Hons) Business Studies with Tourism. These courses consist of a foundation level and, for suitably qualified students, three further levels. The 3-year courses share a common set of modules, with a defined range in the first part of the course and increasing choice of specialisation to suit the type of award. Students may take a one year placement in the third year. After the first year, students can choose to specialise in one of the named degree areas or continue with a broad range of business modules. The final semester is devoted to strategy modules and a personal project

Modular Course?	Yes
Qualifications:	BA; BA Hons
Application Deadline:	UCAS
Commencement Date:	
Entry Requirement:	General requirements to include GCSE Maths and English at C or above, individual course requirements on request.
Applications to Places:	
Registered:	1165
Awards:	

	Duration	EC Fees	Non-EC Fees
Full time	3 years		
Part time	7 years		
Sandwich	4 years		

Degrees in Accounting

BA (Hons) Accounting; BA (Hons) Accounting and Business; BA (Hons) Accounting and Law; BA/BSc (Hons) Accounting IT; HND Business.

Modular Course?	Yes
Qualifications:	BA Hons; BSc Hons; HND
Application Deadline:	UCAS
Commencement Date:	
Entry Requirement:	General requirements to include

GCSE Maths and English
at C or above, individual course
requirements on
request.

	Applications to Places:	
Registered:	n/a	
Awards:		

	Duration	EC Fees	Non-EC Fees
Full time	3 years		
Part time	7 years		

Degrees in Business Enterprise, Innovation and Communications (Stafford Campus)

The courses include: BA (Hons) Business Enterprise; BA (Hons) Business Administration; BA (Hons) International Business Communications; BSc (Hons) Innovation and Business Computing; BA (Hons) Business and Quality Management; BA (Hons) Enterprise and Entrepreneurship. The 3-year courses share a common set of modules, with a defined range in the first part of the course and increasing choice of specialisation to suit the type of award. The final semester is devoted to a series of integrated assignments culminating in a project. Students are not required to attend formal lectures in the final semester and can research their project anywhere in the UK or abroad.

Modular Course?	Yes
Qualifications:	BA Hons; BSc Hons
Application Deadline:	UCAS
Commencement Date:	
Entry Requirement:	General requirements to include GCSE Maths and English at C or above, individual course requirements on request.

	Applications to Places:	
Registered:	1075	
Awards:		

	Duration	EC Fees	Non-EC Fees
Full time	3 years		
Part time	7 years		

Degrees in Economics

There are five awards available in this programme including: BA (Hons) Business and Financial Economics; BA (Hons) Economics; BA (Hons) European Economics; BA (Hons) Leisure Economics; BA (Hons) Economic Studies. Economics is also offered as a single, combined or joint award in Economic Studies. Each award reflects a different perspective and, although there is a common core, the way the information is used and the specific problems addressed differ according to the student's orientation. The degrees focus on major economic issues and the policies that can be used to solve them. The courses consist of a foundation level and, for suitably qualified students, three further levels.

Modular Course?	Yes
Qualifications:	BA Hons
Application Deadline:	UCAS
Commencement Date:	
Entry Requirement:	General requirements to include GCSE Maths and English

	Applications to Places:	
Registered:	300	
Awards:		

	Duration	EC Fees	Non-EC Fees
Full time	3 years		
Part time	7 years		

Degrees in Property and Construction

Courses include: BSc (Hons) Facilities Management; BSc (Hons) Quantity Surveying; BSc (Hons) Valuation Surveying; BSc (Hons) Building Surveying; BSc (Hons) Property and Construction; BSc (Hons) Property with Business Studies. The courses in Quantity Surveying, Valuation Surveying, and Building Surveying and BSc (Hons) Property with Business Studies are approved by the Royal Institution of Chartered Surveyors.

The degrees share a common first level of study with specialisation at 2 further levels. This allows for greater professional integration and offers some choice to transfer registration between surveying programmes at the end of Level 1. The Quantity Surveying award is designed to prepare students for careers where they will provide expert advice on all matters relating to the construction, management, and financing of building projects. The Valuation Surveying award prepares students for careers where they will provide expert advice on all matters relating to the planning, valuation, management, and development of landed property. The Building Surveying award prepares students for providing advice on the construction, maintenance, repair and refurbishment of all types of property.

Modular Course?	Yes
Qualifications:	BSc Hons
Application Deadline:	UCAS
Commencement Date:	
Entry Requirement:	General requirements to include GCSE Maths and English at C or above, individual course requirements on request.

	Applications to Places:	
Registered:	240	
Awards:		

	Duration	EC Fees	Non-EC Fees
Full time	3 years		
Part time	7 years		

Faculty of Management

Faculty of Management

Address:

Stirling
FK9 4LA

Area: Scotland
Phone: 01786 467277
Fax: 01786 467279
Email: management@stir.ac.uk
Website: www.stir.ac.uk/management/

Email Application Available?	No
How to apply by email:	
Total Number of Teaching Staff:	110
Staff Teaching Undergraduate Courses	
Research Rating:	3a
Teaching Rating:	Highly Satisfactory
Additional Rating Information	Accountancy and Finance 4, Highly Satisfactory Business and Manangement 3a, Highly Satisfactory Computing Science 3a, Satisfactory Economics 4, Excellent Mathematics 3b, Highly Satisfactory
Male:Female Student Ratio	47:53
Head of Business School	Professor Leigh Sparks
Head of Undergraduate Studies	
Admissions Contact	Ms Kate Davidson

About the School:

The Faculty of Management at the University of Stirling is one of the largest University centres of management education in the UK. The University was established in 1967, and has a reputation for its flexible and innovative approach to teaching and research. The University is situated just outside the historic town of Stirling, and is considered one of the most attractive campuses in Europe. The Faculty comprises the Departments listed below, which run their own programmes and combined programmes.

About Undergraduate Studies:

The key to undergraduate study at Stirling is flexibility. As well as a broad range of single and combined Honours programmes in Management subjects, students can also combine study of Management with subjects from other areas, such as education, sociology,

or modern languages. As well as four-year Honours programmes, it is also possible to complete a three-year General degree.

Facilities:

The University has an impressive range of outdoor and indoor sports facilities on campus. These include a swimming pool, squash courts, fitness room and a sports hall, and both grass and all-weather outdoor pitches. The University is home to the Scottish National Tennis Centre, with indoor and outdoor courts. The Students' Association provides a range of social facilities and societies, and the MacRobert Arts Centre on campus offers theatre, films, exhibitions, concerts and dance.

Departments/Faculties:

Accounting, Finance and Law
Computing Science and Mathematics
Economics
Entrepreneurship
Marketing
Management and Organization
Sports Studies

Links with Academic Institutions:

The University of Stirling has links with many other academic institutions. For example, undergraduates have the opportunity to spend one or two semesters on exchange in a European or North American University. For postgraduates, the MSc programme in International Business is run by Stirling, CERAM (France) and Groningen (Netherlands). Students on this programme have the opportunity to spend a semester at each of the three institutions.

Links with Industry:

A number of the Faculty's programmes, at undergraduate and postgraduate levels, give students the opportunity to undertake a placement or project within a company or organisation, as an integral part of the educational experience. Executive level programmes are a key element in several Departments.

General Undergraduate Courses

Business Studies

Four-year Honours or three-year General degree; also available as a part-time programme by daytime or evening study.

Modular Course?	Yes
Qualifications:	BA; BA Hons; Joint Honours
Application Deadline:	
Commencement Date:	September
Entry Requirement:	Higher BBBB A-level BCC
Applications to Places:	11:1
Registered:	122
Awards:	68

	Duration	EC Fees	Non-EC Fees
Full time	4 years	£1000	£5950
Part time	flexible		
Sandwich			

Marketing

Four-year Honours or three-year General degree; a specialised programme in Retail Marketing is also available.

Modular Course?	Yes
Qualifications:	BA; BA Hons; Joint Honours
Application Deadline:	
Commencement Date:	September
Entry Requirement:	Higher BBBB A-level BBC
Applications to Places:	10:1
Registered:	77
Awards:	94

	Duration	EC Fees	Non-EC Fees
Full time	4 years	£1000	£5950
Part time	flexible		
Sandwich			

Accountancy

A four-year Honours (three year General) programme giving significant exemption from the professional examinations of the Institutes of Chartered Accountants in Scotland, England and Wales, and Ireland; also CIM and CIPFA.

Modular Course?	Yes
Qualifications:	BAcc Hons/General
Application Deadline:	
Commencement Date:	September
Entry Requirement:	Higher BBBB A-level BBC
Applications to Places:	10:1
Registered:	104
Awards:	54

	Duration	EC Fees	Non-EC Fees
Full time	4 years	£1000	£5950
Part time	flexible		
Sandwich			

Economics

Four-year Honours and three-year General degree programme.

Modular Course?	Yes
Qualifications:	BA; BA Hons; Joint Honours
Application Deadline:	
Commencement Date:	September
Entry Requirement:	Higher BBCC A-level BC/CCC
Applications to Places:	6:1
Registered:	89
Awards:	39

	Duration	EC Fees	Non-EC Fees
Full time	4 years	£1000	£5950
Part time			
Sandwich			

Computing Science

Four-year Honours and three-year General degree programme. Specialised programmes in Business Computing and Software Engineering are also offered.

Modular Course?	Yes
Qualifications:	BSc; BSc Hons; Joint Honours
Application Deadline:	
Commencement Date:	September
Entry Requirement:	Higher BBCC A-level BC/CCD
Applications to Places:	7:1
Registered:	86
Awards:	23

	Duration	EC Fees	Non-EC Fees
Full time	4 years	£1000	£7850
Part time			
Sandwich			

Additional Courses

Sports Studies, Mathematics, and an extensive range of combined Honours courses involving Management subjects.

Modular Course?	Yes

Specialist Undergraduate Course

Management Science

Modular Course?	Yes
Qualifications:	BSc; BSc Hons; Joint Honours
Categories:	

Human Resources Management

Modular Course?	Yes
Qualifications:	BA; BA Hons; Joint Honours
Categories:	Human Resources

Entrepreneurship

Modular Course?	Yes
Qualifications:	BA; Joint Honours
Categories:	Small Business

Retail Marketing

Modular Course?	Yes
Qualifications:	BA Hons
Categories:	Retailing

Business Law

Modular Course?	Yes
Qualifications:	BA; Joint Honours
Categories:	Business Law

Strathclyde Business School

Strathclyde Business School

Address:	McCance Building
	16 Richmond Street
	Glasgow
	G1 1XQ
Area:	Scotland
Phone:	0141-548 2787
Fax:	0141-552 0775
Email:	sbs@mis.strath.ac.uk
Website:	http://www.strath.ac.uk/Faculty/ SBS/

Email Application Available?	No
How to apply by email:	
Total Number of Teaching Staff:	340
Staff Teaching Undergraduate Courses	
Research Rating:	5
Teaching Rating:	Excellent
Additional Rating Information	Research 4: Economics, Information Science, Law; 3a: Environmental Planning Teaching Highly Satisfactory: Environmental Planning, Law, Hotel School; Satisfactory: Accounting and Finance, Economics
Male:Female Student Ratio	41:59
Head of Business School	Professor Douglas Pitt (Dean)
Head of Undergraduate Studies	
Admissions Contact	Sandra Branney (Admissions and Student Support Officer)

About the School:

Strathclyde Business School is the largest Faculty in the University. It has nine main subject Departments offering the full range of undergraduate and postgraduate programmes, research and consultancy, and five specialist units. The School puts a particular emphasis on combining excellence with relevance, with interests wider than most business schools. This gives the School strength in depth across a broad range of disciplines relevant to business education.

The School in particular, and the University in general, have built a high reputation for the quality of their staff, teaching, research and graduates, as well as their strong links with business and industry, and internationally.

About Undergraduate Studies:

The School is a major innovator in business and management education, and offers an in-depth study of selected disciplines from a range of business subjects, or a choice specialism, or an interdisciplinary approach. Courses address not only the subject's knowledge base but also a range of generic, cognitive and subject-specific skills central to a sound business education.

Facilities:

Glasgow is a vibrant, dynamic, cosmopolitan, cultural capital and is host to some of the most exciting arts and cultural activities in the world; there are art galleries and exhibitions, opera, dance, theatre, cinema, clubs and music concerts, but the city is also within reach of some of Scotland's most spectacular scenery.

The University has an active Students' Association and over 100 clubs and societies, in addition to the excellent sports facilties for a wide range of sports. The Sports Union has over 40 affiliated sections: past and current members have adhieved recognition at Scottish, British, Olympic and World level.

The University's accommodation has been developed as a Campus Village, right in the heart of the city, there is also a Student Advisory and Counselling Service, Student and Occupational Health Service, a Chaplaincy Centre, theatre and the Collins Art Gallery.

Departments/Faculties:

Accounting and Finance, Economics, Environmental Planning, Human Resource Management, Information Science, Law School, Management Science, Marketing, Scottish Hotel School, Fraser of Allander Institute for Research on the Scottish Economy, Scottish Local Authorities Management Centre, Interface Studies Unit, Strathclyde Graduate Business School, European Policies Research Centre.

Links with Academic Institutions:

The School participates in a number of student exchange programmes and articulation agreements with UK and overseas institutions. There are links with institutions/ business schools in Spain; Italy; France; Germany; Austria; The Netherlands; Denmark; Finland; Sweden; Norway; Estonia; Singapore; Malaysia; Iran; and North America as well as UK collaborations, for example the Glasgow Graduate School of Law developed with the University of Glasgow.

Links with Industry:

The Strathclyde Business School Council and Departmental Advisory Panels provided a forum for the discussion and development of ideas with representatives of the business community. The School has .many links with industry: in addition to research contracts and consultancy, companies are involved in student placements and may contribute to programmes.

Student Testimonials:

"My degree was a key stepping stone in obtaining my professional qualification. Because Strathclyde has a dedicated Business School, I could choose from a wider range of subjects than the narrower dictate of the professional syllabus - allowing me to keep final career choice options open in earlier years and to enjoy other subjects, such as marketing."

Technology and Business Studies offers a unique combination of knowledge and skills, and employers are interested in the concept of the degree."

The course combines a good all-round education with the ability to specialise. I chose design as my specialism; however opportunites exist to pursue careers in computing, management, environmental science or town and country planning."

General Undergraduate Courses

BA degree in the Strathclyde Business School

Students choose four distinct subjects from the broad range offered by Departments in the first year, together with classes in computing and statistics. Students then select two of those principal subjects to be studied in depth in the second and third years. After qualifying for the Pass degree, students may be admitted to a fourth year for the degree with Honours in one or both of the principal subjects. Students must take their first principal subject from the following Business subjects: Accounting, Business Law, Environmental Planning Studies, Finance, Human Resource Management, Law, Management Science, Marketing, Tourism. Students may take their second principal subject from the above or from the following subjects: Economic and Social History, Geography, Politics, Psychology, Modern History, Modern Languages, Sociology, Mathematics and Statistics.

Modular Course?	No
Qualifications:	BA; BA Hons; Joint Honours
Application Deadline:	15 December
Commencement Date:	24 September 1999
Entry Requirement:	AABB at Higher grade, including English and preferably Mathematics, and reflecting a broadly-based education. GCE Advanced Level: BBC (or AB): if English and Mathematics not offered, must include as a minimum GCSE English Language and Mathematics.
Applications to Places:	6
Registered:	403
Awards:	325

	Duration	EC Fees	Non-EC Fees
Full time	3 or 4 years	£1,000	£6,290
Part time			
Sandwich			

International Business and Modern Languages

Modular Course?	No
Qualifications:	BA Hons
Categories:	Finance; Marketing; International Business; Economics

Technology and Business Studies

Modular Course?	No
Qualifications:	BSc; BSc Hons
Categories:	Marketing; Computer Science, Electronic Technology, Manufacturing Engineering, Management Economics, Management Science

Hotel and Hospitality Management

Modular Course?	No
Qualifications:	BA; BA Hons; Joint Honours
Categories:	Human Resources; Marketing; Hospitality; Business Law; Tourism; Economics

Environmental Planning

Modular Course?	No
Qualifications:	BA Hons
Categories:	Environmental Planning

Law

Modular Course?	No
Qualifications:	LLB, LLB Hons
Categories:	Law, European Law, Law and a Modern Language

179

Sunderland Business School

Sunderland Business School

Address:	St Peter's Campus
	St Peter's Way
	Sunderland
	SR6 0DD
Area:	North East England
Phone:	0191 515 2311
Fax:	0191 515 2308

Email:

Website:

Email Application Available?	No
How to apply by email:	
Total Number of Teaching Staff:	91
Staff Teaching Undergraduate Courses	84
Research Rating:	n/a
Teaching Rating:	Satisfactory
Additional Rating Information	
Male:Female Student Ratio	60:40
Head of Business School	Professor Graham Henderson
Head of Undergraduate Studies	Professor Hugh Brayne
Admissions Contact	Mike McDonnell

About the School:

Sunderland Business School has in excess of 3000 full and part-time students, with growing numbers of EC and overseas students providing a strong international flavour. To cater fully for the growing number of students, the Business School has recently re-located to the new St Peter's Campus which provides state-of-the-art teaching and study facilities, including three lecture theatres, library and learning resource centre complete with video and computing facilities. New student accommodation is also conveniently located.

About Undergraduate Studies:

The Business School works in collaboration with employers to offer programmes which are tailored to the needs of organisations. This means there is a strong emphasis on practical applications and the use of a great deal of live project work. The Institution is also committed to the improvement of teaching and learning through the use of a wide range of learning resources which are made available to students.

Facilities:

St Peter's Campus is conveniently located, close to the city centre, and yet only a short walk from the sea front. The Students' Union has facilities close by and provides representation and advice on all activities affecting students. The University also has its own sports and fitness centres with facilities for a wide range of sports.

General Undergraduate Courses

Business Studies Programmes

The School offers a wide range of Business Studies Programmes including: BA Business Studies; BA Economics; BA Accounting and Business; BA Accounting and Economics; HND Business and Finance. All students on business programmes study core modules at level 1 or 2 in marketing, law, business environment, organisational behaviour, financial and management accounting, business decision making and information systems and at level 3 there are a further 2 core modules in 'business planning and control' and 'strategy and policy'. Students then supplement these core modules with a range of specialist and/or option modules appropriate to their particular area of study. The modules are delivered through a combination of methods including lectures, seminars and workshops. A number of courses provide opportunities for placement or for study and placement abroad. For example, BA European Business/Diploma Betriebswirt and BA European Business/Licenses-Matrises includes a final year studying in a European institution for a dual qualification.

There are also Shortened versions of BA Business Studies and BA Business Administration aimed at mature students who have the skills to complete the modules in a shorter time and who may have previous qualifications.

Modular Course?	Yes
Qualifications:	BA; HND
Application Deadline:	UCAS deadline
Commencement Date:	
Entry Requirement:	14 points or equivalent from 2 or more A-levels.
	Advanced Level GNVQ merit.
Applications to Places:	6:1
Registered:	c. 1500
Awards:	

	Duration	EC Fees	Non-EC Fees
Full time	3-4 years	£1000	£5840
Part time	4-5 years	£1000	£5840
Sandwich			

BA (Hons) Business Studies/ BA (Hons) Business Administration

This course provides a broad business education with a strong vocational focus and appeals to students aiming at a specific career or those who wish to explore the wider choices. The Business Studies course includes a placement year.

Modular Course?	No
Qualifications:	BA Hons
Application Deadline:	UCAS deadline
Commencement Date:	
Entry Requirement:	14 points or equivalent from 2 or more A-levels. Advanced Level
Applications to Places:	7:1
Registered:	
Awards:	

	Duration	EC Fees	Non-EC Fees
Full time	Various	£1000	£5840
Part time			
Sandwich			

BA (Hons) International Business; BA (Hons) International Business with a Language

This course offers specialist options in European Business and includes the study of a language - French, German, Spanish, Russian or Japanese. At least 30 weeks will be spent on industrial placement in the appropriate country to develop both language and business skills.

Modular Course?	No
Qualifications:	BA Hons
Application Deadline:	UCAS deadline
Commencement Date:	
Entry Requirement:	14 points or equivalent from 2 or more A-levels. Advanced Level
Applications to Places:	7:1
Registered:	
Awards:	

	Duration	EC Fees	Non-EC Fees
Full time	Various	£1000	£5840
Part time			
Sandwich			

Accounting and Business

Regiestered: 80

	Duration
Full time	3 years

Business Administration

Registered: 220

	Duration
Full time	3 years

Business Economics

Registered: 85

	Duration
Full time	3 years

Business Studies

Registered: 370

	Duration
Sandwich	4 years

Business and Human Resource Management (IPD accredited)

Registered: 90

	Duration
Sandwich	4 years

Business and Legal Studies (ILEX accredited)

Registered: 120

	Duration
Sandwich	4 years

Business and Management Studies

Registered: 120

	Duration
Sandwich	4 years

Business and Marketing

Registered: 160

	Duration
Sandwich:	4 years

Economics

Registered: 70

	Duration
Full time	3 years

Swansea Business School

Swansea Business School (Swansea Institute)

Address:	Mount Pleasant
	Swansea
	SA1 6ED
Area:	Wales
Phone:	01792 481 124
Fax:	01792 481 127
Email:	**sbs@sihe.ac.uk**
Website:	**www.siph.ac.uk**
Email Application Available?	No
How to apply by email:	
Total Number of Teaching Staff:	55
Staff Teaching Undergraduate Courses	
Research Rating:	n/a
Teaching Rating:	Excellent
Additional Rating Information	
Male:Female Student Ratio	45:55
Dean of Faculty of Business:	Olive Hopker
Head of Undergraduate Studies	Stephen Griffiths
Admissions Contact Business School Secretary	

About the School:

Swansea Business School was created in 1995 through the merger of the former faculties of Business and Management and Finance, whose work had been recognised as 'excellent' in the 1994 Quality Assessment exercise. The Business School is part of the Faculty of Business of the Swansea Institute of Higher Education whose predecessors have a tradition of providing quality education since before 1900. Current provision includes full and part-time programmes at higher national, undergraduate and postgraduate levels, together with a portfolio of professional qualifications and research degrees.

Facilities

The School is a small institution with a reputation for a friendly atmosphere, and it boasts a team of highly committed, qualified and experienced staff. Swansea is located on the doorstep of an area of outstanding natural beauty in this very attractive part of South Wales with its beautiful beaches and spectacular mountain scenery. The Institute has an active Students' Union with a wide range of facilities available, including access to the local leisure centres and Morfa Stadium.

General Undergraduate Courses

BA Business Administration

This full or part-time degree has a vocational basis and is aimed at the generalist who requires a general background in all functional areas. A specialist flavour can be adopted by selection of optional modules. Core areas cover the essentials of business including Economics, Accounting, Quantitative Methods, IT, Organisational Behaviour, and Marketing.

Modular Course?	Yes
Qualifications:	BA University of Wales
Application Deadline:	UCAS deadline
Commencement Date:	September
Entry Requirement:	Determined by Admissions Tutor, but normally 2 A-level passes or equivalent, with ability in English and Maths. GNVQ, IB, professional qualifications and mature students also considered. Entry with advanced standing possible.
Applications to Places:	6:1
Registered:	250
Awards:	

	Duration	EC Fees	Non-EC Fees
Full-time	3 years	£1000	£5800
Part time	On request	On request	On request

BA Business Studies

This programme is similar to that followed by Business Administration students, but includes a 1-year placement in an organisation which can be in the UK or overseas, including USA.

Modular Course?	Yes
Qualifications:	BA University of Wales
Commencement Date:	September
Entry Requirement:	Determined by Admissions Tutor, but normally 2 A-level passes or equivalent, with ability in English and Maths. GNVQ, IB, professional qualifications and mature students also considered. Entry with advanced standing possible.
Applications to Places:	6:1
Registered:	300
Awards:	

	Duration	EC Fees	Non-EC Fees
Full time	4 years	£1000	£5800
Part time	On request	On request	On request

BA Business Education

This full-time programme carries qualified teacher status and graduates are entitled to apply for appropriate teaching or lecturing posts where Business Studies specialists are required. The first two years concentrate on the business skills needed, while the last two cover Education and Professional Studies, with teaching practice in a variety of secondary schools and further education colleges. By the end of the course, students should be competent, lively and knowledgeable practitioners.

Modular Course?	No
Qualifications:	BA University of Wales
Application Deadline:	UCAS deadline
Commencement Date:	September
Entry Requirement:	Determined by Admissions Tutor, but normally 2 A-level passes or equivalent, with GCSEs or equivalent in English and Maths. GNVQ, IB, professional qualifications and mature students also considered. Entry with advanced standing possible.
Applications to Places:	6:1
Registered:	70
Awards:	

	Duration	EC Fees	Non-EC Fees
Full time	4 years	£1000	£5800

BA Accounting

This programme, available on a full-time or a part-time basis, is aimed at students seeking to become professionally-qualified accountants through a degree which offers exemptions from professional examinations. Students can develop interests in areas such as Audit and Taxation.

Modular Course?	Yes
Qualifications:	BA University of Wales
Commencement Date:	September
Entry Requirement:	Determined by Admissions Tutor, but normally 2 A-level passes or equivalent, with ability in English and Maths. GNVQ, IB, professional qualifications and mature students also considered. Entry with advanced standing possible.
Applications to Places:	6:1
Registered:	90
Awards:	

	Duration	EC Fees	Non-EC Fees
Full time	3 years	£1000	£5800
Part time	On request	On request	On request

School of Business and Management

School of Business and Management

Address:	Middlesborough
	TS1 3BA
Area:	North East England
Phone:	01642 218 121
Fax:	01642 342 839

Email:

Website: **www.tees.ac.uk**

Email Application Available?	No
How to apply by email:	
Total Number of Teaching Staff:	55
Staff Teaching Undergraduate Courses	
Research Rating:	n/a
Teaching Rating:	n/a
Additional Rating Information	
Male:Female Student Ratio	52:48
Head of Business School	Dr M Nick Hodge
Head of Undergraduate Studies	Adrian Evans
Admissions Contact	Dave Wall/Janet Blee 01642 342 807

About the School:

The School of Business & Management offers a range of courses at diploma, degree, postgraduate, and post-experience level. The areas of study include business, finance, management, marketing, human resources, and information technology.

About Undergraduate Studies:

Undergraduate studies at Teesside is a wide ranging modular programme leading to a number of specialist awards. You can study or work abroad in a number of locations in the USA or Europe as part of your programme. The programme provides the opportunity to receive a strong academic grounding and the chance to study for relevant professional qualifications in Accountancy, Human Resource Management and Marketing (depending on options chosen). HND and top up programmes are also offered. Contact the School for details.

Student Testimonials:

"One of the most important things about the course is that in the final year you can study for the Chartered Institute of Marketing Diploma. Its an important professional qualification so I'm taking advantage of that. The staff are helpful and easy to get hold of when you need to talk to them, and I would say that the resources provided are excellent....The facilities here are very good indeed, and the new Learning Resource Centre lets you have access to loads of PCs so you don't have to buy your own."

General Undergraduate Courses

BA (Hons) Business Studies

This four year thick sandwich course provides students with the opportunity to study a broad range of Business related areas including, Marketing Human Resource Management, Economics, Accountancy, IT and Strategy. The focus is on a sound academic underpinning, skills development and the application of theory to real business situations. The placement period in the third year is an opportunity to put learning into practice in and organisation in the UK or abroad. There are options to study a language, entrepreneurship or leisure management.

Modular Course?	Yes
Qualifications:	BA Hons
Application Deadline:	UCAS deadline
Commencement Date:	September
Entry Requirement:	10 points
Applications to Places:	3:1
Registered:	80
Awards:	75

	Duration	EC Fees	Non-EC Fees
Full time			
Part time			
Sandwich	4 years	Standard	Standard

BA (Hons) Accounting and Finance

This three year course provides exemption from the foundation stage of the professional Accountancy examinations. You will study a broad business related curriculum and specialist accounting options chosen from a range including audit, taxation and the public sector.

Modular Course?	Yes
Qualifications:	BA Hons
Application Deadline:	UCAS deadline
Commencement Date:	September
Entry Requirement:	10 points
Applications to Places:	3:1
Registered:	60
Awards:	45

	Duration	EC Fees	Non-EC Fees
Full time	3 years	Standard	Standard
Part time			
Sandwich			

BA (Hons) Marketing, BA (Hons) Human Resource Management

These two courses provide the opportunity for students to specialise in an area of business, developing the knowledge and skills related to the area but within the broader business context. Professional accreditation from the Chartered Institute of Marketing and The Institute of Personnel and Development (Grad IPD) is available for students who choosing the appropriate study pathway.

Modular Course?	Yes
Qualifications:	BA Hons
Application Deadline:	UCAS deadline
Commencement Date:	September
Entry Requirement:	10 points
Applications to Places:	3:1
Registered:	80
Awards:	50

	Duration	EC Fees	Non-EC Fees
Full-time	3 years	Standard	Standard
Part time			
Sandwich			

BA (Hons) International Business Studies

This four year course provides students with the opportunity to study a broad range of business related areas including, Marketing Human Resource Management, Economics, Accountancy, IT and Strategy in an international context including the chance to study or work in Europe or the USA.. The focus is on a sound academic underpinning, skills development and the application of theory to real business situations.

Modular Course?	Yes
Qualifications:	BA Hons
Application Deadline:	UCAS deadline
Commencement Date:	September
Entry Requirement:	10 points
Applications to Places:	2:1
Registered:	30
Awards:	New course

	Duration	EC Fees	Non-EC Fees
Full time	4 years	Standard	Standard
Part time			
Sandwich			

BA (Hons) Leisure Management (subject to approval)

This new degree course allows students to study a range of business and management issues in the context of leisure in general or the specialist pathways of sport, hospitality or tourism. It is designed to meet the growing need for service sector managers with considerable specialist knowledge of the leisure industry. Students will take part in live projects with local leisure industry organisations.

Modular Course?	Yes
Qualifications:	BA Hons
Application Deadline:	UCAS deadline
Commencement Date:	September
Entry Requirement:	10 points
Applications to Places:	n/a
Registered:	10
Awards:	New course

	Duration	EC Fees	Non-EC Fees
Full time	3 years	Standard	Standard
Part time			
Sandwich			

Department of Business and Management

Department of Business and Management

Address:	Allt-Yr-Yn Campus
	PO BOX 180
	Newport
	NP9 5XR
Area:	Wales
Phone:	01633 432 432
Fax:	01633 432 850
Email:	**uic@newport.ac.uk**
Website:	**www.newport.ac.uk**
Email Application Available?	No
How to apply by email:	
Total Number of Teaching Staff:	27
Staff Teaching Undergraduate Courses	27
Research Rating:	n/a
Teaching Rating:	Satisfactory
Additional Rating Information	
Male:Female Student Ratio	50:50
Head of Business School	Monica Gibson-Sweet
Head of Undergraduate Studies	Dave Orford
Admissions Contact	Karen Fishlock

About the School:

The Department of Business & Management, located on the Allt-yr-yn campus of the University of Wales College, Newport was established in 1993, building on more than 25 years' experience in delivering business, management and professional studies courses. 2679 students were enrolled in 1997/98 on a wide variety of courses which are continuously developed to provide a unique, up-to-date portfolio, offering flexibility, access and choice. Students' feedback has consistently pointed to a supportive and challenging atmosphere maintained by tutors and support staff.

The Department of Business & Management is a major provider of part-time education in Wales and has extensive franchising arrangements with partner colleges. The school has developed a reputation for its professional Accountancy provision and flexibility in course design with a supporting Research Centre and overseas links.

Facilities:

The campus is 10 minutes walk from the centre of Newport, 10 minutes by train from Cardiff, and close to 530 square miles of varied countryside with something to offer for all recreational and leisure interests. Every first year full-time student is offered accomodation in the student's village at the University College's Caeneon Campus, some 2 to 3 miles outside Newport. The Caeneon campus offers sports, club, bar and multi-gym facilities while both Caeneon and Allt-yr-yn campuses provide shops, common rooms and student support services.

General Undergraduate Courses

Undergraduate Business Programme

This modular, semester-based programme offers pathways leading to University of Wales BSc (Hons) awards in: BSc (Hons) Business Administration; BSc (Hons) Accounting & Finance; BSc (Hons) Business & Legal Studies; BSc (Hons) Accounting and Legal Studies.

The Business Administration Degree is designed to provide a broad, balanced business education to Honours degree level and to produce graduates who can become flexible, high calibre business managers. The other degree courses prepare students for more specialised careers in business.

Modular Course?	Yes
Qualifications:	BSc Hons
Application Deadline:	UCAS deadline
Commencement Date:	September
Entry Requirement:	5 GCSE passes to include English
	Language with at least
	2 at A-Level (10 points).
	Advanced Level GNVQ with
	Distinction, BTEC National award
	with Merit/ Distinction
	profile. An approved Access
	Certificate or equivalent
	qualification.
Applications to Places:	2:1
Registered:	240
Awards:	

	Duration	EC Fees	Non-EC Fees
Full time	3 years	On request	On request
Part time	4 years min	On request	On request

HND Business and Finance

This programme provides a vocationally-relevant educational foundation for students to pursue careers in administration and management within commerce, industry and the public sector. Students may acquire either a general business education with a broad option oice or specialise in an elective field. The course tablishes a sound basis for future studies in ofessional fields or at degree level. The programme nsists of 6 core and 6 options modules and offers ecialist pathways in the following areas: Accountancy Finance, Business & Legal Studies and European siness Studies. There are opportunities available for e progression to degree programme at end of a mmon 1st year.

dular Course?	Yes
alifications:	HND
plication Deadline:	UCAS deadline
mmencement Date:	September
ry Requirement:	5 GCSE passes to include English Language with at least 1 at A-Level (12 points). Advanced Level GNVQ with Merit, BTEC National award with Pass/Merit profile. An approved Access Certificate or equivalent qualification.
plications to Places:	2:1
gistered:	140
ards:	

	Duration	EC Fees	Non-EC Fees
l time	2 years	On request	On request
t time	3 years	On request	On request

Registered:			40

	Duration	EC Fees	Non-EC Fees
Full time	3 years	On request	On request

pecialist courses

Degree in Accounting Practice

his course is primarily designed for students who wish pursue a professional accountancy qualification within e framework of an honours degree.
he Accounting Practice Degree will provide students ith the knowledge, understanding and competencies levant to a career in accountancy. The completion of e two year DipHE stage can lead to exemptions from e first 10 papers of the Association of Chartered ertified Accountants (ACCA) examination scheme. The ird year of the Degree provides sound preparation for e final four ACCA examinations.

dular course:	No
alifications:	BSc Hons
plication deadline:	UCAS
mmencement date:	September
ry requirements:	5 GSCE passes to include English Language with a least 2 at A-Level (10 pointa); Adanced Level GNVQ with Distinction, BTEC National award with Merit/ Distinction profile. An approved Access Certificate at equivalent qualification.
plications to places:	

UWIC Business School

UWIC Business School

Address:	Colchester Avenue
	Cardiff
	CF3 7XR
Area:	Wales
Phone:	01222 551 111
Fax:	01222 453 292

Email:

Website: **www.uwic.ac.uk**

Email Application Available?	No
How to apply by email:	
Total Number of Teaching Staff:	100
Staff Teaching Undergraduate Courses	20
Research Rating:	n/a
Teaching Rating:	n/a
Additional Rating Information	
Male:Female Student Ratio	53:47
Head of Business School	Tom Cockburn
Head of Undergraduate Studies	Gareth Jones
Admissions Contact	Jonathan Lowell

About the School:

The faculty is one of four within UWIC, which is a University College of the federal University of Wales, and has a full-time staff of over 100, many of whom are extremely active in research and consultancy.

General Undergraduate Courses

BA Business Studies

Modular 3 year course. Students can specialise in one of a number of designated pathways, eg human resource managmeent, marketing, finance.

Modular Course?	Yes
Qualifications:	BA Hons
Application Deadline:	UCAS deadline
Commencement Date:	October
Entry Requirement:	12 points at A-level
Applications to Places:	10:1
Registered:	75
Awards:	65

	Duration	EC Fees	Non-EC Fees
Full time	3 years		£6250
Part time	3 years		£6250

Warwick Business School

Warwick Business School

Address:	Coventry
	CV4 7AL
Area:	Midlands
Phone:	01203 524 306
Fax:	01203 523 719
Email:	inquiries@wbs.warwick.ac.uk
Website:	www.wbs.warwick.ac.uk
Email Application Available?	No
How to apply by email:	
Total Number of Teaching Staff:	106
Staff Teaching Undergraduate Courses	106
Research Rating:	5
Teaching Rating:	Excellent
Additional Rating Information	
Male:Female Student Ratio	72:28
Head of Business School	Professor R Dyson (pro tem)
Head of Undergraduate Studies	
Admissions Contact	Trixie Gadd

About the School:

Warwick Business School is one of the largest and most highly regarded centres of excellence of its kind in Europe with 17 major degree programmes, a cluster of specialist research centres and about 260 staff. Its teaching spans undergraduate, specialist Masters, MBA and doctoral degree programmes, attracting over 3100 students from around the world. Since its creation in 1967, the School has taught over 12,000 students who now hold challenging jobs around the world.

The School has dual strengths in both research and teaching, with enviable ratings for excellence in both from the Higher Education Funding Council. Its strong emphasis on interdisciplinary and collaborative research enriches every area of activity and complements the flexible and innovative design of its varied teaching programmes. The School has developed strong links with business, industry and the public sector both in the UK and internationally.

The Business School is an integral part of the University of Warwick which is sited on an attractive campus just outside Coventry. The campus is a lively self-contained community with its own shops, banks, health and welfare services, restaurants and major arts and sports centres to cater for all tastes. The University is within easy reach of Coventry with its city amenities and nearby towns such as Warwick, Stratford-upon-Avon, Kenilworth and Leamington Spa.

About Undergraduate Studies:

Competition for places is keen. The School seeks students who are both numerate and literate, who can cope with the necessary quantitative tools to analyse problems, and who can communicate their results effectively. All applications must be made through UCAS.

Facilities:

There are excellent indoor and outdoor sports facilities. An attractive greenfield campus on three adjacent sites includes social facilities to suit all tastes. Warwick Arts Centre on the central campus is the largest Arts Centre in England outside London.

Departments/Faculties:

The School is organised into five subject groups: Accounting and Finance; Industrial Relations and Organisational Behaviour; Marketing and Strategic Management; Operational Research and Systems; and Operations Management. There is also a cluster of seven specialist Research Centres incorporating nine smaller Research Units.

Links with Academic Institutions:

The School has current links with 42 academic institutions for exchange purposes in Europe, North America, South Africa, Singapore and the Far East. Many other overseas organisations are involved in research collaboration. Approximately 15% of staff are from overseas or have overseas qualifications. Around 16 Visiting Fellows from overseas work at the School each year.

Links with Industry:

Many of the School's staff have consultancy links with major national and international organisations. Four of its specialist research centres are funded by consortia, made up of national and international companies. In 1997 over 1800 delegates from the public and private sectors attended Executive Development courses.

General Undergraduate Courses

BSc Accounting and Finance

Designed to provide a broad educational base for an eventual career in accounting and financial management. Depending on option choices, exemptions may be granted by the major accountancy bodies enabling students to become professionally qualified within two or three years of graduation.

Modular Course?	No
Qualifications:	BSc
Application Deadline:	UCAS deadline
Commencement Date:	
Entry Requirement:	Normally 3 A-levels, or 2 A-levels plus 2 AS-levels, GCSE Maths grade A. Appropriate

Applications to Places: 14:1
Registered: 239
Awards:

	Duration	EC Fees	Non-EC Fees
Full time	3 years	£1000	£6795
Part time			
Sandwich			

BSc Management Sciences

This course aims to develop students' ability to analyse a wide range of problems in the management of human, financial and physical resources in both public and private sector organisations. The course develops quantitative and analytical techniques, written and verbal communication skills.

Modular Course?	No
Qualifications:	BSc
Application Deadline:	UCAS deadline
Commencement Date:	
Entry Requirement:	Normally 3 A-levels, or 2 A-levels plus 2 AS-levels, GCSE Maths grade A. Appropriate language A-levels for international courses.
Applications to Places:	14:1
Registered:	204
Awards:	

	Duration	EC Fees	Non-EC Fees
Full time	3 years	£1000	£6795
Part time			
Sandwich			

BSc International Business

This course aims to develop students' analytical and practical understanding of the processes behind the globalisation of business. The programme is taught in conjunction with Warwick's highly-rated departments of French Studies, German Studies, and Italian Studies. Students spend their third year abroad.

Modular Course?	No
Qualifications:	BSc
Application Deadline:	UCAS deadline
Commencement Date:	
Entry Requirement:	Normally 3 A-levels, or 2 A-levels plus 2 AS-levels, GCSE Maths grade A. Appropriate language A-levels for international courses.
Applications to Places:	14:1
Registered:	95
Awards:	

	Duration	EC Fees	Non-EC Fees
Full time			
Part time			
Sandwich	4 years	£1000	£6795

BA German and Business Studies

This course, jointly taught with the Department of German Studies, offers students the opportunity to spend half of their course following management sciences courses and the other half achieving a high level of fluency in the German language, together with a wide knowledge and understanding of contemporary Germany.

Modular Course?	No
Qualifications:	BA
Application Deadline:	UCAS deadline
Commencement Date:	
Entry Requirement:	Normally 3 A-levels, or 2 A-levels plus 2 AS-levels, GCSE Maths grade A. Appropriate language A-levels for international courses.
Applications to Places:	14:1
Registered:	55
Awards:	

	Duration	EC Fees	Non-EC Fees
Full time	4 years	£1000	£6795
Part time			
Sandwich			

BA Law and Business Studies

This programme, jointly taught with the Department of Law, aims to give a firm grounding in the disciplines of law and business studies and to develop a critical understanding of both the legal framework of business activity and the economic and commercial context in which the law operates. Emphasis is given to the many areas of overlapping interest between the two disciplines.

Modular Course?	No
Qualifications:	BA
Application Deadline:	UCAS deadline
Commencement Date:	
Entry Requirement:	Normally 3 A-levels, or 2 A-levels plus 2 AS-levels, GCSE Maths grade A. Appropriate language A-levels for international courses.
Applications to Places:	14:1
Registered:	40
Awards:	

	Duration	EC Fees	Non-EC Fees
Full time	3 or 4 years	£1000	£6795
Part time			
Sandwich			

Watford School of Business

Watford School of Business

---

ddress:	Hempstead Road
	Watford
rea:	London and South East England
hone:	01923 812951
ax:	01923 812584
mail:	**wsb@westherts.ac.uk**
Vebsite:	**www.westherts.ac.uk**
hail Application Available?	No
ow to apply by email:	
tal Number of Teaching Staff:	28
aff Teaching Undergraduate Courses	20
esearch Rating:	n/a
aching Rating:	n/a
Iditional Rating Information	
ale:Female Student Ratio	50:50
ead of Business School	Ms PM Kendall
ead of Undergraduate Studies	Mr M Edmonson
Imissions Contact	WSB Office

About the School:

VSB offers a wide range of full-time and part-time usiness and management education programmes. F/T ndergraduate courses include HND Business/ Marketing/Finance/Personnel and HND in Advertising nd Marketing Communications – with BA (Hons) top-p programmes in Business Admin and AMC, in ssociation with the University of Hertfordshire. The chool has developed a close working relationship with he Advertising and Marketing Communication industry nd is the only HE institution accredited by the nternational Advertising Authority. Vocational post raduate advertising and public relations programmes re also offered.

General Undergraduate Courses

BA (Hons) Business Administration

One year top-up course offered in association with the University of Hertfordshire which enables Watford chool of Business HND Business programme students o achieve a BA. With options in either Marketing, inance or Personnel.

Modular Course?	No
Qualifications:	BA Hons
Application Deadline:	UCAS deadline
Commencement Date:	September
Entry Requirement:	HND with merit profile and 2 distinctions.
Applications to Places:	
Registered:	25
Awards:	25

	Duration	EC Fees	Non-EC Fees
Full time	1 year	On request	On request
Part time			
Sandwich			

BA (Hons) Advertising and Marketing Communications

One year top-up course offered in association with the University of Hertfordshire which enables Watford School HND Advertising and HND Business with Marketing students to achieve a BA (Hons) in Advertising and Marketing Communications. Modules include Strategy, Integrated Marketing Communications, Advertising Effectiveness, Consumer Behaviour and Brand Management

Modular Course?	No
Qualifications:	BA Hons
Application Deadline:	UCAS deadline
Commencement Date:	September
Entry Requirement:	HND with merit profile and 2 distinctions
Applications to Places:	
Registered:	20
Awards:	18

	Duration	EC Fees	Non-EC Fees
Full time	1 year	On request	On request
Part time			
Sandwich			

HND Advertising and Marketing Communications

This course is designed for students who wish to specialise in Advertising as a preparation for careers in the Marketing Communications industry. After completing this programme students can progress to the BA Hons in Advertising and Marketing Communications top-up year, which is offered in association with the University of Hertfordshire

Modular Course?	No
Qualifications:	HND
Application Deadline:	UCAS deadline
Commencement Date:	September
Entry Requirement:	A level, GNVQ or mature student
Applications to Places:	

Registered:		50	
Awards:		50	

	Duration	EC Fees	Non-EC Fees
Full time	2 years	On request	On request
Part time			
Sandwich			

HND Business/Finance/ Marketing/Personnel

HND Business Programme – which enables students to specialise in either Finance, Marketing, Personnel or General Business. This programme leads to the BA (Hons) Business Administration top-up year, which is offered in association with the University of Hertfordshire.

Modular Course?	No
Qualifications:	HND
Application Deadline:	UCAS deadlines
Commencement Date:	September
Entry Requirement:	A level, GNVQ or mature student
Applications to Places:	
Registered:	90
Awards:	90

	Duration	EC Fees	Non-EC Fees
Full time	2 years	On request	On request
Part time			
Sandwich			

Westminster Business School

Westminster Business School

Address:	Admissions & Marketing office
	University of Westminster
	35 Marylebone Road
	LONDON
	NW1 5LS
Area:	London and South East England
Phone:	0171 911 5020
Fax:	0171 911 5703
Email:	mar05@wmin.ac.uk
Website:	http://www.wmin.ac.uk

Email Application Available?	Yes
How to apply by email:	Visit our Web site (http:// www.wmin.ac.uk) and complete the online application.
Total Number of Teaching Staff:	85
Staff Teaching Undergraduate Courses	85
Research Rating:	3b
Teaching Rating:	Satisfactory
Additional Rating Information	
Male:Female Student Ratio	50:50
Head of Business School	Professor J R Shackleton
Head of Undergraduate Studies	Mr T Burke
Admissions Contact	David McGowan

About the School:

Westminmster Business School is a lively and cosmopolitan academic community in the heart of London with over 3000 students (undergraduates, postgraduates and lifetime learners), a large and talented staff and a distinguished record of teaching, research and consultancy.

About Undergraduate Studies:

Study on the Westminster Business School integrated undergraduate modular business studies programme and you will open numerous gateways to business and professional careers. You join one of our mainstream courses, which include BA Business Studies and BSc Business Information Technology, choosing between a three year programme or a four year one (which includes a year of work placement or study abroad - this could be in English). The programme's design lets you transfer easily between courses, enabling you to select the exit degree which closely matches your own career expectations. You will soon discover that this rich study programme reflects the global strengths of London as an international metropolitan centre.

Facilities:

The Students' Union runs clubs which you can join as a student at the University. It is affiliated to the Universities' Athletic Union (UAU) and the Southern England Students Sports Association (SESSA). These organise regional and national competitions. The University also has Open Clubs with both student and non-student members. The clubs make use both of the facilities at Chiswick and those in central London.

Departments/Faculties:

Department of Business Information Management and Operations
Department of Economics and Quantative Methods
Department of Finance and Business Law
Department of Human Resource Strategy
Department of Marketing and Business Strategy

Links with Academic Institutions:

Large number of links with continental Europe.

Links with Industry:

There is an Employers Advisory Council which offers guidance on the development of our programmes. A Business Placement Office organises placements in industry for around 200 students per year.

Student Testimonials:

General Undergraduate Courses

BA (Hons) Business Studies

Classic 4 year degree programme, built around a year in industry, provides students with a good all round grounding in business.

Modular Course?	Yes
Qualifications:	BA; BA Hons
Application Deadline:	
Commencement Date:	September
Entry Requirement:	18 points @ A level plus GCSE English & Maths Grade C or above
Applications to Places:	
Registered:	
Awards:	

	Duration	EC Fees	Non-EC Fees
Full time		£1000	£5850
Part time			
Sandwich	4 Years	£500	£2930

BA (Hons) Business Studies (Services)

Provides students with a good general background for business, but with the opportunity to specialise in three areas of business operations: Financial Services, Retailing and Travel and Tourism

Modular Course?	Yes
Qualifications:	BA; BA Hons
Application Deadline:	
Commencement Date:	September
Entry Requirement:	18 points @ A level plus GCSE English & Maths Grade C or above
Applications to Places:	
Registered:	
Awards:	

	Duration	EC Fees	Non-EC Fees
Full time	3 Years	£1000	£5850
Part time	5 Years	£135	£135
Sandwich	No		

BA (Hons) International Business

Students choose one of the following languages: French, Italian, Spanish, German, Russian, Mandarin Chinese and Arabic

Modular Course?	Yes
Qualifications:	BA; BA Hons
Application Deadline:	
Commencement Date:	September
Entry Requirement:	18 points @ A level, GCSE English & Maths Grade C or above, evidence of language ability. Students wishing to study French must achieve A level French Grade C or better.
Applications to Places:	
Registered:	
Awards:	

	Duration	EC Fees	Non-EC Fees
Full time	4 Years	£1000.00	£5850.00
	(Year 3 - study abroad)		
Part time			
Sandwich			

BA (Hons) Business Information Management & Finance

Degree for students wishing to combining the application of Information Technology and Financial Management, as well as an applied year in industry.

Modular Course?	Yes
Qualifications:	BA; BA Hons
Application Deadline:	
Commencement Date:	September
Entry Requirement:	18 points @ A level, plus GCSE English & Maths Grade C or above
Applications to Places:	
Registered:	
Awards:	

	Duration	EC Fees	Non-EC Fees
Full time	£1000.00	£6145.00	
Part time			
Sandwich	4 Years	£500.00	£3120.00

BSc (Hons) Business Information Technology

Concentrates on the use of information technology in a business. A year in industry is also included to allow students to put into practice the skills learned during the course.

Modular Course?	Yes
Qualifications:	BSc; BSc Hons
Application Deadline:	
Commencement Date:	Septemeber
Entry Requirement:	18 points @ A level, plus GCSE English & Maths Grade C or above
Applications to Places:	
Registered:	
Awards:	

	Duration	EC Fees	Non-EC Fees
Full time	£1000	£6145	
Part time			
Sandwich	4 Years	£500	£3120

Additional Courses

BA (Hons) Business Studies (Part-time Evening Only), BA (Hons) Economics for Business, BA (Hons) Managing Business Information, BSc industrial Systems & Business Management, BSc Environmental Sciences & Business Management, BA (Hons) Business with Italian

Modular Course?	No
Qualifications:	
Application Deadline:	
Commencement Date:	
Entry Requirement:	

Applications to Places:
Registered:
Awards:

	Duration	EC Fees	Non-EC Fees
Full time			
Part time			
Sandwich			

Wolverhampton Business School

Wolverhampton Business School

Address:	University of Wolverhampton
	Shropshire Campus
	Priorslee
	Telford
	Shropshire
	Telford
	TF2 9NT
Area:	Midlands
Phone:	01902 321789
Fax:	01902 321724

Email: **wbs-marketing@wlv.ac.uk**

Website: **http://www.wlv.ac.uk/wbs**

Email Application Available?	Yes
How to apply by email:	via wbs-marketing@wlv.ac.uk
Total Number of Teaching Staff:	90
Staff Teaching Undergraduate Courses	75
Research Rating:	2
Teaching Rating:	Satisfactory
Additional Rating Information	
Male:Female Student Ratio	50:50
Head of Business School	Dr Bryony Conway
Head of Undergraduate Studies	Ms Julie Lydon
Admissions Contact	Marketing and Recruitment Office

About the School:

The School has 3500 students following a wide variety of full-time and part-time programmes at undergraduate and postgraduate level. It has strong international links, exchanges and joint programmes with universities across Europe, as well as the Far East. The University's long experience of modularity and its commitment to access has resulted in extensive opportunities for flexible study. The School has a unit which facilitates the accreditation of prior learning where appropriate. The Shropshire Campus at Telford is one of the newest in the UK, with purpose built facilities and a strong technological base for learning provision and support.

Facilities:

At each of its four major campuses across the region the University offers a range of sports facilities. At both Compton Park and Telford students can enjoy social facilities supported by the University and the Students Union. In the wider community Wolverhampton offers a wide range of shopping, leisure and entertainment opportunities, including a vibrant club scene. Telford is amongst the UK's most successful new towns and offers a wide range of amenities in a modern urban setting. The region offers a wealth of cultural attractions, including the Ironbridge Museum, and also has much to offer to those who are interested in outdoor pursuits.

Departments/Faculties:

Academic staff of the School are organised into four major Divisions: Business Enterprise & Strategy; Marketing, Economics & Tourism; Finance, Information & Operations; Human Resources, Organisation & Management. Divisional teams provide the base of expertise to support the School's major programmes in Business Education, Postgraduate & Professional, and Research & Consultancy. In addition to the Divisions there are number of specialist units and centres, for example the Management Research Centre.

Links with Academic Institutions:

The School maintains a wide range of links with other acadmic institutions. In recent years the Management Research Centre has established collaborative links with other research centres, complementing the longstanding involvement of the School international student exchange networks and in collabaorative ventures with overseas partners. Within the region the School also seeks to collaborate with FE Colleges to widen access to HE.

Links with Industry:

The School is proud of its origins as a former Polytechnic, and continues to work closely with private enterprise and public organisations across the West Midlands region and beyond. Activities include provision of Management Development Programmes to major employers, Business Research and Consultancy, Work Placements and Teaching Company Schemes.

General Undergraduate Courses

Modular Degree Programme

The Business School offers a range of specialist and modular degree programmes in a variety of attendance modes – sandwich, full-time or part-time. Modular Degree programmes offer all the following subjects, full-time or part-time either as a major, minor or in combination with any subjects listed in the University Modular Degree Scheme: Business; Economics; Marketing; Human Resource Management; Accounting; Information Management; Tourism; BA (Hons) Accounting and Finance; BA (Hons) Hospitality and Licensed Retail Management; BA (Hons) Business Economics.

Modular Course?	Yes
Qualifications:	BA Hons

	Duration	EC Fees	Non-EC Fees
Full time	1 year	£1000	£5750
Part time			
Sandwich			

Application Deadline:		UCAS deadline
Commencement Date:		
Entry Requirement:		GCSE Maths, English grade C or equivalent, plus 16 points at A/AS-level. BTEC HNC/HND 4 Merits. Advanced GNVQ Distinction or equivalent.
Applications to Places:		
Registered:		780
Awards:		

	Duration	EC Fees	Non-EC Fees
Full time	3-4 years	£1000	£5750
Part time			
Sandwich			

BA (Hons) European Business Administration

This course features half of years 2 and 3 in a partner institution outside the UK, with a possible double award of a UK degree plus an equivalent from the partner institution.

Modular Course?	No
Qualifications:	BA Hons
Application Deadline:	UCAS deadline
Commencement Date:	
Entry Requirement:	GCSE Maths, English grade C or equivalent, plus 16 points at A/AS-level. BTEC HNC/HND 4 Merits. Advanced GNVQ Distinction or equivalent.
Applications to Places:	
Registered:	120
Awards:	

	Duration	EC Fees	Non-EC Fees
Full time			
Part time			
Sandwich	4 years	£1000	£5750

BA (Hons) Business Enterprise; BA (Hons) Business Administration

These courses feature a strong emphasis on learning by doing and this equips students with the essential skills and expertise needed by employers.

Modular Course?	No
Qualifications:	BA Hons
Application Deadline:	UCAS deadlines
Commencement Date:	
Entry Requirement:	From HND or equivalent
Applications to Places:	
Registered:	220
Awards:	

HND Business and Finance

Modular Course?	No
Qualifications:	HND
Application Deadline:	UCAS deadlines
Commencement Date:	
Entry Requirement:	
Applications to Places:	
Registered:	200
Awards:	

	Duration	EC Fees	Non-EC Fees
Full time	2 years	£1000	£5750
Part time			
Sandwich			

Other members

The following institutions are also members of the Association of Business Schools;

Ashridge
Ashridge Management College

Berkhamsted
Hertfordshire
HP4 1NS
Phone: +44(0) 1442 841000
Fax: +44(0) 1442 841036
Email: info@ashridge.org.uk

Website: http://www.ashridge.org.uk

Cranfield School of Management
Cranfield University

Cranfield
Bedford
MK43 0AL
Phone: +44 (0) 1234 751122
Fax: +44 (0) 1234 751806
Email: m.williams@cranfield.ac.uk

Website: http://www.cranfield.ac.uk/som

Derbyshire Business School
University of Derby

Kedleston Road
Derby
DE3 1GB
Phone: 01332 347 181
Fax: 01332 622 741
Email:

Website: http://www.derby.ac.uk/schools/business

Further Education Development Agency

Merlin Place
Milton Road
Cambridge CB4 4DP
Phone: 01223 420579
Fax: 01223 423389
Email: gpeeke@feda.ac.uk

Website: www.feda.ac.uk

University of Glamorgan Business School
University of Glamorgan

Pontypridd
CF37 1DL
Phone: 01443 480 480
Fax: 01443 482 380
Email:

Website: www.glam.ac.uk

University of Glasgow Business School
University of Glasgow

Department of Management Studies
59 Southpark Avenue
Glasgow
G12 8LF
Phone: 0141 339 8855
Fax: 0141 330 5669
Email:

Website: www.gla.ac.uk

Henley Management College
Henley Management College

Greenlands
Henley-on-Thames
RG9 3AW
Phone: 01491 571 454
Fax: 01491 410 184
Email:
Website: www.henleymc.ac.uk

Keele University School of Management
Keele University

Darwin Building
Keele University
Keele
ST5 5RG
Phone: 01782 583 089
Fax: 01782 584 272
Email: mnb01@keele.ac.uk
Website: www.keele.ac.uk

Leicester University Management Centre
University of Leicester

University Road
Leicester
LE1 7RH
Phone: 0116 252 3991
Fax: 0116 252 3949
Email:
Website: http://www.le.ac.uk/lumc/

Faculty of Business and Management
University of Lincolnshire and Humberside

Cottingham Road
Hull
HU6 7RT
Phone: 01482 440 550
Fax: 01482 463 828
Email:
Website: http://www.humber.ac.uk/hbs

London Business School
London Business School

Sussex Place
Regents Park
London
NW1 4SA
Phone: +44 171 706 6859
Fax: +44 171 724 7875
Email: mba-info@lbs.ac.uk
Website: http://www.lbs.ac.uk/

Manchester Business School
University of Manchester

Booth Street West
Manchester
M15 6PB
Phone: 0161 275 6333
Fax: 0161 275 6489
Email:
Website: www.mbs.ac.uk

The Management Unit
University of Reading

Building 22
London Road
Reading
RG1 5AQ
Phone: 0118 931 8591
Fax: 0118 931 6539

Email: mgt_unit@reading.ac.uk

Website: http://www.dataware-sys.com/MGT

Sheffield Business School
Sheffield Hallam University

Business and Information Technology Centre
City Campus
Howard Street
Sheffield
S1 1WB
Phone: 0114 225 2820
Fax: 0114 225 5268

Email: sbspgdinfo@shu.ac.uk

Website: http://www.shu.ac.uk/school/sbs

Sems - University of Surrey
University of Surrey

Sems
University of Surrey
Guildford, Surrey
GU2 5XH
Phone: 01483 259347
Fax: 01483 259511

Email: sems@surrey.ac.uk

Website: www.sems.surrey.ac.uk

Thames Valley University School of Management
Thames Valley University

Wellington Street
Slough
SL1 1YG
Phone: 01753 697 750
Fax: 01753 697 591

Email:

Website: www.tvu.ac.uk

Ulster Business School
University of Ulster

Ulster Business School
University of Ulster
Shore Road
Newtonabbey
BT37 0QB
Phone: 01232 368882
Fax: 01232 368948

Email: ca.lavery@ulst.ac.uk

Website:

Matrix of Schools and Courses

School	Undergraduate General	Undergraduate Specialist	Certificate in Management	Diploma in Management Studies	Professional qualifications	MBA full-time	MBA part-time	MBA distance/OL	Specialist Masters full-time	Specialist Masters part-time	Specialist Masters distance/OL	Research degrees	Doctor of Business Administration	Executive programmes
Aberdeen Business School; The Robert Gordon University	✔	✔	✔	✔	✔	✔	✔		✔	✔		✔		
Anglia Business School; Anglia Polytechnic University	✔	✔	✔	✔	✔	✔	✔		✔	✔		✔	✔	✔
Aston Business School; Aston University	✔	✔		✔	✔	✔	✔	✔	✔	✔	✔	✔		✔
School of Management; University of Bath	✔	✔				✔	✔					✔		
The Birmingham Business School; The University of Birmingham	✔	✔		✔		✔	✔		✔			✔		✔
Bolton Business School; Bolton Institute of Higher Education	✔	✔	✔	✔			✔		✔	✔		✔		✔
The Business School; Bournemouth University	✔	✔	✔	✔			✔		✔			✔		✔
Bradford Management Centre; University of Bradford						✔	✔	✔	✔	✔		✔		✔
Bradford Business School; Bradford and Ilkley Community College	✔	✔	✔	✔	✔				✔			✔		✔
Brighton Business School; University of Brighton	✔	✔	✔	✔	✔	✔	✔		✔	✔		✔		✔
Bristol Business School; University of the West of England	✔	✔	✔	✔	✔	✔	✔		✔	✔		✔		✔
Buckinghamshire Business School; Buckinghamshire Chilterns University College	✔	✔	✔	✔	✔		✔	✔	✔	✔	✔	✔		
The Judge Institute of Management Studies; University of Cambridge	✔			✔		✔			✔			✔		✔
Canterbury Business School; University of Kent at Canterbury						✔	✔		✔			✔		✔
Cardiff Business School; University of Wales, Cardiff	✔	✔				✔	✔		✔	✔		✔		✔
Business School; University of Central England in Birmingham	✔	✔		✔		✔	✔		✔	✔		✔		
Faculty of Business and Social Studies; Cheltenham and Gloucester College of Higher Education	✔	✔	✔	✔	✔	✔	✔		✔	✔		✔		✔
City University Business School; City University	✔	✔				✔	✔		✔	✔		✔		✔
Coventry Business School; Coventry University	✔	✔	✔	✔	✔	✔	✔		✔	✔		✔		
Croydon Higher Education Centre; Croydon College	✔	✔	✔	✔	✔					✔				

Matrix of Schools and Courses

School	Undergraduate General	Undergraduate Specialist	Certificate in Management	Diploma in Management Studies	Professional qualifications	MBA full-time	MBA part-time	MBA distance/OL	Specialist Masters full-time	Specialist Masters part-time	Specialist Masters distance/OL	Research degrees	Doctor of Business Administration	Executive programmes
Leicester Business School; De Montford University	✔	✔	✔	✔	✔	✔	✔	✔	✔	✔	✔	✔	✔	
Dearne Valley Business School; Doncaster College	✔	✔	✔	✔	✔					✔				
Dundee Business School; University of Abertay Dundee	✔	✔	✔			✔	✔	✔	✔	✔		✔	✔	✔
Durham University Business School; University of Durham			✔			✔	✔	✔	✔	✔		✔	✔	✔
School of Management; University of East Anglia	✔		✔			✔			✔	✔		✔		
The East London Business School; University of East London	✔	✔	✔	✔	✔	✔	✔		✔	✔		✔	✔	✔
Edinburgh University Management School; University of Edinburgh						✔	✔		✔			✔		✔
European Business School London; European Business School London	✔	✔	✔											
European School of Management - Oxford; European School of Management						✔				✔				
University of Exeter Centre for Management Studies; University of Exeter		✔	✔			✔	✔		✔	✔		✔		✔
Faculty of Business; Glasgow Caledonian University	✔	✔	✔	✔	✔	✔	✔		✔	✔		✔		✔
Business School; University of Greenwich	✔	✔	✔	✔	✔		✔			✔		✔		
School of Management; Heriot-Watt University	✔					✔	✔	✔	✔	✔	✔			
Business School; University of Hertfordshire	✔	✔	✔	✔		✔	✔		✔	✔		✔		
Huddersfield University Business School (HUBS); University of Huddersfield	✔	✔	✔	✔	✔		✔	✔	✔			✔	✔	✔
School of Management and School of Accounting Business and Finance; University of Hull	✔	✔	✔	✔			✔	✔	✔	✔	✔	✔	✔	✔
Kingston Business School; Kingston University	✔	✔	✔	✔	✔	✔	✔			✔	✔	✔		✔
Lancashire Business School; University of Central Lancashire	✔	✔		✔		✔			✔	✔		✔		
The Management School; Lancaster University	✔	✔		✔		✔			✔	✔		✔		
Leeds University Business School; University of Leeds	✔			✔		✔			✔	✔		✔		
Leeds Business School; Leeds Metropolitan University		✔	✔	✔	✔		✔		✔	✔		✔		✔

Matrix of Schools and Courses

School	Undergraduate General	Undergraduate Specialist	Certificate in Management	Diploma in Management Studies	Professional qualifications	MBA full-time	MBA part-time	MBA distance/OL	Specialist Masters full-time	Specialist Masters part-time	Specialist Masters distance/OL	Research degrees	Doctor of Business Administration	Executive programmes
Liverpool Business School; Liverpool John Moores University	✔	✔	✔	✔	✔	✔	✔		✔	✔		✔	✔	✔
London Guildhall University Business School; London Guildhall University	✔	✔	✔	✔	✔	✔	✔					✔		✔
Loughborough University Business School; Loughborough University	✔	✔		✔			✔		✔	✔	✔			✔
Luton Business School; University of Luton	✔	✔	✔	✔	✔	✔	✔	✔		✔	✔			✔
Faculty of Management and Business; Manchester Metropolitan University	✔	✔	✔	✔	✔		✔		✔	✔	✔			✔
Department of Business and Management, Crewe+Alsager Faculty; Manchester Metropolitan University	✔	✔	✔	✔	✔		✔			✔		✔		✔
Manchester School of Management; U.M.I.S.T.				✔		✔	✔		✔			✔		✔
Middlesex University Business School; Middlesex University	✔	✔				✔	✔		✔	✔		✔		✔
Napier University Business School; Napier University	✔	✔	✔	✔	✔		✔	✔	✔			✔		✔
Faculty of Management and Business; Nene University College	✔	✔	✔	✔	✔	✔	✔		✔			✔		✔
School of Management; University of Newcastle upon Tyne	✔	✔	✔	✔	✔	✔	✔		✔	✔		✔	✔	✔
Business School; University of North London	✔		✔	✔	✔	✔	✔		✔	✔				
Newcastle Business School; University of Northumbria at Newcastle	✔	✔	✔	✔	✔	✔	✔	✔	✔	✔	✔	✔		✔
University of Nottingham Business School; University of Nottingham	✔	✔				✔	✔		✔	✔		✔	✔	✔
Nottingham Business School; The Nottingham Trent University	✔	✔	✔	✔	✔		✔	✔	✔			✔		✔
Open University Business School; Open University			✔	✔				✔						
Said Business School, University of Oxford; University of Oxford	✔		✔	✔		✔				✔		✔		✔
School of Business; Oxford Brookes University	✔	✔	✔	✔	✔	✔	✔	✔	✔			✔		✔
Department of Management & Marketing; Univeristy of Paisley	✔	✔												

Matrix of Schools and Courses

School	Undergraduate General	Undergraduate Specialist	Certificate in Management	Diploma in Management Studies	Professional qualifications	MBA full-time	MBA part-time	MBA distance/OL	Specialist Masters full-time	Specialist Masters part-time	Specialist Masters distance/OL	Research degrees	Doctor of Business Administration
Plymouth Business School; University of Plymouth	✔	✔	✔	✔	✔	✔	✔	✔		✔		✔	
Portsmouth Business School; University of Portsmouth	✔	✔	✔	✔	✔	✔	✔	✔	✔	✔		✔	✔
Queen's School of Management; Queen's University, Belfast	✔					✔	✔		✔	✔		✔	
School of Business; Royal Agricultural College		✔		✔		✔			✔	✔		✔	✔
The Management School; University of Salford	✔	✔	✔	✔	✔	✔	✔			✔	✔		✔	✔
Sandwell College; Sandwell College				✔									
Sheffield University Management School; University of Sheffield	✔	✔	✔	✔		✔			✔	✔		✔	✔
Department of Management; University of Southampton		✔	✔			✔	✔		✔	✔		✔	✔
Southampton Business School; Southampton Institute	✔	✔	✔	✔		✔	✔	✔		✔	✔	✔	
South Bank Business School; South Bank University	✔	✔	✔	✔	✔	✔	✔		✔	✔		✔	
Business School; Staffordshire University	✔	✔	✔	✔	✔	✔	✔		✔	✔		✔	✔
Faculty of Management; University of Stirling	✔	✔				✔	✔	✔	✔	✔		✔	✔
Strathclyde Graduate Business School; University of Strathclyde	✔	✔				✔	✔	✔	✔	✔	✔	✔	✔	✔
Sunderland Business School; University of Sunderland	✔	✔	✔	✔	✔	✔	✔	✔	✔	✔		✔	
Swansea Business School; Swansea Institute of Higher Education	✔	✔	✔	✔	✔	✔	✔		✔	✔		✔	✔
Teesside Business School; University of Teesside	✔	✔		✔					✔	✔		✔	
Department of Business and Management; University of Wales College, Newport	✔	✔		✔		✔	✔						
UWIC Business School; University of Wales Institute, Cardiff	✔					✔	✔					✔	
Warwick Business School; University of Warwick	✔	✔				✔	✔	✔	✔	✔		✔	✔
Watford School of Business; West Herts College	✔			✔									
Westminster Business School; University of Westminster	✔	✔	✔	✔	✔	✔	✔	✔	✔	✔	✔	✔	✔
Wolverhampton Business School; University of Wolverhampton	✔	✔	✔	✔	✔	✔	✔			✔		✔	✔

Index